AF291341

A LIFE *Appreciated*

First published 2022

Copyright © Tim Ralph 2022

Published under licence by Brown Dog Books and
The Self-Publishing Partnership Ltd, 10b Greenway Farm, Bath Rd,
Wick, nr. Bath BS30 5RL

www.selfpublishingpartnership.co.uk

ISBN printed book: 978-1-83952-418-9

Cover design by Kevin Rylands
Internal design by Andrew Easton

Printed and bound in the UK

This book is printed on FSC certified paper

A LIFE *Appreciated*

FROM SPAIN TO NORWAY ON A BIKE

TIM RALPH

In memory of my late wife, Rowenna, who left this life too soon and who gave me the desire to live every day to the full.

To my wife, Anne, who showed me again the joy of life, friendship, and happiness. And my daughters, Sarah, and Helen, who ensure my feet remain firmly planted in reality.

Contents

The Route from Spain 2 Norway

FOREWORD
By
Robert Mads Anderson

When Tim and I stood atop Everest together, the sun was blazing, the wind was little more than a breeze, it was rather early in the morning. It was an ideal time, as first ascensionist Sir Edmund Hillary said, to 'look beyond' to other great adventures.

Tim had also just completed his Seven Summits, that rather magical ascent to the top of the world on each of the seven continents. He very much has a passion for grand adventures.

In this book, he has stepped out of his crampons and into his bicycle cleats, bringing his tale of riding the length of Europe to life. And what a tale it is.

In *A Life Appreciated*, Tim undertakes one of the most fascinating journeys on our planet, though the history, cultures, geography and people of Europe. He rides a rather astounding 7,946 kilometres, from the southern tip of Spain all the way to the remote and wild northern tip of Norway. To add just a bit to the challenge, he throws in a few extra mountain roads and passes, collecting a host of added metres, adding up to over 10 ascents of Mount Everest.

When you start your journey with the Spanish Iberian Eagle overhead and finish riding amongst reindeer, you know you have been on an incredible bicycle ride. Riding alone, Tim inevitably opens himself up to both meeting others and learning more about himself, from drafting behind racers who wonder why he is still close behind them (needless to say, Tim is rather fit and fast, even on a touring bike), to dawn rides through landscapes that simply make one very happy to be alive.

The experiences from the road: from wild camping to the breadth of people he meets, has created within these pages a cultural tour de force of Europe. Accompanied by a host of photographs, we are led through a cornucopia of European highlights, yet viewed with an eye to endless delights that have just been stumbled upon around the corner – a great way to travel and discover the world.

While the physical accomplishments of the ride alone are immense, it is in capturing the small moments that this story really envelopes us in the journey. From a steaming coffee in the morning amidst a field, to a quiet lunch in a local café, to tucking the tent in behind a hedgerow for the night, we are brought into the moments that encapsulate Europe, from the inside looking out.

Travelling by bicycle also almost subconsciously awakens all the senses. Vistas open up, birds sing, streams flow past and the welcoming smell of a good café arrives before you even see it. Europe has always been about awakening all the senses and what better way than on a bike, experienced vicariously through turning the pages of this book.

We experience the crisp mountain air of an alpine pass and the rocketing descents back to the valleys below. In Norway, Tim descends under the earth, in the multitude of dark, wet and troll-inhabited tunnels of northern Norway, before finally pedalling out on the final kilometres to Nordkapp.

This book inspires us to look beyond and set off on our own adventures. And, while few of us will ever ride the length of Europe, in these pages we can savour and experience the true adventure first hand.

Robert Mads Anderson
Author of Nine Lives – Expeditions to Everest
www.explore7summits.com

INTRODUCTION

Sir Edmund Hillary said, "It is not the mountain that we conquer, but ourselves." Our battle as perceived by others is a physical one, but for those of us who do these things, the psychology is as important, borne in part from preconceived concepts arrived at via readings of recollections of the forefathers of adventure. Accounts of expeditions that were achieved without incident, mishap or disaster are less known than those that either achieved notable success or befell disaster. We have only to think of the English climber Joe Simpson and his incredible story of misfortune and good luck in his book called *Touching the Void*, or the story of Tom Simpson, Britain's first superstar cyclist who tragically died while cycling up Mont Ventoux in France on July 13th, 1967. Without William Fotheringham's book, *Put Me Back On My Bike*, (which Simpson never actually said), few outside the cycling fraternity would know the story.

Those of us who are addicted to adventure draw much from the experiences of others, but as a mountain never presents itself as the same beast from one season to another, likewise no cycle road trip is like another. We gain much from research and would be wise to plan for the unexpected. There is no true map of what lays ahead of us. I have climbed Everest without incident but have nearly died on a seemingly less arduous mountain. I cycled up two of the three routes on Mont Ventoux in a day without incident, but unbeknown to me at the time, nearly lost the sight in my left eye whilst cycling across America. Life is a lottery.

WHY DO I CYCLE?

I am motivated to stay fit and healthy because quite frankly – I want to prolong my life. Cycling for me has proven to be the best sport to achieve and maintain good levels of fitness. In the past there has been athletics, badminton, squash, rugby, kayaking, long distance hiking and climbing, all enjoyed to the point of obsession, but none so beneficial as cycling.

I rarely relish the thought of going for a ride. Perhaps because I know my mind will challenge my body to a duel. Rides for me are more enjoyable having punished my body and achieved good results, an objective that is becoming less achievable as the years pass. I loathe the idea of performance drop-off, even if there is a valid reason, such as the inescapable ageing process.

There is also another type of enjoyment, knowing that however many hills are climbed, and distances covered it is all down to personal effort, both physical and mental.

More obvious pleasures from cycling are the feeling of freedom and self-reliance, a strong part also being the immense adrenaline rush of pushing the limits on long ascents and fast descents, knowing that a small error will have consequences, and that feeling of contentment through exhaustion achieved when arriving at the summit of a long, hard climb.

Cycle touring is different. The emphasis is not on performance. Primarily for me it is the freedom it offers. Being able to travel at a chosen pace, in chosen locations is a privilege. I have cycled in so many different countries, in idyllic weather and dangerous weather, seen incredible sights and met incredible people, seen so many cultures and slept in many different and unusual places.

What motivates me? A desire to live and seek out the new, to meet different people and see different cultures within their own countries.

This is why I ride a bike.

"It is the unknown around the corner that turns my wheels." Heinz Stucke

DON'T SUBSTITUE MEMORIES FOR DREAMS
Alastair Humphreys from his book, 'Moods of Future Joys', "One of the appeals of bike travel is that you arrive slowly.... By bike you experience the proximity or distance between different people and places that forms some of the ways they interact, or do not interact, and consequently how the very history of our planet has unfurled."

As we travel through life the attraction to reflect increases, restrict this to moderation and continue to realise your dreams. If I were to live for a hundred years, I would still not have fulfilled all my desires, but would depart this life with reflective contentment, gratitude, and satisfaction. This was my positive thought as I descended into Gibraltar airport.

Descent into Gibraltar.

CHAPTER ONE
Out of the Starting Blocks

**"There are no foreign lands. It is the traveller only who is foreign."
Robert Louis Stevenson.**

With the tyres submerged beneath the blown sand, I pushed the laden bike towards the start of my adventure. The sand stung as it blasted against exposed skin of arms and legs. A film of salty seawater had provided bonding for the sand to form a thin layer of armour that covered anything in its path. The wind was strong with gusts powerful enough to unbalance me. With the sand airborne it was painful to turn the head in any direction other than downwind. Soaring high above were several windsurfers, their feet strapped to the board beneath them. Others skimmed the waves using them to launch their sails rapidly upwards. This initiation had not been planned nor anticipated. Even before mounting my bike for the epic journey north, I was experiencing one of many uncomfortable moments that would present themselves in the weeks to come.

I was in Tarifa, the most southerly town in Spain, in fact in Europe, and was about to embark on an 8,000-kilometre unsupported cycle ride to Nordkapp in Norway, the most northerly point in Europe. Previously I had cycled several long-distance routes, most notably across America with a good friend. That 4,000-mile trip had been completed in forty days on road bikes with credit cards and little else. That had been a lightweight and speedy trip. This one was to be a solo effort, involving as much wild camping as possible; self-sufficiency was the objective. It is a blessing that we do not possess the ability to see into the future.

To address the 'Why do this?' question and not to have to re-visit it would make me a happy cyclist. A response would either attract a short, probably wholly inadequate answer or one that was boringly complex. Perhaps as you turn the pages you may understand the attractions of such an adventure, or (and I am sure there are many of you), who will have your belief in the lunacy of the project confirmed. *"But something must have drawn you to do this ride,"* I hear you say. Having travelled and climbed around the world, I was shocked to find out one day how ignorant I was of countries nearer to my home in the UK. At about the same time as this revelation, my wife bought me a ticket to go and see a presentation given by a far more experienced cycle trekking addict called Andrew Sykes. A brief chat with him after his excellent talk confirmed that an embryo of an idea had been planted squarely in my frontal lobe. Whereas Andrew had cycled in many parts of Europe, his speciality was touring, whilst I preferred the speed of road bikes. However, the duration of this trip was going to be longer than the Seattle to Boston cycle, the aim being to embrace both the culture of different countries and as many classic cycle climbs on the route. The credit card would take a serious hammering if the American approach were to be adopted. So, the decision was made to ride an old hybrid cycle I had used for a Lands End to John O'Groats ride eight years previously.

The Trek 7700 cycle was stripped down to its nakedness, looking forlorn and covered in sea salt and sand, and positioned between two overfull waste wheelie bins to the side of a petrol filling station in Tarifa. I had retreated from the sandblasting experience back into the streets of Tarifa and was musing on how quickly a pristine and perfectly prepared outfit could be trashed by the weather. If the sand and salt were not removed, rust and mechanical problems would soon develop. The middle-aged, seriously under-tanned, lycra-clad old git, who could only just explain his actions to passers-by via the use of limited Spanish, caused some amusement. How different it had been on landing in Gibraltar a few hours earlier. With the bike boxed and the charity I was supporting, YORKSHIRE CANCER RESEARCH, clearly labelled, positive comments had been heard; now comments had a mixture of sympathy and bewilderment.

Having chosen not to cycle the notoriously dangerous A7 from Taraguilla to Tarifa, I had dragged the bike box from the airport to the bus station, some 700m (only boxed cycles are permitted on the buses) and having arrived in Tarifa, assembled the bike, and loaded it, then cycled through the sun-drenched, windswept town to the Calle Segismundo Moret, a short narrow peninsula that leads to the Isla de Las Palomas. The southernmost point of this off-limits island is the absolute southern point of Europe and the point at which Andrew Sykes started his journey after painstaking efforts in securing permission to access the island. I admired his tenacity, but it was not for me. So, my journey commenced on the north side of the locked gates to the island. The bike was now again pristine, or so I thought. During the next 8,000 km sand from the Mediterranean would continue to emerge from parts of the bike and its accessories. The initial kilometre of my 8,000 had been a 'baptism of fire', or should I say, of wind, sand, and saltwater. Every journey starts with the first step, or in this case, the turn of the pedal. I was on my way north and would be cycling through ten countries and climbing over 95,000 metres.

With the bike cleaned, I finally hit the road. Unabated wind speeds that would have needed considerable care when coming from the side, and brute strength when head on, were now pushing me along at 40 km/h. In the pleasant afternoon sun and with few vehicles on the road, finally the feeling of having started this adventure sunk in. I kept to the N340, passing the turnoff to Bolonia, and heading northwest with a broad smile on my face and a following wind. Turning southwest to hit the coast at Zahara de los Atunes, now the side winds threatened to part me from the bike, failing that it would have me pushed into the path of a rare passing vehicle. Zahara was a typical beautiful small Spanish seaside town with pristine white-painted homes and a similarly white-painted church with a small turret supporting a single bell that was silhouetted by the setting sun over the Atlantic Ocean. This was going to be a great trip. After the even smaller town of Barbate, I started to look for a place to sleep alongside the A313. A lean-to structure attached to a disused restaurant overlooking what was once a pleasant garden provided my first lodgings in Spain. No need for a tent, just a bedroll, and a sleeping bag. Normally my first night under the stars or in a tent is a restless affair. Not so this evening, even the occasional vehicle passing metres away could not disturb this contented cyclist.

The following morning, having crossed the N340 at Vejer de la Frontera, I bought a breakfast of baguette de jamon and, with an injection of strong caffeine, continued north on the peaceful A396. The city of Seville was to be my first objective, but for now, I was enjoying the peace and tranquillity of the 'less trodden' roads of southern Spain.

The peaceful country roads some 50 km east of the motorway that connects Cadiz with Seville allowed my mind to wander and relax. The warm weather, cloudless skies, and undulating countryside were welcoming. My second night was spent under a hedge elevated on the side of a hill east of the tiny town of Espera.

Daily Blog: *As ready as I will ever be. April 1st*

So, the bike has been serviced and the ageing old git who is to ride it has also had the necessary checks, including facet joint injections for spondylolisthesis and degenerative lumbar spinal stenosis. As Piers, my consultant expertly inserted the injections, my mind was thinking of the pain relief this procedure has given previously, the thought detracted slightly from the discomfort. The following day's dose of 'discomfort' was provided via an emergency extraction of a tooth by my new and very competent dentist. I am reminded of the Monty Python's 'Black Knight' sketch: 'It's only a flesh wound.' Pain is what it is – think of the Cycling Rules – Rule Number FIVE needs to prevail.

I am as ready as I will ever be. Training has not gone to plan, The Beast from the East and all that, storms, and high winds, but this trip does not demand immediate ultra-fitness. With 8,000 km and around 95,000 m of elevation, initial levels of fitness are not so important.

I took the bike and full rig for a short ride the other day. Cragg Vale (the longest continuous climb in England that is on my doorstep) has never been climbed as slowly. However, the bike was balanced and following a little fine-tuning by Dave Kaye of Cycle Fast in Halifax, is now spot on. The rig weighs around 30 kgs, which includes the trek bike, tent, sleeping bag, and other absolute essentials.

With more snow forecast for Easter weekend, it may be interesting getting to Manchester airport on Easter Sunday.

Daily Blog: *Out of the starting blocks – slowly. April 2nd*

Sitting in a restaurant in Arcos de la Frontera eating the first of many chicken salads. This one sets the bar high for all others that will surely follow in the weeks to come. Memories of Andy's and my daily fix of salad whilst travelling across America cross my mind.

The flight path into Gibraltar went around the Rock, which was topped with a broad-brimmed hat of cloud that caused some turbulence just before landing. An opportunity for a few atmospheric photos was not missed. With a laid-back stroll through customs pushing the 33 kg bike box on a trolley, nothing could be easier. This was a short-lived pleasure, as I was told trollies could not be taken across to border control. Carrying both a pannier and the bike box was beyond me. How long can a cardboard box be dragged along a pavement before it wears through? The bus station is about 700 m from the border control – it made it, but my arms are a little longer now. I was pleased to catch the 11.30 am bus to Tarifa, the next being 3 pm. This was the last set time that needed to be met until I meet up with Anne, my wife, in Lourdes at the end of the month. Whilst waiting for the bus to depart, a young guy started chatting with me. Dan Acomb, a medical student from Bristol University, was taking time out for some climbing. He was catching the ferry from Tarifa and heading to Morocco, then down to Toubkal, a mountain I had taken Helen, my youngest daughter to several years ago. Wish you well, Dan, good to meet you.

In Tarifa I took a leisurely hour building the bike and, having attracted a few strange looks from two couples when emerging from the toilet, who had seen me enter in normal clothes and who displayed obvious surprise at seeing the morphed lycra-clad replacement, I 'mounted up' and rode off into the sunset. Well, into town and to the start point.

The adventure starts.
Sandblasted and covered in salt.

Now, Easter Sunday in Tarifa was a little windy! There is a causeway that leads out to the Isla de Las Palomas. On the right of this causeway, windsurfers were launching themselves 15 m into the air, quite a sight! On the left side, the sand was being blown across the causeway, only to be replaced further out by random sea spray. Should I abandon the idea and just cycle from the town? I didn't! The sand was painful on the legs, arms, and face. Pushing the loaded bike took considerable effort, cycling was certainly not possible. We can dodge the waves, oh! no, we could not. Both the bike and rider were drenched but we did start at the beginning, although unlike Andrew Sykes, I did not get permission to enter Las Palomas and unlike him, my bike was both sand plastered and washed with saltwater. The bike was unloaded and thoroughly washed at the first fuel station on the outskirts of Tarifa.

Finally, I cycled away from Tarifa. The wind alternated. From behind it gave me an easy 40 km/h, heaven. From the right side, it tried its hardest to push me into overtaking traffic, hell!

Not since Luke and I cycled Land's End to John O'Groats, another south to north ride, have I ridden such a loaded cycle and the crosswind was challenging. After a couple of hours, I turned off the N340 and headed to the upmarket coastal town of Zahara de los Atunes and then on to the not so 'upmarket' town of Barbate, where a fantastic Easter procession was parading through the town. Barbate's claim to fame was being the holiday destination of General Franco. Having eaten here, I was now on the lookout for a place to 'wild camp'. A most unlikely location presented itself in the form of a disused country pub and dance floor. Having a massively deep external lean-to roof and terracotta tiled floor, no tent was needed.

I had placed my bedroll at 90 degrees to the wall, so my makeshift pillow would not 'walk' during the night. A good idea at the time. Now, nocturnal creatures like the security of edges and corners. So, a mouse running the wall edge did not hesitate to scramble over me, much to both our surprises. It is amazing how large and terrifying a mouse can be when it wakes you at two in the morning! and equally disturbing when it repeats the exercise an hour later.

The first of many nights.

The route for the second day took a steady upward elevation to Medina Sidonia and onto Arcos de la Frontera, both classic Spanish hilltop towns of notable beauty. The countryside was of rolling hills, ever gaining in height with far-reaching views. Not long before the day was done, I came across a shepherd tending his flock of a hundred or so goats. He was very animated, but my Spanish being two points off pathetic, I could only guess at what he said.

A friendly goat herder.

The final push up to Malduenda El Algarrobillo was weirdly into the wind. My second campsite required a tent. Pitched and tucked into a deep hedge with numerous rabbits as company, I could feel their eyes on me, I had a special view south west across to Gibalbin. I did have a human visitor during the night, but he chose not to disturb me, leaving only his size ten boot prints in the soil outside the tent.

And the second night.

Spain is waiting.

It had rained during the night, also little had dried from the previous day, but the initial dampness of my cycling gear soon warmed with body heat. Heading down to Las Cabezas de San Juan, my phone rang! 'This is the telephone engineer, are you at home?' 'Well, no, I am on a bike somewhere in Spain, but my wife is. Here is her number and give her my love.'

I should have put wet weather gear on, I was going to get soaked and remain wet for the rest of the day. As it happened after breakfast in Las Cabezas, the weather improved and remained sunny and windy all day, drying all the gear.

Today was a short day and I could easily have made Seville. I am ahead of my schedule, still having spent plenty of time sightseeing in Las Cabezas and Utrera. I am camping next to a canal with a railway line and a motorway that runs into Seville. It is a sunny spot and only three people have passed in the last three hours. Two ancient Land Rovers with about ten greyhounds being towed in their wake attached by leads was an unusual sight. They looked as though they were enjoying their evening walk.

FACT FACTORY: Francisco Franco (1892-1975) ruled Spain as a dictator from 1939 until his death. He frequently spent holidays in Barbate, which like so many other towns, has disassociated itself from his memory by renaming many of its streets and buildings. Franco shared similarities with Hitler, one of them being each only had one testicle. He also put Spanish clocks back one hour to correspond with his Nazi allies. To this day Spain remains under Central European Time and not GMT.

'How easy it is to make friends in Spain.' George Orwell

I had arrived at my campsite just outside Seville having cycled through a housing estate. Knowing that I could not continue riding towards the city without further reducing the chances of finding a place to pitch my tent, I aimlessly meandered around, hoping for a suitable spot. Leaving the busy main road had been a good idea but negotiating the deep rainwater gullies that edge the road at slow speed had not been wise and, not for the first time, resulted in me falling off and removing previous scar tissue from my left knee. With dried blood down my leg, I pitched the tent in a small field of barley, next to a canal, and having washed the blood from my leg and reminded myself that vigilance and concentration would help in avoiding me becoming a Spanish road death statistic, I enjoyed a relaxed evening.

The following morning, I arrived early in Seville. The roads were busy but not manic, allowing me to absorb the sights. The Plaza de Americas followed by the Plaza de España cannot fail to impress. I walked around the Plaza de España not quite knowing where to look first. Surprisingly, it is not as old as I thought it to be. Completed for the World Fair in 1929 as the centrepiece, this semi-circular architectural masterpiece blows the mind with its magnificence that seems to wrap itself around you. There are bridges that cross a moat, each bridge representing the four ancient Spanish kingdoms of Aragon, Castile, León, and Navarre. With a tower at either end, the style is a combination of Moorish and Renaissance, with red brick and azulejos brightly coloured ceramic tiles. There are 48 alcoves each with benches that are individually dedicated to a province in Spain. Decorated ceramic tiles detail the name, coat of arms, a map, and some history of each province. This is an impressive building that invites the visitor, whether from Spain or further afield, to just stare with dropped jaw.

My senses were treated to another pleasure as Peruvian pipe music could be heard coming across the plaza. I make no secret of my love for the South American seaboard countries of Peru and Cusco, Bolivia and Copacabana on Lake Titicaca, Ecuador, and Quito and Chile with the beautiful Torres del Paine and the 'frontier' city of Punta Arenas. I have climbed many times there and the sound of Peruvian pipes to me are like bagpipes to a Scotsman. I listened to the music played by a gentleman dressed in his national costume and, knowing that the Plaza de España faced towards the new world that the early Spanish had set out to colonise, my mind conjured thoughts of again climbing volcanoes. Colonisation was frequently brutal, intentional killings and death from diseases brought from Europe. By the mid-1500s, under the crown of Castile and executed by the conquistadors the Americas were absorbed into the Spanish empire, that is all except Brazil that was British America. Today the influence of the Spanish in these countries remains profound and deeply embedded. Happily, many of the ancient cultures were not totally lost. South America historically has been the home to many ancient cultures, from the Caral Supe from 3,000 to 2,500 BC, the Nasca from 1 to 700 AD, and of course the Inca from 1250 to 1532 AD (their demise was about the same time as the conquistadors arrived in Chile).

After visiting several other places, I hunted out my bed for the night. I had booked two nights in a pension, to enjoy a further full day in this special city. Unfortunately, this was not to happen. Two nights became one and spent in the company of young ladies who produced a cacophony of noise. This sounds exciting, it was not.

Daily Blog: A shower and a shave today. April 3rd

I have arrived in the vicinity of Seville too soon, not that time matters when your only concern is where the next meal is coming from, and can a safe place be found to pitch a tent and secure an undisturbed night's sleep.

Last night's meal was from a shop. Bread rolls, cheese, yogurt, and a litre of good beer, it had not been a hard day in the saddle. The 'campsite' took some finding. Urbanisation had reduced the opportunities of finding a suitable place. I cycled through a less than impressive housing area and down to a canal, both a railway line and the AP 4E5 motorway were only 500 m away, this was not promising. I ate my evening meal and drank the beer, no one walked the canal path for several hours, and having pitched the tent on barren land amongst a cereal crop, was not disturbed all night and thankfully the traffic reduced, and the trains stopped. My only visitors were two vehicles each with a horizontal bar mounted behind them, which in turn had about ten leads attached each to a Greyhound being exercised. The drivers of each waved and shouted greetings. An excellent night's sleep was had.

The morning arrived with a heavy dew, and much was stowed wet in various locations within the cycle panniers. My packing is meticulous and although still being perfected, most items are being placed in the same location each morning.

The ride into Seville required some concentration; unlike a near miss I had had yesterday, all drivers were considerate.

A Life Appreciated

My first jaw-dropping moment was a view of Plaza de Americas, followed by the Plaza de España, where a Peruvian piper was playing his pipes and some 50 horses pulled their carriages for tourists.

Plaza de Americas.

Plaza de España.

Plaza de España.

There was no rush to find my lodgings for the night; just as well as it was hidden in the depths of the old town. The next few hours were spent indulging in viewing beautiful architecture, Torre del Oro and the Catedral and Jewish Quarter, to name two.

Finally locating my pension for the next two nights and having hauled my bike up the internal stairs, I was informed that cycles were not permitted on the premises. The proprietor found me alternative accommodation and eventually I located it, but just for one night; there was no room at the inn for the second night. This afternoon I have spent six hours sightseeing in beautiful Seville. Tomorrow I will be heading north to Monesterio. The weather is set to be hot.

I probably have not done justice to Seville. It is an amazing city, vibrant, fashionable, multi-cultural, obviously proud of its status, and surprisingly clean. Yes, there are street beggars, but even they seem happy and certainly from what I saw were gracious for the regular coins given them.

FACT FACTORY: Seville, as an Arabian-esque city of beauty, has been the location of several classic films, the 1962 film *Lawrence of Arabia* with Peter O'Toole and Omar Sharif and as the Kingdom of Dorne in *Game of Thrones*. More recently the Plaza de España featured in the film *Star Wars Episode 11: Attack of the Clones*.

The impressive Seville Cathedral is one of the largest in the world. After

his death in 1506 Columbus was buried first in Valladolid, Spain, then taken to Monasterio La Cartuja in Seville. The remains were again moved to what is now the Dominican Republic before Spain lost control, when they were moved to Havana, Cuba, before returning to rest in Seville after Cuban independence in 1898. Even after death, Columbus managed to travel more than most during their living lives.

Daily Blog: Escape from Seville. April 4th

Not that anyone would want to escape from this wonderful city. However, my accommodation had failed to say that they did not take cycles, although the proprietor did find me alternative lodgings for one night, a shared dorm with six girls. For a younger man, this would have been manna from Heaven. One snored, two arrived back after a night on the town at 1.30 am, one had a nightmare and one, (and I will not give her bunk location) was capable of a fart to be proud of.

The fifth day of this epic journey started with negotiating the city's one-way streets that never go in the desired direction. Having crossed one river, I found myself on what seemed to be a motorway, but cyclists are permitted, perhaps as entertainment for other vehicle users. (Ten points for removing the cyclist from his bike without killing him). The second river was bridged using a footpath beside the now fenced off motorway. This footpath – having crossed the river – just stopped, disappeared! Hauling the bike over the chain-link fence and joining the traffic, which would have taken me to the N630, was not possible. The path just entered a field and went nowhere. Seeing a dirt track that ran beside the river bridge, I carried the bike over rough ground to it. This bike does not get lighter! Cycling under the bridge I had just used to cross the same river, I continued along the dirt track, it passed a derelict building surrounded with debris and rubbish. A lady was sweeping a small patch of a football pitch-sized area, strange. Cycling through a massive flood tunnel I was surprised to see a near-perfect nonslip green-coloured cycle path. This ran for about 3 km before bringing me back on a major dual carriageway with multiple intersections. Then equally as quickly I was on the N630. This road was to be my route for many kilometres. From this point the day improved, the frustration of the morning soon evaporated. Now on the N630 cycling heaven had been entered.

With the adjacent toll-free A66-E803 dual carriageway running parallel about a kilometre away, which took most of the traffic, the N630 had only the occasional vehicle. It also had an excellent surface.

Once on the N630, I have never seen so many cyclists. Pelotons of five to twenty, triples, doubles, and solo riders, all on road bikes. Cycle snobbery was very apparent. Riding a road bike, as I normally do, nearly always attracts an acknowledgement from other road cyclists, but if you are riding a hybrid or touring bike, these thoroughbred roadies rarely acknowledge your existence. I took pleasure in emphasising the 'HOLA' and other Spanish greetings. Perhaps I am being unfair because at least twenty of the hundred plus did acknowledge my existence. As I cycled further north away from Seville, the cyclists became fewer until there were none. There are those who enjoy the fast but short-lived rides and those who ride for longer with stamina. The joke about the young bull's comments to the old bull regarding the heifers comes to mind.

The initial side and headwinds dropped, and the temperature rose to nearly 28 degrees. The sun shone and the world was good. The theme of the day was elevation gain, which was achieved by numerous undulating hills. Long steady climbs of around 6 to 8%, with shorter descents, an elevation of 750 m was obtained. With far-reaching views over thousands of hectares of ancient olive trees, the cycling was a delight. Alpine pastures with numerous flowers providing a kaleidoscope of colour. In other fields beneath the olive trees, well-fed suckler herds of cattle grazed with their calves, with neck bells ringing. Later the unmistakable odour of pigs, large black Iberian sows, and boars so famed in this area. I cycled over a Roman bridge, now with a not-so-Roman road surface of tarmac.

That night I found a wild camping spot, beside the N630, South of Monesterio. A solitary vehicle would pass every few hours, but I was out of sight under an old oak tree listening to the crickets in the trees and two horses shaking their heads to rid themselves of flies.

Even my first puncture of the trip, which happened as I cycled around Monesterio looking for a supermercado, did not dent my mood and yes, it was the rear wheel that necessitated unloading the bike. As so often is the cause, it was one of those multiple thorns that have spikes protruding in all directions.

My lasting memory of this day will always be coming across a son, Rodriguez, who was pushing his wheelchair-bound father on the hard shoulder of the road up one of the numerous long inclines. My Spanish is limited, but I understood that it was the wish of his father to make a pilgrimage along the Camino de Santiago. They were not the only two I saw that day, there were two other solitary hikers. What utter commitment and what love this father and son must have for each other, astounding.

Daily Blog: *A truly rural night's sleep. April 5th*

Dusk was short and soon after in the dark the crickets fell silent, as did the bells around the necks of nearby sheep and cattle. Presumably, they too had decided to sleep. Apart from the low droning of dwindling traffic on the A66, I looked forward to an undisturbed sleep. I awoke around 2 am to the quiet breathing of two large animals very nearby. If they were cows, there would have been more and all jostling for a closer inquisitive look at my tent. Then both took off at a canter, horses, and agile ones at that. Within minutes they cantered back, snorting with curiosity. I opened the tent to look up at two large horses. The moonlight shone on a beautiful dapple grey and a chestnut. Only a tumbling limestone wall and a thread of wire separated us. Packing the tent away in the morning there was half-chewed grass that had been snorted on the tent.

The night the horses visited.

After breakfast, with last night's puncture repaired and the weather perfect, I set off for a fast ride to Mérida.

I was now truly in Iberian pig country. First established when oak trees adorned the rolling hillsides, but not a single tree or acorn in sight now. The free-range piggery and the associated odours gave way to fields of small olive trees and acres of young vines growing in red soil. Still at about 700 m above sea level (ASL), this was ideal wine grape country.

There was an unusual amount of horse evidence on the road. Later the sound of singing, beautiful singing, travelling across the meadows, the voices of three or four singers in harmony. Soon I passed three 'traveller' caravans, although they were more like carts, with about twelve people, all happy, some still singing. Some shouted a greeting as I cycled past.

Happy travellers.

Just beyond them at the top of a hill, there were two cyclists. They were on a tandem, dressed for arctic conditions and I am sure I saw the hot and cold taps attached to the kitchen sink that was protruding from the third pannier on the left of the bike.

They both waved with tired resolve as I passed. Some choose to travel heavily. Perhaps taking everything you might just need on a long bike ride is not such a good idea.

The Spanish continue to like their bullfighting, although largely now banned. Bullfighting rings are places of homage and today I saw two. The first in Almendralejo, where I also had the second-best chicken salad to date, and then the very impressive bull ring in Mérida, where I met a German cyclist heading to Madrid. His hometown is Hamburg, but he will be off cycling the French Atlantic coast when I arrive in Hamburg to meet up with my wife weeks ahead of now.

Almendralejo bull ring.

Mérida bull ring.

I was pleased with my cycling today, 110 km with an average speed of 27 km/h. The weather again was near perfect. However, as I write this in the dark of my tent the rain is lashing down. The first properly wet night of the trip.

To finish on an upbeat note. Mérida has a wealth of Roman ruins and was the ancient capital of the province of Lusitania.

The impressive Roman aqueduct at Mérida.

The remains of the portico.

I am coming to the conclusion that posting regular blogs isn't achievable. Although I am writing them most nights, whilst I am wild camping they cannot be posted and although lazing around in a cafe, hooked into their Wi-Fi during the day, is an admirable pastime, it does not eat up the miles. So, it is likely that several blogs will get posted together when an opportunity arises.

FACT FACTORY: The most important Roman site in Spain, Mérida, originally called Emerita, in Extremadura, was awarded UNESCO World Heritage Status in 1993 owing to its outstanding Roman archaeological ensemble. Although inhabited since prehistoric times, the Romans founded the city of Emerita Augusta back in 25BC and it went on to be one of the most important cities of the Roman Empire.

CHAPTER TWO

Snow is Falling in Béjar

'A bicycle is a curious vehicle. Its passenger is its engine.' John Howard

My onward journey ever in a northerly direction until I reached La Vega (Riosa) south of Oviedo, some 550 km 'up the road', continued on the N630. My first classic cycle climb awaited me. Alto del Angliru is a 1,573 m climb that solicited the comment from Marzio Bruseghin, the Italian professional cyclist, *'What is the point of cycling up a mountain that it'd be quicker to go up by foot?'* As with all cycling classic mountain climbs, this one is steeped in history. In particular, the horrendous Cueña les Cabres at a gradient of 17.5% nearing the end of the climb, both attracts disgust and gladiatorial response. It does not do well for the brain to dwell too soon on matters that will present themselves further up the road. Enjoy the present and indulge the senses. Besides, Alto del Angliru was only the first of at least fourteen lung bursting classic climbs that lay ahead. But for now, the terrain was flat, with only vultures soaring above my head.

Cycling to the vanishing point.

Vultures circle above me.

Still on the flatlands west of and parallel to Madrid, there were the towns of Caceres, Salamanca, Zamora, and Benavente to see. Caceres is another of Spain's World Heritage Sites. One of fifteen such cities in the country. Caceres certainly merits this coveted status with its historic mixture of cultures from the Bronze Age, through the Roman, Goth, and Arabian eras. In the 13th century, the city changed hands between the Arabs and Spanish on several occasions, with the sword, rather than negotiated diplomacy being the modus operandi. Not surprisingly, it is an immensely fortified town, having a wall over a kilometre long that surrounds the old town. Caceres has always been on an important trade route and hence a political centre. Today the mellow stone buildings with pantile roofs, flint cobbled streets, and walkways provide a calmness, enhanced further by no modern-day traffic in the centre. This cyclist wandered around absorbing the sights and the obvious history that exuded.

Today was to be a long and varied one and one that would see the spectrum of moods capable of being expressed by a long-distance cyclist. From the pleasures of seeing beautiful countryside and historic buildings bathed in warm sunlight to the resigned fate of knowing you were to be drenched to the skin. The blog describes this in detail. Passing the town of Plasencia and onto Bejar, where I succumbed to having four walls and a roof over my head. That roof, together with others, would be covered with snow in the morning.

Masochism is a certain type of enjoyment derived from personal pain. If I did (although I have never) derive such pleasure, today would have been the day I gave it up. When you are climbing, whether in the Scottish winter, waist deep in wet snow or high on a Himalayan peak or in Antarctica with temperatures seriously below zero, it is more comfortable than first being soaked through, then snowed on and placed in a wind tunnel that is your descent off a snow-covered road, whilst straddling a bike with a puncture you cannot fix because although you can see your fingers, you cannot feel them. '*Am I applying the brakes or am I not?*' My feet, unclipped, plough through the snow inches from the road surface beneath, trying to keep the bike upright as it skids from left to right. I escaped the direct fall of the snow by 'sheltering' in a tunnel that takes the main road above, but the wind remained lazy, choosing to drive through me, rather than around. I arrive in Salamanca. My enthusiasm has been deflated. I know this is another wonderful Spanish city. I am cold to the core. I am in perfunctory mode. Annoyed with myself, I try and draw on positives. Salamanca is another World Heritage city. It has the oldest university in Spain, wonderful buildings, and a mosaic of history. I arrived in the Plaza Mayor de Salamanca, a massive, empty, rain-soaked but still impressive square. I needed warmth. The pleasant weather of the morning had changed to heavy rain, to snow then hailstones back to rain. I was shivering involuntarily as two police officers walked past me with more than a curious look. People were sheltering under the cover ways that side the plaza. This was a tourist mecca and consequently a mecca for thieves. If I left my bike outside the ever-beckoning bakery to get those needed calories on board, would the bike be there on my return? I watched my still numb fingers receive orders from my befuddled brain and on the third attempt successfully locked the bike to a drainpipe that was so choked with rain, water ran down the outside of it. I returned with expensive food that I ate for energy, not taste. I find it hard to remember where I slept that night.

Daily Blog: *Cycling on the Sabbath. April 6th*

My church this morning was a beautiful, isolated spot beside the N630. Twisted windblown trees growing from limestone outcrops. Hidden from the rarely used road, I was about 15 km north of Caceres. The scene was perfected by an abandoned ancient horse-drawn cart on the skyline.

The art of staying near your route without being observed is an acquired one.

Before moving on, Caceres is worthy of a note. As with several towns I have entered, the initial impressions have not been favourable, 'fly tipping' is an epidemic and there are many abandoned and derelict buildings. However, the town centres are a window into history. Caceres, with its narrow cobbled and flinted streets and multi balconies to the houses on either side, leads you to a medieval world, the Ciudad Monumental, most worthy of the World Heritage Site status it holds.

Packing up in the morning has evolved into a precise affair. The night's downpour has given way to a fresh and cumulus-clouded sky. A cold start, but one of those mornings when you are privileged to be alive. I had intended a longer ride today, to Béjar. It was a day that included a variety of weather, scenery, and modern architecture. The architecture was the unfinished rail bridges of what is sometime in the future going to be the Linea de Alta Velocidad Madrid to Portugal line. A wonderful incomplete high level bridge hangs in the balance overlooking the Embalse de Alcantara, an area that looks similar to the Lake District in the UK. Further on past Plasencia there are smaller structures before an abrupt end to any construction is reached, it is as though the project has been mothballed. Does it remind anyone of the UK's Advanced Passenger Train (APT) that was to run the West Coast? Only our Government continued to spend millions up to its final test runs before abandoning the project, and we wonder where our wealth has gone!

The incomplete Linea de Alta Velocidad Madrid to Portugal line.

Two photos taken in Plasencia.

The scenery of the Sierra de San Bernabe still clad in winter snow was impressive, as was the climb to the summit of Puerto de Vallejera some 1,200 m near the end of the day's ride. Then the heavens opened again, not surprising with a prevailing SW wind and Sierra de Tormantos sitting at 1,800 m.

As I was cycling up one of the numerous bends nearing the top, not so far from Hervas, a cyclist was descending in a very controlled manner. Surprisingly, he was the sole occupant of a tandem cycle. The heavy rain, my shortness of breath, and inability to rapidly find the Spanish for, 'she's fallen off,' or even, 'he's fallen off,' probably would not have been seen as helpful.

A long and varied day was had on this eighth day of my journey. I have wild camped for seven of them. It is not that I do not like being soaked to the skin, cold, hot, and all points in-between. My clothes need washing, as do I. The bike needs some maintenance and so do I. The energy power pack needs charging, I am suffering from withdrawal symptoms with no means of uploading Strava or my blogs and cannot contact several people. I have ridden about 140 km today and climbed about 2,000 m of elevation. So, with a forecast of wet weather tomorrow, it will be a day of domestic chores. Anne has booked me into an excellent hostel, the Hostal Extremeño in Béjar. The rain continues.

Daily Blog: *Snow is falling in Béjar. April 8th and 9th*
Strange waking up in a bed surrounded by four walls and not feeling the cold wet tent rub on your bald patch as you sit up. Oh, and everything is dry. Looking out of

the window over Béjar most sounds are muffled by the snow. Today was a good day to choose to do maintenance chores.

The weather forecast for the next five days is decidedly unfavourable, with precipitation guaranteed together with a high windchill factor. Some character building is needed for speedy descents. Let us hope the snow has been cleared from the roads. This is not what was expected, but to arrive in Norway to see the last of the Midnight sun, an early departure from Tarifa was necessary. I hung on to the memories of warmth and culture of a few days ago.

Alfred, my travelling companion.

Yes, Alfred is with me. This chap has travelled with me to many countries and has cycled many miles and climbed many mountains. He has been to the summit of Everest at 8,848 m above sea level and read a book whilst floating on his back in the Black Sea at 413 m below sea level. He also hitched a ride with Andy Hill and me across America. Made and given to me by my mother shortly before she died, he is a reminder that life can be short and painful and we should live it with endeavour, compassion, and determination, as did my mother.

I have just returned from a tour around Béjar. Certainly not a pretentious town. It has some old architecture, mainly Catholic churches. The old town square is large, bordered by a school with a grand facade, a church opposite, four-storey apartments sit facing each other across a 100 m square. On one side, the iron railed balconies and window shutters are decaying.

Functional Béjar.

The town has two parts, the modern, which is functional and services the needs of visiting skiers, whereas the old part is just that. Four and five-storey buildings, all with large, shuttered windows and balconies. Many are for sale. Large heavy timber entrance doors, more akin to stable doors that have been worn down where hands have opened and closed them over the centuries. With some buildings having collapsed in a terrace, orange sprayed foam has been applied to the gables to prevent further decay. Roofs of others have fallen in, allowing ancient timber beams to slowly rot. There is a frankness about this town that says, 'We live in an old town, not beautiful enough to attract tourists to make sufficient funds to repair derelict buildings, but this is our town, and we are proud of it.'

Don Quixote.

Now Don Quixote la Mancha has been hanging around in various forms in Spain since 1605. His gesture says it all: 'You may not think Béjar is as impressive as Plasencia or Salamanca, but we think it's great.'

It would be remiss of me not to mention the hostel I stayed in. Hospitable, warm, excellent breakfast and an incredible evening meal, with a very generous jug of red wine. The Hostal – Restaurante Extremeño between the old and new town of

Béjar should be your choice if visiting this area, and all for 20 Euros a night.

And an update regarding the snow; it has gone from the town. However, the surrounding hills look decidedly wintery.

FACT FACTORY: *Don Quixote de la Mancha*. This novel is in two parts: the first was written by Miguel de Cervantes in 1605, and the second he added in 1615. These works are considered to be the first modern novel, written first in Spanish, and then translated into English by Thomas Shelton. It is about a middle-aged gentleman from the region of La Mancha in central Spain. Obsessed with the chivalrous ideals touted in books he has read, he decides to take up his lance and sword to defend the helpless and destroy the wicked. After a first failed adventure, he sets out on a second with a somewhat befuddled simple farmer called Sancho Panza, who he persuades to accompany him as his faithful squire. Alonso Quixote does not see the world for what it is, preferring to live the life of the knightly characters in the numerous books that have brainwashed him.

Daily Blog: *I am giving up masochism, the enjoyment is too much! April 10th*
Well, bike and bloke have arrived in Salamanca. It was only a 75 km ride, but one that reminds you that the weather will make all the difference. Now I am sitting drinking a beer and unashamedly tucking into a pizza, looking out at some inspiring architecture, whilst people watching.

Was it only this morning that I left Béjar? As the proprietor shook my hand, saying he thought I was a little crazy, I most definitely was having second thoughts about the sanity of cycling in such a deluge. Uphill through the 'newer' town, uphill to the industrial area, uphill to… well, you get the idea. It was not that steep, just the rain was incredible, and I was getting hot, yes hot. It was to be vastly different later.

I climbed to 1,204 m, or so the large sign on my left informed me. Although still raining at a rate that would have most seeking out Noah and asking for a passage in the Ark, I was, as anyone who has cycled with me will confirm, looking forward to the downhill dash.

My fingers were numb and swimming in water that had collected inside the waterproof over-mitts. My 'will always keep your feet dry' overshoes had not collected a single point for effectiveness. My toes squelched in my shoes.

A little after the summit I pulled over under some fir trees and layered up with two more lightweight jackets. Put my sun! glasses on to stop the 'rain' from stinging my eyes, inadvertently left my lunch for the squirrels and was about to head down at speed when a van, perhaps the only vehicle I had seen for an hour, slowed, the driver opened his window and said something in Spanish, pointing with enthusiasm down the valley. In the time I had stopped, the rain had become snow and was falling heavily. As I started to descend, any speed would not have had a happy ending and I realised the driver had been urging me to get to lower ground as soon as possible.

The snow was 50 mm deep, slushy, and getting deeper by the minute. The first bend, a right-hander, nearly had me off, as the rear wheel skidded out. It was not a great idea to have my shoes cleated into the pedals. Both feet were now skimming the freezing slush. A solitary car came up past me, a 4×4. Although on the wrong side of the road, the tyre tracks provided improved traction for my tyres. Had the weather been different this long downhill multiple bend descent would have had me trying to hit 70 km an hour, instead, 10 was tops. The vehicle tyre tracks went off down a side road, leaving me again to negotiate the virgin snow. By now the whole of the rear gear mechanism on the bike was iced up. There was a thin sheet of ice covering my outer jacket, ice clogged the brakes, and was even clinging to the sides of the wheels. Luke (a friend who first introduced me to 'proper' cycling), will remember well our wet trip to Wales the previous year and the Scottish trip with both him and Andy. This exceeded that discomfort. I had not been as cold on the summit of Everest some 7,000 m higher.

Cold and numb but down from the mountain.

After descending the conditions improved considerably.

I stopped several times to de-ice the 'important bits'. On one of these occasions, I noticed the rear tyre was almost flat. Oh bother, what an irritation, how inconvenient and other expletives spilled from my mouth. My fingers were numb, totally without feeling. There was no way that I had the ability to remove the rear wheel and change the inner tube. Pump it up! and ride – with care. Pumped it up again a few km down the road. Note the word 'down'. The snow stopped snowing and soon the road was dry! I pumped the tyre a further three times before arriving in Salamanca.

The weather improved. The sun came out, for five minutes, then disappeared behind a seriously dark grey brooding mass. Could I reach Salamanca before that cloud ejected its contents?

My bell started to ring. Yes, I have a bell. This bike is not a thoroughbred racer, it is designed for endurance and perhaps if necessary, pavement cycling, particularly in Denmark and Germany, (a bell is always appreciated by pedestrians). What was ringing my bell? Definitely, not Chuck Berry. Hailstones! Causing a near-constant soft ringing. Clattering on my helmet, trying to penetrate my cheeks and the signpost said 5 kms to Salamanca. Game, set and match to the weather today.

Maintenance of bike and body.

A 'four-walled tent' with heating. I will get back to wild camping, but a re-occurrence of pneumonia is not on the list of 'must haves'.

Even when shivering and in dire need of caffeine and a hot shower, Salamanca is a beautiful town. The Plaza Mayor has a slight feel of St Mark's square in Venice. There is a wealth of medieval buildings, too numerous to be mentioned or for me to visit in one late, cold, and wet afternoon. This is a city to be revisited.

Wet, cold, but still a wonderful city. Plaza Mayor del Salamanca.

The plan for tomorrow, 11th April, is to arrive in Zamora. It had been to carry on to Benavente. However, this unseasonably cold and wet weather has impacted the mileage. We will see what the day brings.

FACT FACTORY: The city of Salamanca is situated on the top of a 'mountain' next to the Tormes River. The old city was declared a World Heritage Site in 1988 by UNESCO. The university dates back to 1218 and is the oldest university in Spain and the third oldest in Europe.

Daily Blog: *What a difference a day makes. April 11th*

Pulling the shutters away from the window in my room this morning in Salamanca I did not have high expectations for good weather. My lovely wife has, since the deluge, followed by snow on the Puerto de Vallejera, kindly booked me some accommodation.

The sun welcomed me, but opening the window was a shock. How cold!

Sitting in Lupys restaurant in Benavente this evening, having eaten an unusual salad, that needed additional food to follow, I am happy with today's effort. The first ride from Salamanca to Zamora was 64 km and was followed by a second to Benavente of 70 km. The second ride proved hard, as a strong wind blew in from a NW direction and with panniers, the bike certainly does not 'cut the air'. This reduced my average speed and had me wishing for that hot bath I eventually got here in Benavente. Whilst Anne was on the phone giving me the address of my accommodation, I was looking across the road straight at the hostel. It could have been anywhere in the city. I only had to carry the bike up to the third floor.

The old faithful N630 continues to be my vein through Spain. Today consisted of rolling hills of arable land. Pigs were still very apparent, their odour invasive at times, even when kept in massive indoor buildings. Slaughterhouses abounded. However, strangely there are still the enormous and immensely proud steel black bulls on prominent hill crests. I asked myself, 'Where are the massive and proud boars?' Maybe pigs do not carry quite the same impact or carry the same importance for advertising a brand of brandy.

An Osborne Bull, the origins of this advertisement for a brandy are lost in the mists of time.

For at least 40 km north of Salamanca I continued to see walking pilgrims on the Camino de Santiago, probably around 50 strung out, in ones and twos in various states of fatigue, all wrapped up well against the cold. I admire their tenacity and willpower. This stretch of the route is not inspiring. It was a cold and bright morning, that was to cloud over with threatening dark angry grey clouds.

Another puncture! The hard shoulder consists of sharp gravel clippings – think the idea came from a 'cyclist hater'. The N630 is usually void of traffic and when vehicles do approach, they are excellent in giving a wide berth. Sometimes though it is necessary to travel on the 'bed of nails' that is the hard shoulder when an overtaking vehicle is approaching at the same time another is oncoming. With the last inner tube used, it would have been a hindrance to get another puncture. I did get to Zamora and bought two more tubes. The guy in the shop also kindly lubricated the bike chain after yesterday's ice hammering.

Zamora is no Salamanca but has its own charm. Quieter, with many churches. I had my lunch overlooking the main square. Zamora was also attractive enough *to draw Laurie Lee, the English poet, novelist, and screenwriter, best known for his autobiographical trilogy that included 'Cider with Rosie' in 1959. He then continued to Madrid and then travelled south, just before hell broke loose in Europe in the mid-1930s. Spain also had its horrible Nationalist/ Republican war that put Franco, the Nationalist, in power till his death in 1975.*

Inside the cafe from which I saw an old lady robbed.

It was a shame whilst I was inside the café eating my lunch I could not get to an old lady before she got into a taxi. She had dropped several banknotes on the pavement, which were then swooped up and immediately pocketed by a younger lady even before the taxi door had been closed. I wonder whose needs were the greater!

The landscape was not that appealing today and concerns about a further puncture persisted until the realisation that if it happened it would be no great deal and there is little that can be done to avoid one. I did notice that shards of broken wall tiles had been seemingly thrown at many of the Camino road signs. These slithers would slice through any tyre. You must ask yourself what goes on inside the heads of some people. That said, to date, everyone had been polite and respectful.

My newly acquired pastime whilst eating the miles away is to try and cycle only on the solid white line. I remember Andy Hill saying that given the massive distances covered, any marginal reduction in friction on the tyres by cycling on a smoother surface will benefit on wear and tear. So, for an added incentive, I imagined the white line was hundreds of metres up in the air, suspended, with thin air on either side. Try as I might, I failed to remain just on the line and 'fell to my death' many times.

The weather forecast still looks terrible for the next few days. Hopefully, I will move on to León tomorrow. The first of the cycling classic climbs I intend to do is the Alto del Angliru, scheduled in a few days. Today the whole mountain range was blanketed in snow.

CHAPTER THREE
The Only Way is Up

'It is not the goal but the way there that matters, and the harder the way the more worthwhile the journey.' Wilfred Thesiger

This unseasonal weather could not persist, but it did. Zamora, Benavente, and finally León. Spain was supposed to be warming up for the summer. In England, Anne and others told me they were enjoying mild spring-like weather with the sun shining regularly. I had started this journey on April 1st, All Fools Day, but it had not been a foolish decision, more one dictated by the time needed to arrive in Nordkapp before the last of the midnight sun disappeared for the year. Although cycling in warm weather is preferable, I am not averse to inclement weather providing it is not persistent day after day. The rain, snow, hail, and headwinds were making a few inroads on my positive outlook. This adventure was hatched from a desire for enjoyment, not a desire to catch pneumonia. I had already succumbed to pneumonia following an unplanned overnight stay sitting on a climbing rope with Sean, a regular climbing partner, near the top of the Matterhorn, following un-forecasted high winds that had slowed our traverse from the Italian side over into Switzerland. I had no desire to again succumb to pneumonia.

The following day, April 12th was another cold day. I arrived in León having been chased by a dog that was proud of his teeth and had an intention of using them. My mind had found a good place, with the first thousand kilometres of my journey cycled and my first classic climb approaching; the flatness of today's ride would soon be a distant memory. Caffeine, and plenty of it, drunk behind the glass looking out into the rain that washed the streets of León, had warmed me again. A blanket of contentment and tiredness spreads over me. A tiredness from the energy of trying to keep warm, of cycling fast, keeping the legs pumping, the blood circulating and all the time burning calories.

After my coffees, how many, I cannot recall, I went for a walk around this architecturally blessed city.

León's Cathedral, the Catedral de Santa Maria de Regla de León, was originally built on the site of Roman baths where King Ordoño II's palace had also been. Work started in the 13th century and was completed in the 16th century. It is a stunning example of French Gothic architecture and contains 1,800 m of the world's finest stained glass. It is a hugely impressive structure made more so with large open expanses around it, allowing full admiration.

Although the old convent of San Marcos is now a five-star hotel, the church, originally consecrated in 1541, remains, and there is also an archaeological museum. Built by Fernando the Catholic and gifted to the city, today it is considered to be the best Spanish Renaissance building in the country.

The Plaza Mayor is another treat for the eyes. Surrounded by colonnade arches, this plaza is in the centre of the city. Brightly painted, beautifully designed, it was originally constructed in 1672 and called Plaza Pan to reflect the large number of bakeries on the plaza, now replaced by many cafes.

With thought association running amok, it was time to eat again. A city this size should have many restaurants catering to all tastes. Maybe I was not vigilant enough, but not one of the numerous bars served anything but tapas and as nice as they are, real food was needed. The rain returned. However, my meanderings took me to the Boccalino guesthouse and restaurant, with a menu that would not be out of place in Paris, London, or New York. Overlooking the San Isidoro Square even the weather could not detract from the beauty of the buildings and the statues. On the ubiquitous television that hung on the wall, was a programme about Western Australia, where my youngest daughter and family have accomplished so much since emigrating. The food was exquisite, as was the wine, knowing that as wet as I may get returning to my hostel, I could enjoy another hot shower and a warm bed. For the last few nights, I had retreated into hostels, tonight was a functional, dry, and warm small room in the city centre. I would return to wild camping that I had enjoyed so much when starting this trip, when the weather improved.

Daily Blog: *So flat and so straight. April 12th*
The serenity of the N630 was shattered today. Riding through the outskirts of

Benavente last night, maybe I should not have been surprised. Every available space was occupied by a truck, scores of them, parked on the hard shoulder, side streets, and on the wider pavements.

A flat ride of 75 km did not warrant an early start, but I had not anticipated the 'scenic' route around a massive industrial area before getting on a busy dual carriageway that was the N630 until it branched off. Strava, my cycling phone app, must have shown my efforts to escape like a bunch of knitting. Gone was the largely well-maintained surface, replaced with pitted broken tarmac or concrete. The surface resembled an aged matriarch elephant's skin. Within minutes the trucks started passing. Unusual, maybe a coincidence. The coincidence continued for the next 70 km! Maybe the parallel dual carriageway now required a toll to be paid and they were using the N630 as a 'freebee'. Trucks outnumber all other vehicles. Although making a serious mess of the road, every driver to the very last one, drove cautiously, not passing if there was an oncoming vehicle and always giving maximum clearance when they did.

A familiar odour was apparent for a stretch of the route. These piggies weren't confined in 'sweat barns'. They had smiles on their dirty faces, as they rooted in the mud. They were being managed using a method called The Roadnight system, named after Doctor Roadnight back in the late 1960s. He recognised the benefits of rearing pigs the natural way and save only for a corrugated field shelter for each sow, the whole conception, birth, and growth to point of slaughter is natural. Thanks, Mr. Ferguson, for teaching me this at agricultural college. The knowledge has been amazingly useful over the decades.

In the distance, the snow-covered hills could now clearly be seen. Not once today was I warm, my feet did not belong to me, my face uncomfortably cold with a dripping nose. Wonder what it is going to be like once above the snow line, if this dense cloud and cold wind persist? The forecast is for better weather next week; it cannot come fast enough.

Today has not been one of the better ones. Flat, boring, bum numbing, freezing, chased by a dog, that given his commitment to catching me, had not eaten for a while. Fortunately for me, he is still hungry. I should not be too fed up. Although I have cycled about 1,000 km, it is still only the beginning of a fantastic adventure.

The weather will improve, I will get back to wild camping and I will smile again.

I arrived in León mid-afternoon and since looking around my mood has lightened. I am again caffeine loading, looking out of a cafe window, and through the rain I can see the impressive Junta building.

The following are a few photos taken on my earlier 'walk-about'.

The Junta de Castilla y León.

Now that is what you call low flying.

San Marcos.

Inside San Marcos Museo, one of several informative museums in León.

Evidence that some artists do have a sense of humour. It would appear that Don Garcia Ramirez did, (note the dog bottom left).

Daily Blog: The only way is up – followed by an adrenaline-charged descent. (Friday) April 13th

As I looked at the burnt roll of bread with processed cheese and ham glued to it, I wondered where all the quality locally grown pork had gone. No self-respecting deceased pig had ever graced this breakfast bar. However, last night's meal had been a delight. If ever visiting León, a meal at the Boccalino guesthouse and restaurant is thoroughly recommended.

It must be the norm that whatever our careers have been, we still gravitate to that area, even having been retired for some years. From a fire safety perspective, last night's hostel is a multiple fire death scenario waiting to happen, with a single means of escape from all floors, each with many bedrooms, many with dead-end travel distances, and all aiming to get the escapee to a protected staircase. However, that staircase had every single door latched open at all levels. So, having made your miraculous escape to the ground floor i.e., not suffocated in the smoke, you would still have to pass open double doors leading into a bar and the open kitchen (probably the seat of the fire). Strangely, I slept very well. Anyway, enough of being pedantic, or not!

The climb out from León was refreshing. The sun shone and the cool air brought a smile to my face. Up onto rolling countryside, gradually gaining height to La Robia, onto La Pola de Gordon and up to the summit point at Puerto de Pajares. It was to be a climbing day.

The Boccalino restaurant.

The snow-covered mountains in the distance were today's destination. Not cutting through the Tunel de Negron on the AP 66 but the old faithful N630. The few towns such as Villamanin were void of life. Earlier, with 60 km to the next town and having only eaten a piece of burnt bread, cheese that had not originated from any animal and 'not' pork, fuel levels were insufficient. Opposite a church in a small hamlet was a brilliant bar, it did not look any different from any other, but getting back on the bike after a massive slice of deep cheese and mushroom omelette and a coffee to blow your head off, the hill ahead was a mere mound.

The church opposite the café of 'salvation'.

Road tunnels, I cannot readily recall having cycled through any during my cycling career. Near La Pola de Gordon was the first, Lucia at 277 m length, followed by La Gotera at 206 m. However, none of these were remotely near the lengths of some of the Norwegian tunnels that were later to present themselves.

The first of many tunnels encountered. Here painted on a garage door.

As I approached Busdongo de Arbas the clouds, having built rapidly, unzipped a cascade. The routine is now well practised. Remove phone from handlebar and place into waterproof case. Existing jacket off, 'totally' waterproof jacket on. Check that the bum bag with cash and cards is secure under my jacket. Activate wipers on sunglasses, (if only). Wish I had changed the high UV lens for nil protection that allows you to see where you are going. Ask again why in mid-April in Spain it rains so heavily and so often. Start laughing – hysterically. Get cycling!

Yesterday was boringly flat, today there is variety. I love the mountains, their beauty, their challenges, just being in amongst them excites me. The train track that runs nearly parallel with the road at times, is protected from avalanches by concrete tunnels that run for thousands of metres. The hills are that steep the cows face uphill to graze, so they do not have to stoop to eat.

The summit at Puerto de Pajares 1,879 m ASL.

There had been an impressive temperature inversion in the morning, with the clouds trapped in the valleys and the snow-covered peaks reflecting the sun. Now the whole mountain range was being drenched and the mist is heavy. What followed, not even the rain could spoil, an exceptionally long and rapid descent following numerous bends and curves. A real adrenaline rush! Being able to see any upcoming traffic and nothing catching me from behind, I cut the corners. Just the downpour and 20 kg of luggage behind my bum kept the speed down. I had a big smile behind my drenched buff that was glued to my face. Down to Malvedo, where the N630 disappeared. The A66 was not for cyclists or horses. A big sign said so! However, the AS242 took me into Mieres.

I had intended to camp tonight, but nothing was dry, and I was drenched to the skin. Anne very kindly found two hotels with vacancies, both expensive. I chose the Hotel Mieres del Camino. Most things are now dry, I have had a hot bath and this MAG (middle-aged git) feels ready to cycle up the Alto del Angliru tomorrow with its height gain of 1,266 m, average gradient of 10%, and max. of 23.5%. I hope the weather plays ball. It is also one of my son-in-law's birthdays. Scott, have a fantastic day and enjoy your birthday surprise.

Tomorrow, after the climb my direction of travel will change from north to east. Twelve days of cycling, with a rest day in Salamanca, have seen me travel from Gibraltar to Mieres.

CHAPTER FOUR
Today Embodies the Reason I Cycle

'What's the point of riding up a mountain that it's quicker to go up by foot?' Marzio Bruseghin talking about Alto del Angliru. This climb is not a stranger to the Vuelta a España.

Having cycled up through Spain and experienced unusual weather, persistent rain, snow, and days of headwinds, I had arrived in the Asturias mountains and was looking forward to some climbing. Although my journey was about visiting many European countries, I had always viewed it as an opportunity and a challenge to cycle as many of the classic cycle climbs as possible and had designed the route to include that objective. In Spain, I intended to cycle the Alto del Angliru, Lagos de Covadonga, and Puerto de Urkiola.

Daily Blog: *Today embodied the reason why I cycle. April 14th*
With the sun shining on Riosa far below in the valley, the winding lane could be seen for miles below, dry, and free of traffic, an invitation to open the throttle. Retracing my upward route, I had limited time to admire the surrounding countryside, as I leaned left and right, straightening the tight corners as best I could on the descent. Pushing my speed to the limit, with maximum concentration, the adrenaline surged through me: this was living. It took only minutes to return to La Vega.

It had been a different tale heading up the Alto del Angliru. This classic and most beautiful of mountains has had various cyclists such as Cav (Mark Cavendish), Conta (Alberto Contador), Wiggo (Bradley Wiggins), and many others dripping their sweat on the tarmac. Testimony still stands with their names written large and bold on the road surface. This was the first of ten cycle climbs I had planned to do. Planned and taken from Daniel Friebe and Pete Goding's inspiring book entitled 'Mountain High - Europe's greatest cycle climbs'.

I had to work hard on the final steeper sections. The maximum grade is 23.5% and the average is over 10%. However, the 12.5 km climb is a long one with little let-up throughout the 1,578 m altitude gain. I had ridden from Mieres – a bit of a warm-up first, but that too had been uphill.

These cycle climbing routes are fantastic. They are the real reason I cycle. The pure enjoyment of pushing to a personal physical limit and achieving a goal is indescribable. Then when at the top, there is the descent.

I am never going to cycle up and down any of the planned climbs on this trip a second time. So, beating a PB (personal best) is not the objective, it is the thrill of reaching the summit and the fast descent that is addictive. Being on the edge, just safe, but get it wrong and it is going to hurt!

Cycling uphill, it was easy to take in the beauty of the valley. Houses clinging to steep hillsides. The backdrop of high cliffs with snow-covered mountains beyond. Cattle and sheep gently ringing their neck bells as they grazed.

As I got nearer to the top, two cyclists overtook me: oh, to have youth again. Then a car drove past, all three occupants cheered me on. They parked the car on a particularly 'vertical' hairpin bend and started taking photos of this puffing, panting, sweating middle-aged git. The third person to overtake me was the son of the driver. We chatted in five-word sentences as we rode a little together before he left me. He was twenty-five years young! and used the climb for training. How I pine for youth!

All four of us riders, although not cycling together, had a rude awakening about 1 km from the summit. Snow! Well, to be precise, an avalanche had covered the road and damaged a section of the protection barriers. The snow contained rocks and was reasonably deep. Too deep to push a cycle and too long to carry one over it. Having put so much effort into the climb, we reluctantly had to admit defeat, but to have cycled in the Sierra del Aramo was a pleasure to remember for years to come.

The avalanche above the Cuena les Cabres, a leg-busting section of the climb in the Sierra del Aramo.

Below are some more photos taken during the climb of 1,573 m up the Alto del Angliru.

Two typical bends that ensure the lungs stay open.

Keep on going up! Somewhere on that ridge behind the hill in the foreground is the summit of the climb. Whilst the eyes are delighted with the views, the calf muscles scream.

A happy chap. A break to appreciate the views during the spectacular descent.

The way back down.

A Life Appreciated

Tomorrow I head east for the first time, aiming to arrive in Cangas de Onis, ready for the second climb, the Lagos de Covadonga on Monday.

Daily Blog: ***Started the day with a climb and finished with a climb. April 15th***

With a substantial breakfast inside me, I cycled through the deserted Sunday morning streets of Mieres and having passed the town square, where last night I had seen an excellent display of period dancing, all to medieval musical instruments, I turned up the AS111 road.

Traditional dancers in Mieres.

The road twisted and turned as it climbed. To the right in a deep and narrow valley, there were several residential tower blocks, dwarfed beneath me, looking just like a miniaturised urban conurbation out of character with its surroundings. The views back to the snow-capped mountain that had been yesterday's exercise looked superb. The AS111 could be known as the Viaduct Road. There were many of them and a few road tunnels.

Several viaducts on the AS111.

I have bought food for the day in Mieres from a bakery. As I was leaving the shop, the owner, who had been interested in my journey, asked me to wait as he wanted to give me something. He returned minutes later with a bread roll, just one roll. Generosity is always proportional to what the giver can afford. Thanking him, I left. Since biting into that roll, I understand why he wanted to give it to me. Hidden within was a calorie overload that would boost any cyclist up the steepest of hills.

A charitable surprise.

I have finally said farewell to the N360. It had been my artery through Spain for nearly 1,000 km. It has made navigating easier. Today I had expected route finding to be more involved, but few problems presented themselves. The country lanes over the tops via San Julian were a delight and Nava was a vibrant town.

Several km was done on the N634 before turning off at Romillo for a steep climb and a fast ride down into Cangas de Onis. Cangas is probably the best small town I have passed through. It again had a vibrant atmosphere and well-maintained buildings without the usual crumbling structures scattered amongst occupied properties. The centrepiece is the old bridge.

The medieval bridge in Cangas de Onis.

Having bought some bread and cheese I cycled on. I could do with a large meal, but although my Garmin was telling me that I had consumed 3,500 calories today, all the restaurants were 'up-market' and remarkably busy and would frown on a middle-aged man in lycra, wanting a table for one. However, up the road, there was an ideal restaurant, La Palmera. I chose kid and chips. The 'child' did not complain too much, and I have to say it tasted succulent, probably far better than the mature goat that was also on offer. I also had an excellent piece of cheesecake and, only anticipating riding a few more km, a couple of beers. This meal hit the spot and I headed up the road for Covadonga.

On either side of the road, there were well-kept houses, several hotels, and more restaurants. Coaches, many of them, going in the opposite direction. I saw the best example of the many storage barns, called horreos, on stilts.

A decorative horreo en route to Covadonga.

This area has a quite different feel about it, more show, upmarket, touristy than anywhere since Salamanca.

Now fed and with supplies for breakfast, the aim was to find a place to set up camp. After a look around Covadonga with many other tourists and a chat with three local police officers who wanted to know where I had been, I cycled back down to the roundabout that would take me around the corner and up to my campsite, hopefully not too far up the road.

Covadonga.

CHAPTER FIVE
From the Mediterranean to the Biscay Bay

'All journeys have secret destinations of which the traveller is unaware.'
Martin Buber

I headed up the road that led to the Lago de la Ercino, my intended climb for tomorrow. The road was a near constant 10%. The climb was through a heavily wooded area on steep ground and very wet, with no suitable flat ground for a tent. Up and up, with a full load on the bike. I came across a deserted mountain hut that promised a place to camp. However, looking further with limited furniture and a primitive cooker, it was obvious it was occasionally used. I carried on, eventually finding a place just off the road behind a small field barn. An hour ago, I was listening to cowbells, the last of the bird song, and some foxes barking. Before the rain, followed by hail drowned out all other sounds.

I aimed to finish the Lagos de Covadonga climb the following day, with its maximum gradient of 15% and an elevation gain of 962m rising to 1,135 m above sea level.

April 16th was a dry morning and intending to descend the same route, I had hidden my panniers behind a few rocks near the field barn, hoping that the workmen digging the road up since daybreak would not have seen me. I had shortened the length of the 14 km climb by cycling more than anticipated the previous evening. The real climbing started about 5 km into the ascent, about where I had camped. Past the roadworks, surreal in such an isolated location, through a handful of cattle aimlessly wandering on the road and up on past a tiny smallholding, where a dilapidated cottage surrounded by various animals was evidence of rural poverty.

Nearing the top, the climbing is not constant, indeed there is a descent. With no mountain mist, the views were sublime. Looking down on Lago de Enol, one of the three Lagos de Covadonga that includes the 'phantom' Bricial lake, which only appears twice in a decade, I was hailed by two middle-aged gentlemen. A short chat with them confirmed that they were also equally in awe of the scenery. Arriving at the top of the climb, there is no sense of being at the top. The lake is ahead of you and a natural amphitheatre of mountains provides the backdrop. Turning around and cycling around the now numerous coaches parked in the car park, I descended, being careful not to meet upcoming coaches on hairpin bends and skidding on what cows always leave on roads.

The Basque country is beautiful, mountainous, and lush. Such vibrant growth of vegetation can only come from high levels of precipitation, similar, but on a grander scale to where I live in Yorkshire. Basque mists are also frequent, so I was fortunate to have so few of them. Having cycled the 400 km from Covadonga via the national parks of Los Picos de Europa, Saja-Besaya, and Ojo Guareña to Mañaria, I arrived on 19th April and readied for my third classic climb of the Puerto de Urkiola. Although not so high at 752 m, with an altitude gain of 524 m, the punch is delivered at the top of this 6 km ride at a 10.7 degree gradient, although there are several preceding sections at 9.8.

Tensions in the Basque country kept the Vuelta a España from including this beautiful climb in Spain's premier cycling event for 33 years.

Arriving in Pamplona I was aware that this would be my last night in Spain before crossing into France. Spain had delivered a full spectrum of weather, from gloriously warm sunny days to some incredible persistent headwinds, snow, hail, and rain. I had glimpsed some architectural wonders and experienced a wealth of differing countryside. My path had also crossed others both on their journeys of vacation and pilgrimage and those going about their everyday life. Spain has so much to offer. Looking at the map of Europe, knowing that I was only three weeks into my adventure to northern Norway, a realisation of the effort still needed to achieve the goal hit home that night.

FACT FACTORY: Each year on July 6th at 8 am the Basque town of Pamplona reinforces its status as the Bull Running capital of the world. The distance run is about 900 m and over the years has seen much blood spilled on the streets as the enraged bulls heading for the bull ring toss and gore any runners that are not fast enough to escape their horns. The practice first started in the 14th

century, but only became world famous when, in 1926, Ernest Hemingway wrote *The Sun Also Rises*.

Daily Blog: *Just a wonderful day. April 16th*
The rain stopped just before dawn. I was in no rush to get up, finally emerging from the sleeping bag at 8.30 am, just as a roadworks team arrived to replace rotten timber safety barriers that sometimes prevent vehicles from taking a shorter unplanned route down the mountain.

My campsite en route up Lagos de Covadonga before the rain arrived.

I packed up, in cleated shoes, slipped on the hillside a few times, finally hid my two panniers and tent, and headed off up to the Lago de la Ercina. What a spectacular route. A few taxis and coaches were negotiating the tight bends. Later in the day, crowds would arrive. Up and up and round and round, beautiful views everywhere. I said hello to two guys of generous proportion, who replied in English, well sort of, they were from Maryland USA, and were also enjoying the scenery a few metres from their vehicle.

A temperature problem of a different type.

Just a sample of the views.

Lago de Enol.

I arrived at Lago de Enol. This was the point at which there was a second descent before the final climb to the route's end. The espresso and massive chocolate dough ring were much enjoyed at the restaurant that serviced the needs of the hungry adventurers who poured from the coaches.

The climb's end.

By this time there were about twenty minibuses in the car park, with an equal number of walking sticks allocated to each bus. Time to descend. I layered up and took off. Even put the GoPro on to record the twists and bends and having the road in your sight for miles below, as it snaked back down to Covadonga and beyond. A car in front of me realised that they were having to brake for many bends in case of upcoming traffic. A bike is narrower, so he kindly let me overtake, (I think). I did not forget to stop and collect my gear. The driver who had allowed me to overtake shouted what sounded like encouragement, at least he looked happy. I also suspected from the smiles on the roadworkers' faces they both knew where the gear had been stowed.

Rural poverty.

Within minutes I was back in the same restaurant as the previous evening, this time the kid was off the menu, so I opted for tuna salad.

Now I have raved about the N630 and sadly our paths have now parted. Another gem has been found, the AS114. Equally deserted of traffic, it takes you through some spectacular country with two notable hill climbs and descents. On the second long run down, unbeknown to me until they overtook at the bottom, I had had a police escort, again the non-driver gave the thumbs up sign. The police around here are friendly. There were also some beautiful villages such as Benia de Onis, Poo, (yes, Poo), well to give it its full name, Poo de Cabrales and Las Arenas, where I bought my evening meal in a supermarket, after which I headed off to find a camping spot.

Last night the area was too steep, wet, and wooded, tonight, well there was a spectacular gorge. The road ran to the right of a torrent of a river with massively high limestone cliffs on either side. Think Gordale Scar in Yorkshire, England and multiply many times. Try as I might I could not find a suitable site to stop and neither did I care. I was heading down the Gargantas Gorge and enjoying every second. Eventually, the gorge broadened, and I found a piece of flat and dry land next to an arched bridge that had the river beneath, again much like an enormous version of The Strid near Bolton Abbey in North Yorkshire.

View from my tent.

It is nearly dark as I write this. A few ducks have flown down the river gorge. An owl is giving it 'rock all'. Both relaxing to hear, shame about the dog barking.

It is completely dark now, only an owl calling. Think I will sleep well tonight.

Tomorrow could see me camping on a beach. Every day (and night) is so different.

Daily Blog: *From the Mediterranean to the Biscay Bay – now we are underway.*
April 17th

Woke after a great night's sleep, packed up, had breakfast, and continued down the beautiful, gorged valley. The steep limestone cliffs had kept the morning sun out, so it was cold, buff covering as much of my face as possible. The river was quieter and wider now and getting bigger.

'*This river was big, I want you all to know*', (thank you Jimmy Nail and Mark Knopfler for a great song). I was fortunate to have ridden beside it as a raging torrent until it became a placid deep, slow-moving river. You could say, the bike and I, 'Nailed' it, although it was not the River Tyne.

Today was to be a 100 km day and a 3,750-calorie day, not that they would be replaced. There were two hills of notable elevation, the toughest to mark the end of the day.

There was a sense of knowing that the sea would be viewable from the hill that climbed out of Panes. There was San Vicente de la Barquera below. This marked the point at which I had cycled from the southern tip of Spain to its northern shore. The journey to Norway has really started now. San Vicente is a mixture of old fortified buildings on a small hill adjacent to the estuary and rows of modern houses built on the opposite hillside.

San Vicente from the AS114.

Later I passed through the wonderful village of Riocorvo, south of Torrelavega, very picturesque. There were many cyclists around today and two invited me to slipstream. By tucking in close behind a cyclist in front of you, less energy is needed to displace the air and there is a beneficial vortex effect. Whoever they were, thanks.

I have never heard of two road racers inviting a touring cyclist to 'jump on the back'. They either felt pity or took longer to catch up with me than anticipated.

Quaint Riocorvo

The picturesque village of Riocorvo

As I headed away from Riocorvo, a quaint medieval hamlet, I had a navigational problem. Where was the narrow lane that cut the corner to the CA170? In the end, I had to go the long way round. Just before the last and long climb started up the CA170, I noticed the remains of that little lane. Not much left of it, as the opencast quarrying had claimed it. I was glad not to have tried to cut that corner. I would have had to retrace my route and still climb the hill.

The hill was long and drained my reserves, not steep, just never-ending and I had not been able to find quality food during the day. Reaching the top, my usual zest to make haste down eluded me. I was happy to let gravity do its thing. I needed to eat and to find a shop to get breakfast for the morning, and it was getting late. I rode around two villages but found no shop. Eventually, I ate at a bar, chips and salad, the best they could do. Still, I did find a shop and now have breakfast. After a further 8 km, with a shopping carrier bag swinging on the handlebars, I have found a lovely camp spot, near the incredibly named village of Entrambasmestas, again set between a road and river. The tent is pitched on the disused approach to a ford across a fast-running river, where I earlier had a very 'refreshing' bath.

Daily Blog: *Bad days are needed. April 18th*

Woke up this morning feeling good!

Whilst getting dressed in the usual prone seesaw style that is necessary in a small tent, I noticed I had company. Three ticks, not the kind you get from a teacher when you have correctly answered a question, but those little creatures that want to get to know you very well. They do not see a problem burrowing their heads beneath your epidermis and taking your blood; after all they in turn may give you something, Lyme disease or encephalitis.

My meticulous planning had not been so fastidious. No tick remover had been packed, so a pair of scissors was used to good effect and helped bleed the sites to minimise the chances of the tic 'gift' remaining. All sorted, let the day commence. Usual routine of getting rid of my rubbish, dropped in one of the numerous trolley waste bins in the villages, turned onto the main road and started cycling, up and up.

Then the realisation that there was a hefty southeast wind, my direction for the day which was a rare diversion away from the more usual northerly direction. It blew all day, save for the last two hours. Due to this wind, many of the downhill sections had to be worked to maintain double figure speeds.

I stopped at the bottom of a hill, it looked just like a normal hill, the road curved round to the right and out of sight. Sitting outside the cafe before the climb with six traffic police officers and three cars was a strange feeling. Again, during the day, I saw several police motorcyclists. Must be a good road to drive and ride, perhaps a training route. It occurred to me that there is a higher presence of police on Spanish roads than in the UK.

Now the climbing started. Fortunately, to a point, ignorance is bliss. Yes, I knew there was a hill, but this one was relentless and went through several small villages including San Miguel de Luena and Bollacin, as it gained an altitude of 1,011 m in a single stretch over the Sierra del Escudo. I am willing to say that on two occasions it was easier to push the bike. Sweat was dripping from nose, ear lobes and elbows, like water cascading off statues in village fountains before councils were obliged to save water.

As I continued, I noticed heavy smoke. Controlled burning was in progress south of me and soon the atmosphere was thick with the stuff. With lungs heaving for maximum oxygen intake, this involuntary passive smoking was going deep into my lungs.

Finally, I reached the top. With lungs full of smoke, the average speed had been 7 km/hr.

The descent passed Embalse del Ebro, a hard-won prize, but nonetheless one that was enjoyed.

Today I applied plenty of sunblock. However, on each occasion a hill climb resulted in it being washed off. This evening I have scorched cheeks, knees, and forearms. Another irritant was the flies, some with the tenacity and persistence of their Australian cousins and lastly, I managed to eat something that resulted in several rapid unscheduled stops. Normally not too inconvenient, but mainly open surrounding ground and wearing bib cycling shorts, that require the removal of upper clothing, there were times of extreme haste.

Enough of this moaning. It was a hard day, but we do need these days to appreciate the good ones. Besides in hindsight, it was not so bad. Something was accomplished under reasonably difficult conditions. There was the wonderful ride over rolling hills with trees clinging to near vertical cliffs. Blossom on the fruit trees and a variety of raptors both quartering their ground for prey and others rising on the

afternoon thermals, and there was the beautiful ride down through yet another gorge, with a few road tunnels leading into Ora.

A couple of shots of old Ora.

Tonight's place of rest, and recuperation.

Now it is dark, I am in the tent, fed (sort of), warm, and ready for tomorrow. The aim today was to get to Miranda de Ebro. By the time I arrived in Oña, there was not much left in my legs. So, a large meal would have been great, like the meat and pasta followed by tart, that was lunch. The restaurant owner said, 'We don't start cooking till 9 pm.' Tonight's tea was an apple, some cheese and four yogurts. Today's stats were: over 80 km travelled, nearly 2,000 m of gained elevation, and 3,800 calories (by Garmin) consumed. Think the reserves are being drawn on. I will sleep well tonight.

Daily Blog: *A short day in the saddle. April 19th*

Another excellent 'camp' site. I awoke to the sound of bird song. No breakfast today and limited water as I rode the 45 km to Miranda. How I thought I would arrive here last night is a mystery. The N232, after the village of Oña, took me over rolling hills of arable land. To the south were the snow-capped Sierra Cebollera. The road was straight for much of the ride, with few villages and no facilities. I was working off the energy values of an apple, a lump of cheese and four yogurts, all eaten last night. Where had all the tapas bars gone? Then I heard a large van driving around, sounding its horn. People came out to buy food stuffs from this mobile shop. However, it was too mobile and had driven off before I could get to it.

The scenery was easy on the eye, not dramatic, just peaceful, blossom on the few trees there were, cereal crops already 150 cm tall, oil seed rape adding a splash of yellow, and the birds just sung their hearts out. Then the N232 combined with the N1. I needed to check that I had not made a mistake. This could have been the M1 in the UK. So many large trucks, probably about 5:1 trucks/cars. Their side wind as they passed ensured I stayed to the right of the hard shoulder. Hot and very hungry, having done 30 km, I branched off into Pancorbo to see what I could find.

I only had a black coffee, a Coke, and a packet of crisps. The Coke and coffee, or caffeine and caffeine entering the blood stream was like an injection of fresh oxygenated blood. I felt as though I had been at high altitude for weeks and just returned to sea level. The newfound energy was appreciated.

Back onto 'Truck Highway', N1. No photos, as my full attention was needed elsewhere. Gone was the serenity of the rolling quiet hills of a couple of hours ago.

A tunnel was approaching. Without question both my rear lights went on, as did the front light, and off came the sunglasses. As I went through the tunnel, I have no idea how many lorries were in there, probably eight, but it was deafening. Within 50 m of emerging, the hard shoulder vanished. I am so pleased that I bothered to put a rear-view mirror on my left handlebar. There were several lorries behind me in both carriageways. As the hard shoulder diminished in width, I waved my hand, pointing my intention to come out into the inside lane. This worked well because I am still alive! It also attracted the attention of, guess what, yet another police car. As the vehicle drove past the officer had his window down, waved and gave the thumbs up to me and said something that even, had I understood, would have been lost to the traffic noise. He later circled off the road and passed me a second time, smiling, and waving.

Anne has kindly booked me a room for tonight. Four nights wild camping makes you smelly and unshaven. Although it has not rained everything is wet and getting muddy due to the morning dew. Nonetheless, I gain a lot of satisfaction from this approach of being more self-reliant.

View from hotel room balcony, where the drying tent nearly morphed into a paraglider's wings as the wind took hold of it.

As I lay on a soft bed in a comfortable eighth floor hotel room in Miranda, I am shaved, bathed, the tent is dry, washed clothing is drying and I am off for some food and a beer in town shortly.

I have visited Ciclos Maldonado cycle shop in town. Juan very kindly agreed to clean and lubricate the bike's gearing that have taken a hammering, particularly in the ice and snow. These long descents are also wearing the brake blocks, so thanks Dave, (of Cycle Fast, back home in Halifax) for the spare set. I will fit them in the next week.

I am now taking some R and R in a town park. Several dogs are being walked and, encouragingly, their owners are bagging their 'evidence'. Also, no litter, and I have been here an hour and not heard a single swear word. Indeed, since Gibraltar I have not heard a swear word. Quite something.

The park has several interesting sculptures and obviously the winters are too cold for the trees.

Daily Blog: *Just a great day! April 20th*

Before my ramblings about today, which was an excellent one, an epilogue to yesterday's.

Yesterday, I very nearly overtook my first road cyclist coming into Miranda de Ebro. I had been gaining on him for a while. When within ten metres of him, he turned and saw me. Well, none of us cyclists like to be overtaken. The look on his early 30's face was one of horror, I could not really blame him. What he saw was a middle aged, white-stubbled man in lycra, riding a hybrid cycle with full panniers and a tent bag and enough gizmos on the handlebars to fly an aircraft. The old git's bike weighed five times the amount of the thoroughbreds. Honour was seen to be in jeopardy. I have never seen a backside come off the saddle so fast! His leg muscles nearly exploded in the effort to get more power down on the pedals. He did not look back again, but he remained out of the saddle with the bike being pushed from side to side as he took the first right turn, never to be seen again. None of us road cyclists can truthfully say that at some time we have not reacted similarly. I certainly have.

Today, was a grand day. I left Miranda without difficulty and found the A3126 from Zambrana and headed east. This in turn lead onto the A3130 and Bernedo. A stunning road that had an old castle on a hill and beautifully kept villages, albeit seemingly deserted.

Two deserted villages.

I had anticipated there being no places to buy food en route. Just as well, the best, was a coffee and coke at Bernedo. Followed by my own picnic at a lovely riverside rest area near Maranon.

The route had first climbed up through beech and plane tree woods, with a river having many waterfalls. Then opening out to sweeping rich arable land and in the distance high cliffs framed the horizon in front of a deep blue sky. At Santa Cruz de Campezo I joined the busier A132, now there were two cars every thirty minutes, instead of one. I smiled.

As I am writing this in the tent pitched at the edge of a field, there is a deer only feet away, totally unaware of me. I can see it through the tent inner mesh but dare not move. Never been so close to a wild one before.

Near Maranon.

The headwind today was testing, particularly on the straight A132 into Estella. It would blow hard for twenty minutes then die to nothing for five minutes, only to return. Very unusual.

And tonight's accommodation comes with grazing deer and other woodland sounds, such as snuffling and gentle grunts from unknown animals.

And finally, caterpillars had learnt how to hold hands when crossing the road. If you look carefully, they are not actually attached to each other.

Daily Blog: 'Who will buy this wonderful morning?' April 21st

No need for Oliver Twist. I am listening to the sounds of a woodpecker, cuckoo and any number of small birds singing. The corn crop in the field where I am camping is about 30 cm high, at my eye level and with the tent open I can see that there is a single drop of dew at the very top of each and every blade. About thirty birds with large and deep wing spans, possibly Griffon vultures, all flying extremely low and all at the same height, are coming from the NE, again in exactly the same direction. Their wings are making quiet whirling sounds, some occasionally making gentle guttural noises. It is like a morning migration – an impressive sight. They just keep coming, so many of them and in no formation. Their wing spans are easily two metres. So many more than thirty now, perhaps a hundred. Time to pack up a very wet tent and hit the road.

'Do you remember us from this morning?' a heavily Spanish-accented voice said, as two cyclists came alongside me late this afternoon. Obviously having seen my adventure mapped out on the rear of my shirt, he added, 'You have a long way to go, but today you have been strong.' And with that they said 'Adios' and slowly pulled away from me. It only takes a brief few words of encouragement. I felt on top of the world after that. Just shows the power of encouragement.

This will be my last night in Spain, tomorrow France. Asi que es 'adios' a España y 'hola' a Francia. Ha sido un viaje maravilloso! I have cycled through eight of the sixteen Spanish regions, Andalusia, Extremadura, Castile and León, Asturias, Cantabria, Basque, La Rioja and Navarre. I cannot say that each have been noticeably different, but I can say that my knowledge and understanding of this large and diverse country has improved.

So, what of the last day in the first of nine countries that my route will take me through? You notice much more from a cycle than from a car. Two very elderly men were planting potatoes. They had probably done this every year for decades. One in front of the other, sack full of seed potatoes, each being dropped into a hole without bending, right foot stuffing soil over it and at the same time, light foot pressure was applied. A few metres behind him, the second gentleman was permanently stooped with a spade in his hand, he rhythmically covered each potato from the left then right, taking a measured step forward, like a simplified dance movement. Neither wasted an ounce of effort. Nor did neither look to be younger than ninety years of age.

I soon arrived in Pamplona, but not before the first of two significant hill climbs. The first was the Alto de Etxauri, a classic climb to 840 m. With a thrilling descent, where I achieved terminal velocity on my 'pack mule'.

Effort before the descent.

The nearest my 'mule' will come to flying.

A rapid descent was five minutes away.

Pamplona – never judge a city until you have viewed its centre. What a place, such a contrast to the morning's tranquillity, a vibrant and exciting city. Made even more so as it was Saturday afternoon. Here are a few photos.

Beautiful Pamplona.

This last remaining gate or Bar to the city has a drawbridge that looks functional. The placements for the multiple levels for cannon can also be clearly seen looking down from the battlements.

Moving on from Pamplona, I took the N135 from Huarte. This town must be known for its graffiti, serious art graffiti, much like what can be found in parts of San Francisco and many other cities.

Imaginative graffiti.

The final hill of the day was north of Zubiri, Erro, at 801 m. With another gloriously fast descent.

This evening I am camped next to the N135, which for the past two hours has seen scores of motorcycles 'racing' up and down. Two police bikes with blue lights on went past ten minutes ago and there has not been a motorbike since.

Tomorrow I cross the border into France at Arnéguy, just south of St Jean Pied-de- Port.

Daily Blog: A social day of coincidences. April 22nd

Another great day. The weather was perfect. It reminded me of my youthful days when the month of June was blazing and not wet as it is has become in the UK. Cycling to my first job after leaving school, all uphill to Wood Green farm, where I was a farm worker, i.e. general dogsbody. It did have its perks, though. Not confined in an office and being able to work outside. I took Anne back there a couple of years ago and although the milking herd has long since gone, the rotating circular wall calendar I had made with a numbered map pin, one for each cow to show where she was in her milk lactation, was still mounted on the wall, where I had put it more than 40 years previously. I suppose the herd had been sold and the buildings mothballed for years. How did I get to that thought? Oh, pleasantly warm summer's days enjoying the outdoor life.

Today's first 'lung opener'.

Today I saw and spoke to more hikers on the Camino de Santiago than any previous day. The route from the east to west to Santiago is generally more interesting and diverse than from the south of Spain.

My first coincidence today was meeting a lady from the same town in New Zealand where my friends Wendy and Russell live. Joanne was walking the Camino and then planned to travel the world. We met in Aurizberri Espinal where there was an excellent cafe. Best wishes, Joanne. Do try the western seaboard countries of South America as you travel around the world.

The next coincidence occurred when I stopped for water and thought I ought to buy an energy drink as well. An Australian gentleman was having problems with the internet. We fell into conversation. Jim and his wife, Marianne, (forgive me if I have not spelt your name correctly), were from Fremantle. A place my daughter and her family, who live south of Perth, and my wife and I visit and love to walk around. Jim's nephew also works at the same place as my son-in-law. It was great to meet you guys. Anne and I will look forward to meeting up with you.

Jim from Fremantle, Australia.

Yes, some cycling did get done today, nearly 100 km, 1,500 m of ascent and very nearly 4,000 calories. There were two sustained climbs with prolonged rapid and very enjoyable descents. The speed of one was held up by a large wagon having to brake for each bend. In the end about four motorcyclists and one middle aged git on a cycle, (not on a motor bike), overtook the wagon at the same time. This caused some amusement and for a moment I had a motorcyclist on each side of me, both laughing and smiling at the situation.

As I am writing this it has become dark. I am camping in a field just west of Barcus, near Oloron-Sainte-Marie. It is quite remote with thick forest below. The wild pigs are squealing and grunting. It sounds as though the fights are quite vicious.

The scenery today has been stunning. St-Jean-Pied-de-Port is a beautiful, if over-provided restaurant town. All the buildings are painted white with doors, gable ends and window shutters in ochre red. This colour scheme continued for many kilometres out of the town. Farms are neat and ordered, buildings are in a good state of repair and there is little litter.

Tomorrow I will arrive in the true Pyrenees, Laruns, and the day after, Gourette, to cycle up the Col d'Aubisque. Now, that is going to be a serious test with all the gear on the bike.

The wild pigs have stopped fighting and the owl has started. It had started to rain. If the weather does change for the worst, the Col d'Aubisque may have to be re- considered.

St Jean

- FRANCE -
CHAPTER SIX

Plans Need to be Flexible

'There is no end to the adventures we can have if only we seek them with our eyes open.' Jawaharlal Nehru

Entering France on April 21st I had planned to give eight days to complete a series of classic Pyrenean cycle climbs before Anne arrived in Lourdes for us to have a few days together. The first of these climbs was to be the Col d'Aubisque, an altitude gain of 1,190 m rising to 1,709 m above sea level. I intended to cross from Laruns to Argelès-Gazost. By going up from Laruns the average gradient was higher at 7.2% but the distance was shorter at 16.6 km. An attractive descent of 30 km was beckoning. I cycled to the ski town of Gourette with its impressive outside climbing wall.

Combining my passions on a subsequent visit to the Pyrenean mountains.

This photo was taken in Gourette on a subsequent road bike 'credit card' trip across the Pyrenean mountains when the snow had left the Col d'Aubisque.

On the Col d'Aubisque a year later.

The town was deserted. Entering the only open café I expected to see Will Smith and his dog from the film *I am Legend*. The barman was at pains to say that the Col was shut and that no vehicles could get over the pass due to potential avalanches under the Cap d'Aout.

Most of the larger previous climbs had been achieved without the necessity of carrying all my gear. The full rig weighed over 30 kg and effort had been put into arriving in Gourette. This, coupled with the only alternative to getting to Argelès-Gazost was a considerable northern detour then through Lourdes and south again, much like three sides of a square, made me reluctant to give up on the idea of the climb. Continuing upwards I was approached forthrightly by a gentleman who advised me in a precise manner that it would be dangerous to continue. Reluctantly but pragmatically, I retraced my route and descended rapidly and headed north on the D36 to then go east on the D152 to Lourdes, passing through pretty Saint-Pé-de-Bigorre, then south on the D13 to Argelès-Gazost. As fortune would have it the emergency services had closed off the D918 due to a forest fire. This had been my intended route down from the Col d'Aubisque. So, April 24th had not gone to plan, but in the greater mix of things, it did not matter, not least because my good friend Andy Hill, who was to link up with me in a few weeks, was subsequently to plan a Pyrenean crossing from Biarritz to Perpignan in 2019. The two of us not only climbed the Col d'Aubisque but also repeated the Hautacam, climbed and descended a freezing Col du Tourmalet and the Col de Peyresourde and several others that could be slotted into a meandering and devious climb-'seeking' route across this beautiful mountain range. On reflection, I am pleased that I was unable to do the Col d'Aubisque on this Spain to Norway trip, as the weather would have impacted adversely. However, with Andy we had a perfect day, and both thoroughly enjoyed this fantastic climb and the incredible high ground before the long, picturesque descent to Argelès-Gazost.

Having bought food, I left Argelès-Gazost not knowing that my next visit to the town would be with Andy and spent in relative luxury inside a hotel rather than in a tent, as it would be tonight. The next climb was to be the Hautacam. It had been a long day and I was looking forward to a large meal and a few beers. The beers would not fit into my panniers, so they swung in a carrier bag from the handlebars as I rose out of the seat to pedal ever upwards. A little way up the hill on a steep rising left-hand bend there was a stone wall and a rare piece of flattish grassed land. Drivers would be too engaged with their safety on the bend to see a tent above them. I had to carry the panniers and bike separately up the slope to the grass but was rewarded with a wonderful view southwest across to Turon de Bene and Pont de Meyabat. After a good 'tent wash' the remainder of the evening was spent drinking beer, eating, watching the sunset, and reflecting on how the fortunes of one day can alter so much.

The following morning's weather (April 25th) was not unexpected. A cool mountain mist swirled silently between the trees in the gentle breeze. There was total silence except for the occasional bird song. I was reminded of the fact that the Pyrenees are blessed with some special birds, from the common kestrel, kites such as red, black, and bee-eater, the royal eagle, the extremely rare boreal owl, and even vultures.

After yesterdays' extended day, mercifully today's climb was to be an unfettered climb without any additional weight of panniers. Heading uphill in the murk with visibility down to a few metres, thoughts of a relaxed and warm descent evaporated. Having ridden up around seemingly numerous bends I broke out into the sunshine. The cool air had been a blessing, keeping me feeling fresh, and now with the warming sun and most of the climbing completed I was a happy cyclist. A classic temperature inversion lay beneath me as I cycled towards an open and near-deserted mountain top café.

I had gained about 1,000 m from my camp. The total elevation is 1,223 m, with the summit sitting at 1,653 m above sea level. With an average gradient of 7.5% and several sections at 10%, this had been a relatively easy climb and without any performance-enhancing EPO drugs as used by Bjarne Riis in the 1996 Tour de France. Which was an unequivocal testimony to the illegal beneficial effects of these drugs.

Knowing the descent would be cold I lingered, soaking in the warmth of the sun and the spectacular views. Slowly and silently the mist slid further down the mountain, revealing more distant views. Still early in the morning, this was going to be a special day.

After a chat with the only waitress and two couples, I was ready to go down. With the road snaking below, this promised to be an exhilarating descent. On the way up I had noted that most of the road was clear of loose gravel and other hazards. Cornering technique is second nature, but it is healthy to consciously think about it when pushing the limits. Remembering to keep my body weight over the outside straightened leg to achieve the greatest traction on the bends, I pushed hard, using unnecessary energy, 'wasting bullets', as Geraint Thomas would say, but what joy. The pure delight of being alive, all senses heightened, the excitement of knowing that a mistake would certainly have consequences but finding it irresistible not to succumb to the drug of adrenaline. Not to miss an opportunity to gain a little more speed, I rode the frequent but short straight sections out of the saddle, crouched low with my crutch inches off the crossbar with arms and legs tucked in, reducing the frontal area. Never achievable but aiming to become invisible to the wind.

Having collected the panniers from my 'campsite' the next classic climb would be Cirque de Gavarnie and although I would retrace the whole route north from Luz- Saint-Sauveur, it was necessary to cycle with a full load as I was to overnight.

I travelled down the quiet and picturesque D921 to arrive in Gavarnie in the evening. The climb starts in Luz-Saint-Sauveur, gaining 1,585 m from there to the summit. With 31 km, it is one of the longest climbs on the schedule. With a lower than usual average gradient of 5.1% and a maximum of 11%, this height is gained with a lower heart rate and faster cadence. By arriving in Gavarnie to overnight, I was splitting the climb in two. The evening of April 25th had turned very cool and as I rode through the small town the door to the gite auberge Le Gypaète opened as two people emerged from the obvious warmth. I cannot recall having made a conscious decision but thirty minutes later standing under a hot shower, still washing, now unnecessary, and wearing only a smile of contentment, I had no regrets. Eating the food purchased earlier in the warmth of a large heavily timbered room, listening to a talk being given to a group of youngsters about mountain skills, that unconscious decision had been a good one.

The following morning having stripped the bike to bare minimum I headed out with great expectations. Gavarnie is a natural wonder. Long before it became a UNESCO site in 1997, this natural massive amphitheatre surrounded in the main by 3,000 m peaks and containing France's tallest waterfall, the Grande Cascade de Gavarnie at 423 m and a stone's throw from the Spanish border, was known for its stunning impact on the eye. Not least the 100 m high gaping gap of the Brèche de Roland. Having read much about what I was about to see, I was excited. It was Hippolyte Taine, the naturalist, who said, *'There are only two solutions, you either learn a description by heart or you make the journey.'* For me, the latter has always been the preferred solution.

I climbed the deserted well-paved road in isolation, with an increasing number of snow patches appearing, particularly beneath a towering cliff of rock. In the summer warmth, this area would probably be swarming with vehicles and hikers. Today I saw just one other person, a cyclist descending through the patches of snow that lay on the upper reaches. Surrounded by a world of beauty and silence I cycled on. With no real physical effort needed, it was a joy. This joy was to be short-lived as I arrived at a car park beyond which the snow covered the road. It was obvious that I would not be able to continue. Disappointed, I donned all my clothes for what was going to be a fast and cold descent. As cold as I became it could not distract from the enjoyment, and to learn later that I had reached the end of the trail, which explained the sudden and total blockage of the route beyond the car park, this allayed my previous disappointment.

It is not often a cyclist has an opportunity to cycle thirty continuous kilometres downhill. Arriving back in Luz-Saint-Sauveur I turned right onto the D918 to approach the Col du Tourmalet. Unlike Gavarnie, which has yet to host the Tour de France, the Tour since 1910 has visited and entertained thousands on the Col du Tourmalet. In 2010, the year I had the good fortune to have summitted Everest, the Tour again visited. From the western side, Luz, the last 8 km continuously exceeds 7.5% with the final section being 10%. From Luz, the length of the climb is 18.8 km with an altitude gain of 1,405 m. Refreshments are gratefully available at the summit. My objective was to do a double-crossing approaching from the west, descend the eastern side and continue to the Col de Peyresourde and then retrace back to Lourdes to meet up with Anne on April 29th.

Disappointment struck as multiple signs advised that the pass was closed. Closed just beyond Barèges and with the lessons learned on the Aubisque and the depth of snow on Gavarnie it would be wise to acknowledge that mountain roads in the Pyrenees are closed for a good reason. I had missed out on summiting the Col d' Aubisque, and now the Tourmalet and with insufficient time, Peyresourde. Due to other constraints of this adventure, there had not been the option to delay these climbs until the winter snows had melted. It had been a balancing act of arriving in certain countries at certain times. I was aware that I was cycling very much in the 'shoulder' season. This was in no small part to avoid the summer heat, tourists and infernal flies, midges, and mosquitoes. As it was, by the time I arrived in Norway my body had hosted several ticks and fed a considerable number of insects. It was unknown at the time that the majority of all these climbs would successfully be achieved fifteen months later. On July 30th 2019, the Tourmalet would have its summit shrouded in thick mountain mist. Andy and I would be denied hot refreshments at the closed summit café and would descend with our bodies involuntarily shaking with the cold. It would take an hour and a hot meal in Sainte-Marie de Campan to warm and dry us.

Daily Blog: ***Today's climb was the Col de Marie Blanque. April 23rd***

What a wet night! It hammered down and with thunder, too. In the morning, many visitors of the slug and leech variety were on the outer side of the inner tent. Whilst packing up I stayed in sandals to save getting my cycling shoes soaked in the long grass. Then had to remove three leeches from my right foot; boy, they hang on. If it is not leeches, it is ticks. I do not mind the bigger natural inhabitants, but it is the sneaky, covert little mites that can give you the nasty diseases.

So off and away, UP -wards! There was a thick hill mist that did not burn off till late afternoon, but still, it was hot work.

Sitting writing this in Laruns, looking up at some beautiful mountains, I am slightly concerned for tomorrow as lenticular clouds shroud their tops: this usually is a sign of high winds.

After the initial hill this morning, the run into Oloron-Sainte-Marie was easy and enjoyable in the atmospheric mist.

Mistletoe in the mist.

Fully aware of what awaits.

A French cyclist took this photo of me in Escot at the start of the Col de Marie Blanque climb. His words of encouragement were, 'This is the hardest side to do it from. Are you taking all your gear up with you?' The route links the Aspe valley with the Ossau valley and is 8 km to the top, which is 1035 m ASL, with the last four providing the steepest climbing. I was to cycle this col again the following year with Andy on our trans-Pyrenees crossing from Berlitz to Perpignan.

Liberté, Egalité, and Fraternité – too right, Rafael Alberto! Those who have cycled this classic climb will know what I mean.

And having descended, a look over my shoulder.

Tomorrow a bigger climb, the Col d'Aubisque. The intention is to do a big climb each day now until Anne arrives in Lourdes on Saturday. The weather may have something to say about that, (it did!).

Daily Blog: *Plans need to be flexible. April 24th*

From Laruns it was straight up. Fully loaded the bike and the gear on it weigh a hefty 33 kg. The plan was to cycle up the Col d'Aubisque and down into Argelès-Gazost and from there do several other climbs.

Note the lack of saddle on the larger bike. This is to ensure the rider sustains 100% effort throughout the climb.

After some strenuous work I arrived in Gourette. This is about 12 km into the 16 km climb. A typical 'out of season' ski town and void of any character, not one but two Intersport shops: get the feeling? Maybe a further eighty or so shops and four massive hotels. Think of the film with Will Smith in, I am Legend, or the original, The Omega Man with Charlton Heston. Weirdly, there was a single dog hanging around as well, but not Will Smith's Alsatian. Everything was closed, except one café. I saw four people, one of whom approached me and asked my intentions. I said I was going to Argelès - Gazost, via the Col d'Aubisque. He said that it was closed. I had my doubts as the signs at Laruns had said it was open. I had chosen to go and see for myself when a rare vehicle approached. I flagged him down and the driver confirmed that the col was definitely closed. It was not the Aubisque that was the problem, it was the high, narrow road near the Col du Soulor. The gates were across the road because of avalanches and ice making it impassable.

The only alternative was drastic, involving the circumnavigation from a hypothetical clock face from 8 to 6 - in a clockwise direction! So back down to Laruns, north to Bruges-Capbis-Mifaget, then east to Lourdes, and finally south to Argelès-Gazost. Quite a detour. Added to the complication, there were extensive road works where I wanted to get onto the D35: it was closed. I am only a cycle, surely there is not a problem? I smiled my way through the workmen, most of whom returned my smile and waved me around the road plant, but I did get a puncture, first since mid-Spain.

The route was not as dramatic as the planned mountain crossing but was beautiful and I found Cycle Route 81 into Lourdes and the beautiful Bétharram Abbey.

Bétharram Abbey.

Passing through Lourdes, I kept my eyes shut, metaphorically speaking, as this is where Anne and I are having a few days together before I head off north through France.

Arriving at Argelès-Gazost there was a helicopter ferrying water to a fire high up on the hillside. Obviously, with a career in the Fire Service I had to stop and *have a look. I noticed that the D918, the road I would have come down had the pass been open, was closed and vehicles were being sent back up over to Laruns. How things sometimes turn out for the best!*

The fire near Argelès-Gazost.

Sunset over my wild camp on the Hautacam route.

This evening, having bought my food from a Lidl store, it took a long time to find a suitable camping spot. Cycling some way up the Hautacam, again with a full load and a carrier bag full of food swinging from the handlebars, is an effort after 95 km, 1,800 m of climbing, and 4,500 calories used. I did find a 'sloping' pitch and opened the first of two cans of beer; a smile came to my face.

I have now seen three examples of the famous tradition of completely leaving alone a Pyrenees Mountain dog to 'live' with a flock of sheep. The first time I came across this was when a white animal, the same size as the sheep in the field, started to run in an un-sheep-like manner. To confirm that it was not a sheep, it barked at a middle-aged cyclist riding past. These dogs seem to be left on their own to protect the sheep from attacks.

Reflecting on the day, it initially looked as though it was going off track. It certainly involved more mileage, but in the end, worked out so much better than it could have.

Emerging from the temperature inversion.

What is more, the cafe was open at the summit. A well-stocked and smart building, bathed in gloriously warm, if not hot, sunshine.

Below was the most perfect temperature inversion. It was as though you could walk out onto the cloud and reach the mountains protruding across the valley.

Before descending it was necessary to wrap up.

Daily Blog: An atmospheric climb up Gavarnie. April 26th

The ride south to Gavarnie this afternoon took longer than expected. There were benefits, seeing the town of Luz-Saint-Sauveur and riding up the beautiful Gorge de Saint Sauveur to arrive here in Gavarnie, ready for the final 18 km of the 30 km climb up to the Port de Boucharo. This goes to a height of 2,270 m ASL.

Admittedly I did some of the climb from Luz Saint Sauveur late yesterday afternoon, resulting in nearly 3,800 m of daily elevation gain. Having done the Hautacam earlier in the day, the old legs were moaning. So, when a gite presented itself as I rode into Gavarnie village, the idea of a tent with certain rain forecasted for the night, you guessed, the gite won and, for less than 20 euros including a shower and a beer, it was a wise decision.

The approach to Gavarnie.

The climbing steepens and the temperature falls.

Gavarnie has not been released from winter yet.

I left the gite by 8 am. It was cold, even when climbing the 8 to 10% gradients. What a spectacular road. The mountain was not showing itself, mist prevailed again. The road either zigzagged upwards or clung to the underside of perpendicular towering cliffs or had been chiselled into them.

The switchbacks wait for my descent.

Thwarted, but this was the trail head.

If it were cold going up, what would the wind chill be like coming down? I had eaten the same for breakfast as for dinner last night, chicken, cheese, pasta, fruit and fruit cake and a quart of liquid. Contrary to what I had anticipated, the ride was relatively easy. Having arrived at what I thought was the two-thirds mark of the climb there was no need of signs saying that the road was closed. The snow *covered it up to a depth of two feet and deeper for as far as the eye could see. It was indistinguishable from the remaining snow fields. Only the line of the road marked on my offline mapping system enabled any idea of where it meandered up the mountain. Note: later I was to learn that this indeed was the end of the climb and only a hiking track continued.*

The road appears to be impassable.

It pays to occasionally look behind. What two minutes previously had not existed, miraculously appeared for a few moments before the curtain was again drawn. The snow-covered mountains framed in cloudless blue skies momentarily showed their splendour. What a wonderful view!

Oh, it was cold! I layered up and headed down. There was a little ice on the road and cornering had to be done with caution. But the run back down to Luz was fast. The faster the better, to try and keep warm. Well, sort of, anyway. It is a little self-defeating though, because the faster you go the greater the wind chill factor. With sunglasses on and buff up over my ears and nose, was this a bank robber making his escape on an ecologically friendly means of transport?

I am in Luz now, three cups of coffee downed, I can now feel my feet again. And of the climb? Another beautiful classic. A 30.9 km climb! The height gain is 1,585 m taking you to 2,270 m ASL. This is the altitude where oxygen starts to deplete in the atmosphere.

Tomorrow is to be the final of four classic climbs in the area, the Col du Tourmalet. It will be my personal test of fitness. I have been regularly cycling 80 km a day and usually around 1,800 to 2,500 m of height gain.

The Col du Tourmalet is closed from Barèges and is hardly worth the short ride to that point. Much of the stunning stuff is further east. Friday is now a re-plan day before returning to Lourdes to meet up with Anne.

Daily Blog: The Evening Edition. Subject – finding a home. April 26th

Sometimes it has been awkward to find a suitable campsite. The criteria are more exacting than would first be imagined. It has not to be on obviously private land. It does not want to attract unsavoury types after dark. Ideally you should not be observed leaving the road and scurrying into a field or wood. The ground needs to be dryish, or at least without running water beneath the tent and (one of the most difficult criteria to meet), on reasonably level ground. Oh, and not within line of sight of traffic, unless on a bend above the road, where hopefully the drivers will be looking for on-coming vehicles, but then there are the passengers.

Houses are in the most unexpected places and people love looking out of their windows across fields where they observe someone taking off his vivid reflective yellow shirt (to reveal bib shorts!) and replacing it with a brown one, removing the hi viz pannier covers and stowing them. Looking around, listening then scampering off behind a thick hedge. So, this wild camping caper is an art, if you are going to minimise the chances of being disturbed during the night. Travelling through many different countries, each with different attitudes towards the idea of 'wild camping', is interesting. In countries where the evening meal is eaten later, finding a place to sleep after dark having eaten is usually more testing. For instance, take this evening. 'Sorry sir, we do not start serving "proper" food till 7.30 pm.' 'But I don't know where I'm sleeping tonight,' said in my head. Going on past record, it can take 90 minutes to find a place, frequently up a steep hill. To avoid pitching a tent in the dark, I ate a bread roll and drank a beer and cycled off, yes up a hill, an extremely steep one. Every village I came to, the line-of-sight from houses precluded several possible sites. Between the villages the left side of the roadside went up too steeply and, on the right, dropped away too steeply! The bends in the road sometimes have flat areas but are in full view of cars. It is a little like the 'On The Far Side' joke. Where all the cows are standing on their hind legs talking to each other and the look-out cow on the bend in the road shouts, 'CAR!' Another hazard are electric fences that must be negotiated with care, both when straddling them and lifting the bike over the wire.

Finally, this evening I have pitched my tent on a disused track in a wood, where I am listening to a wild pig, who is remarkably close and has no idea I am here. Now, if I frighten it, it will do the same as it did an hour ago when it was 20 m away, not five. Bark like a demented dog and thunder off through the woods, waking everything within half a mile. I can hear him chewing the roots he has snouted up. He is so close! It is very nearly dark now; hope he moves off soon.

To conclude on this evening's choice of accommodation. Eventually found a good place. Was observed by a passing driver pushing my bike down a track. Thought I would chance it anyway. Further away from the road there was a sign, in French, 'Beware bees'. So frustrating. Fortunately, there was a second track.

The pig seems to have either moved off or is doing what I am doing, being quiet and listening. Later, two owls gently call to each other. The only other sound is the quiet relaxed tones of a few cow bells.

Hoping no vehicle comes down the track.

My view from the top of the camp track.

We needed fuel yesterday. Luke, do you remember doing this in Scotland near the end of our LEJOG's trip?

This Spaniel followed me for some way.

It is Friday 27th April. 26 days of cycling with a rest day on the 10th at Salamanca. It seems an age since that sea salt and sand blasted both bike and rider in Tarifa.

I have not bothered too much about the statistics, there is still thousands of km to cycle. A calculated guess gives me around 22,000 m of climbing, with a guess of 2,000 km cycled. Although looking at the overall route it looks more like 1/5 completed, so perhaps the final total will exceed 8,000 km. How good to know there is yet so much more ahead! I wonder what awaits in the following months.

This will probably be my last blog until I hit the road again on 4th May and head towards Bordeaux and Royan, where David joins me to ride together to Fontainebleau.

I hope my ramblings are providing some amusement and an insight into long distance cycling.

I headed north back to Lourdes, disappointed with the col closures but looking forward to seeing Anne. I arrived in Lourdes two days early. The next classic climbs would not be until I arrived in Belgium and would be quite different, much steeper and much shorter. Andy, who had arranged to meet up with me in Belgium, would accompany me on the Mur de Huy and others in three weeks' time.

Finding a place to wild camp near larger towns is difficult. It is obvious but when you are tired through back-to-back days of hill climbing and you want to be able to walk to a good restaurant and sit at a table rather than on a foam mat either beside a tent or in it listening to the rain, perspectives become distorted. The gods denied any spots where I could be assured of a peaceful night. However, they did think that I had not cycled up enough hills, so directed me to a steep climb south-east of Lourdes, up towards Sere-Lanso. Had the Mur de Huy emigrated south? After a long day, I found a near-perfect spot just off a narrow hilly lane. With lawn like grass and level with views down to Lourdes, it was promising. Setting about my now perfected routine of pitching camp I was unaware of the bees for some time. Then it dawned, a notice half hidden by a tree warned of bees. The air was alive with them. I moved on. That night the tent was pitched in the middle of a little-used track under a canopy of dense trees. The following day was spent idly in Lourdes, drinking coffee and people watching, trying not to look at the sights as Anne and I were to enjoy them together.

The irresistible urge to return up the hill to my previous night's mediocre camp was easily swayed and resulted in a night on a campsite with the tent pitched on short mown grass and a shower and proper flushing toilet. Living the most basic of existence prompts appreciation of things so often taken for granted. That hot shower was beyond welcome. The following day I cycled to where Anne and I had booked our accommodation for the next few days, The Calm and Independent.

Daily Blog: And of Lourdes. April 27th

My first evening here and I am struck by the friendly atmosphere. It is raining and I am eating in a covered pavement restaurant. I am on my own, people watching and listening to conversations. So many people have come from far and wide, different languages can be heard being spoken all around. So many are drawn here by their beliefs and hopes for healing. Handicapped people of all ages in wheelchairs. Young, joyous people, happy-clappy people. So many and all with a belief in an afterlife. And so it has been since Christ's crucifixion.

I have never seen so many wheelchairs together before.

Now blogs are strange things. You can write with a false sense of anonymity, yet you know maybe many will read what you write, maybe no one will read what you write, but it is out there to be read.

Lourdes needs no introduction, known throughout the world as a major Catholic pilgrimage site. What struck me as I had cycled into town was the numbers of coaches, hundreds of them filling an enormous parking area. Initial thoughts that this was going to be a crowd experience that needed patience after my solitary way of life, were proved right. Wherever I walked or stood I was in the way of someone wanting to move 'through' me.

I am that affected by what I am surrounded with, it would not be right not to comment on it. After all, I said from the outset records of events, journeys and long-distance cycle rides need to be inclusive, they become less genuine if they are selective.

For me, unquestioning faith is the easy way out and I am certainly not insinuating that believers are opting out. Oh, those conversations with my Born-Again Christian father. I am truly envious (and is not that one of the seven deadly sins?). I used to 'believe' in a naive way. However, life's events, together with a pragmatic and scientific empathy, changed that. We are born, we live, we die. It is the memory of ourselves that we leave behind that provides temporary immortality, yes, a contradiction. We all have loved ones who have died, but our memories of them do not.

But what is it that causes so many millions of people to believe without question? Aren't we supposed to do just that? Biblical teachings tell us to believe unreservedly, yet in every other aspect of life, we are told to question and seek answers, how bizarre. It is easier for the non-questioning minds, the non-scientific minds, not that all religious people are not questioning, or indeed some are scientists.

Religion through history has either directly caused or been cited as causing an inordinate amount of death, torture, and suffering. What a contradiction that religions advocate humility, forgiveness, and selflessness.

As I look up from writing this, I cannot help but be astounded and, yes, comforted by so many people who believe in something that they know is so much greater than themselves and are happy to be humbled by that power. Willingness to be humbled in this day and age is a dying attribute.

Have I opened my mind too much? Who knows, but something prompted me to think about this. You may think this is all rubbish, you may not, but it may prompt thoughts you have not had previously.

A gentleman not too dissimilar in appearance to Professor Stephen Hawking has just driven himself past in his wheelchair, followed by a young man carrying a large flag proclaiming Christ as the redeemer, and again followed by another young man of similar age using two crutches to enable him to walk. The elderly black couple hand in hand, he wears a white trilby hat, she holds a loudly coloured umbrella, and both wear open smiles. A lady who can hardly walk does so beside her wheelchair, her pained face watched by her wary husband who pushes her chair. Everyone I look at has their own lives, the most precious thing they possess. Their successes, their failures, their families, and their friends.

Strangers smile and say good things to people they do not know. If the ethos of religion makes us kind, caring, and unselfish, then it must be a good thing, but to believe in a life after death is beyond me. I envy those who can genuinely say that whatever happens is meant to. It is not through a lack of trying, yet for me, why should there be anything after this life? Bellowhead's song about a leaf rings true with me. As does Monty Python's, 'Life of Brian's' closing song, 'Always look on the bright side of life'. Some pious people may think it is blasphemous, not so if it provokes meaningful thought.

So many make the pilgrimage, about five million every year.

To conclude from where I sit, buses, cars, and people bustle past, and then there is the isolated serenity of four anglers fishing from the busy bridge. If ever they brought a fish out of the water, it would probably be carried off on one of the numerous white tourist trains that perpetually tour the town. Maybe I am also a 'fish out of water' in Lourdes.

Sorry for the heavy stuff, folks. I did say that this blog would not be sanitised. Being on my own with hours to contemplate anything and everything, the mind does meander.

Yves let me into a beautiful first-floor apartment of The Calm and Independent. I had time to shower, wash my cycling clothes and clean the bike before Anne arrived in a taxi from the airport at 12.30 pm. Yves and I had agreed to keep my arrival a secret, so Anne had no idea that I was already there until I jumped out from behind the bedroom door. Seeing the surprise on her face was a delight.

The food shopping for us sur la bicyclette. Anne took this picture.

The town orientates around the Sanctuaire Notre-Dame de Lourdes. There is no time of year that the streets are not crowded with Catholics from around the globe. Whether you are a believer or not it is impossible not to recognise the impact that a young lady has had on Christians. The town consists of everything needed to support the millions who visit every year. The architecture of Notre Dame is impressive, made visually more so by the massive expanse of the paved area in front of it and the sweeping bifurcated staircase leading to the great west doors. Every evening a service is held for those seeking cures for illnesses. Anne and I were taken aback by the hundreds who, confined to wheelchairs, are wheeled into regimental rows on this area.

With holy water and candles on sale in abundance, there is a mixture of devout belief and an underlying cynicism. Faith over the millennia has been responsible for both much good and terrible evil. The economy of Lourdes thrives.

The Sanctuary of Our Lady of Lourdes and a view of the town from the Château Fort.

Looking down on Notre Dame is Lourdes castle. Sitting atop a rock bypassed by the moving ice of millions of years ago, this site was first used by the Romans, then the Saracens, and later in the eleventh and twelfth centuries it became almost impregnable. It was extended in the 14th century to dominate three other towns nearby that have since disappeared. In 1590 under the reign of Henry IV it imprisoned his opponents and was known as the Bastille des Pyrenees. In 1685 King Louis XIV's architect, Vauban, had only some of his proposed improvements realised and the castle became known as the Château fort de Lourdes. In 1995 it became a Historic Monument and a 'Musée de France' in 2002. It is an amazing place, steeped in history and impressively presented with a touch of the unusual. It has a miniature village within the walls.

Anne and I also took the 100-year-old Pic du Jer funicular up the 1,000 m to the illuminated cross and the starting point for several off-road downhill cycling routes.

It is May 1st, Labour Day, a public holiday to celebrate workers' rights. It kicked off in 1561 when King Charles IX of France received a lily of the valley flower as a good luck charm. He then decided to offer a lily of the valley to the ladies of the court every year at this time of year. At the beginning of the 20th century, it became custom to give a sprig of lily of the valley, a symbol of springtime, to a loved one. Nowadays it is a bunch of lily of the valley or dog rose. Sold tax-free only on May 1st.

Some of the crowd as thousands more join them at the end of the Marian procession.

Last night we went to the daily evening Marian Procession, held at the Sanctuary of Our Lady of Lourdes. Regardless of any religious connections, although it is impossible to divorce this incredible event from religion, it was a spectacular gathering of over 4,000 people, a thousand of whom were in wheelchairs. There are people from all corners of the world, and this happens nightly from April to October. As it becomes dark the thousands of candles carried become brighter, and the changing lights illuminating the castle become more impactive. A massive projected light image of Bernadette Soubirous is cast onto the castle wall. It was this young lady at the age of 14, the eldest of nine children, who saw the first apparition of the Virgin Mary that became known as the Marian Apparitions. Doubted at first, later recognised to be authentic. Now you cannot walk a hundred metres in Lourdes without seeing the famous photograph of Bernadette. She lived from 1844 to 1874.

This very profound event that we saw last night further compounds the dichotomy of belief and non-belief.

Whilst Anne and I thoroughly enjoyed our time together there was a need for me to get back on the road. I was meeting up with a friend, David, who I had first met through another good friend, Neil Stutchbury. Neil and I had met in Nepal a few years previously and had since climbed together in several countries, our ice climbing exploits being the most notable. David Cronk is also a good friend of Neil's and together the three of us have had some great trips. David being a cyclist too had asked to spend a week cycling in France with me and it was at Royan, north of Bordeaux, that we intended to meet. Whilst I have been retired from the fire service for a few years and Neil recently from a high-powered job in London, David was a GP in Cambridgeshire and only had limited vacation time, so I was happy that he had chosen to spend it with me. Although we had not known each other for long, an incident whilst the three of us had been doing a winter climbing traverse of the Aonach Eagach ridge in Scotland, during which Neil took a death-defying spectacular fall, had from my perspective drawn us all together even more than had the incident not happened.

FACT FACTORY: A staggering six million people a year visit Lourdes. This is mainly due to the sighting of The Virgin Mary by Bernadette Soubirous in the Grotto of the Apparitions in 1858.

Daily Blog: Rejuvenated, enthusiastic, clean-shaven, and not smelly. May 4th
The bike is clean and in excellent working order; so too is its rider. We are heading north, sadly away from the wonderful Pyrenees, but with high expectations of different, calmer, albeit less dramatic scenery.

It would be remiss of me not to thank our hosts in Lourdes, Yves and Anne (Yves' wife), whose fantastic accommodation we have stayed in for the past six nights. The 'Calme et Indépendance', Route de Bagnères, Lourdes is faultless. Fully equipped kitchen, lounge/diner. Great bathroom and bedroom, it is the place to stay when in Lourdes. Our thanks to you both. We thoroughly enjoyed our stay.

Our fantastic accommodation at Lourdes.

I would also like to thank Aurélien of Bike & Py, a cycle shop and cafe on Esplanade du Paradis in Lourdes, for fine-tuning the bike gears and brakes after all the work done both climbing and descending the Pyrenean mountains.

Whilst we were at Bike and Py we met a couple from Holland who had cycled from Lisbon to Lourdes and were heading home via Paris. Bernadette and Paul, it was good to meet you, albeit for a short time. I have looked at my route and unfortunately, you live some way northwest of it. If ever you wish to cycle the hills of Yorkshire please drop us a line.

Sightseeing with my best friend.

The 1/10th sized model medieval dwellings of regional buildings in the Basque area. A surprise within the Lourdes Château de Fort grounds.

Anne has always been orientated to the 'older' man. We were visiting the caves above Lourdes. She said he required a shower, like her husband a few days previously.

Last sunny day together for a while.

Looking south to the Pyrenees and those classic cycling climbs. Seems more than a few days ago I was on them. The Tourmalet is still closed, as more snow arrived two days ago.

Well, it is the morning of May 4th, with lycra donned, clean-shaven and renewed vigour, I am heading up to Royan to meet up with David, who is riding with me to the Paris area.

CHAPTER SEVEN
A Day of Variety

"I Want To Ride My Bicycle
I Want To Ride My Bike
I Want To Ride My bicycle
I Want To Ride It Where I Like."
Freddie Mercury

Anne's flight back to the UK was not until the evening, so it was she and Yves who waved me off that morning from Lourdes. I felt fit and strong. Now heading north away from the mountains the weather was warmer and more stable. The ground was increasingly less hilly. Cycling was effortless as I kept to the D910 and then took the first opportunity at Pontacq to cycle the quieter roads of the D42 and D211 to Aire-sur-l'Adour. Unlike mountainous regions, these 'flatlands' have a labyrinth of country lanes with boundless opportunities for wild camping. May 4th had been a great cycling day ending with finding a peaceful place to sleep under the stars. The joys of self-reliance, anonymity, and freedom.

Having achieved most of and attempted all but one of the intended Alpine climbs before arriving in Lourdes and relaxing with Anne away from the bike, it was as if I could look further and appreciate the greater picture. There was no longer a need to focus on immediate goals. Riding northwards through Spain, the mountains had been waiting for me. I am certainly no 'spring chicken'. Youth evaded me many years ago and has been replaced by sciatica, spondylitis, glaucoma, and a bout of pneumonia following an unscheduled night on a Matterhorn traverse. Knowing that the hardest climbs were now behind me and that my body had benefited from the effort involved, I relaxed and took a broader perspective of what lay ahead. The emotional wealth of travelling is immense and although always appreciative of it, my mind was now freed to indulge to its content.

The following day was equally enjoyable. My arrival in Garein, a small, quintessential French village, had coincided with a flower and crafts show. Stalls surrounded the Église Notre-Dame de Garein and the local streets, selling a variety of homemade quality foods and crafts. Although hundreds of people were there, a family atmosphere was apparent. I stopped in Sabres for an excellent lunch that only came about as I had been refused entrance to the first restaurant on entering the village. Whether it was the lycra I was wearing or the lack of fluency with the language, I did not care. Life was good, I was happy and the sulking person who refused my custom must live with themselves all their lives.

On through Trensaca where the two saints, Martin and Eutrope, seemingly could not decide on the design of their church, incorporating a mixture of a Rapunzel type tower attached to a high single stone gable end with a roofed gallery on the rear side. It looks as though the architect wanted to include everything. Either that or the original height of the church had been reduced.

Confusing architectural desires.

I stopped for an evening beer in Marcheprime. Maybe it was the beer, maybe the disappearance of the quaint villages and the straight boring D5 road, but soon afterwards my legs started saying they had done enough for the day. There was forest on either side of the road, ideal for a campsite. I pushed the bike some two hundred metres down a track and found a suitable place to pitch the tent. What is it with mosquitoes, do they wait and watch until their victim has half achieved their intention before attacking? I have empathy for Canadian Moose who submerge themselves in water to try and escape the swarms that feed on them. Returning to the road at a speed that would impress Mo Farah, I cycled on to the roundabout at Le Temple and pitched the tent at a speed not yet seen, behind a graveyard wall. Mosquitoes can also communicate or fly extremely fast. They were only marginally fewer here than in the forest and through the night could be heard as they hit the outer tent. Throughout the whole 8,000 km trip, mosquitoes would only be a real nuisance on two occasions, this being the first.

At Carcans I turned off the direct route to Point de Grave and travelled up the western side of Étang d'Hourtin. This is a beautiful area of sand dunes and pine forests. The weather was perfect, and I felt alive. Several cyclists were around. With many people shouting welcomes to each other, there was a friendly atmosphere. Three road cyclists passed me and, having seen the route of my journey printed on the shirt, wished me well. I sort of fell in behind them and whilst their speed was greater than mine, drafting them was a benefit not to be missed. It must have looked a little odd with three keen cyclists on road bikes being tailed by an older guy on a hybrid bike loaded with panniers. I followed them for miles beyond Hourtin-Plage, before thinking that I am not appreciating the countryside enough and was again using unnecessary 'bullets'. I thanked them as they continued on their way.

FACT FACTORY: *Tiger mosquitoes, Aedes albopictus (Stegomyia albopicta), from the mosquito (Culicidae) family, also known as (Asian) tiger mosquito or forest mosquito, is a mosquito native to the tropical and subtropical areas of Southeast Asia; however, in the past few decades, this species has spread to many countries through the transport of goods and international travel and are known to carry the Zika virus.*

Daily Blog: In quite different terrain. May 4th - evening

It felt alien to be cycling away from Lourdes, knowing that Anne was going to be there until her flight departure that evening. The six-night break had been everything we had wished for. Now it is time to continue this journey to Nordkapp, which has only just begun.

I left Lourdes at 10.30 am and after several short stops, including shopping, arrived at my field-side accommodation, somewhere near nowhere at 5 pm. Just outside Mont-de-Marsan.

Bronze statues in Mont-de Marsan.

Mont-de-Marsan had some interesting bronze statues lined across the bridge over the river Midou. Although the 'diving figure' seems to be permanent, the nudes examining themselves appear to have since been removed.

I cycled over 100 km today. It was a near-perfect day. No sun, cool and quite different from anything so far on the route up from Tarifa. Although there was a little headwind throughout the day, it was easy to cope with.

The countryside soon became less hilly as I rode north. Arable fields flanked by undulating hills covered with natural ancient deciduous woods. The soil was rich, either ploughed or rotavated, ready for planting. The first cut of silage had been taken from grass fields whilst the barley was tall and green. There were one or two large pig farms and battery hen houses and a few cattle, but predominately it was arable.

What struck me was the neatness of both the farms and, almost without exception, the houses. No grand country mansions, but rural dwellings designed and maintained to high standards. No smelly farms with yards full of broken machinery.

Now the day certainly consisted of two halves. A quiet and tranquil morning, with several hills, one short one of 24%, that opened the lungs. Perhaps seeing twenty vehicles. Whilst this afternoon on the D824, vehicles were passing at speed nearly continuously. Only a few wanted to see how close they could get to me. The vast majority were cautious and curious.

There has not been anything outstanding today to warrant putting a photo on this blog. Just very pleasant countryside, which is hard to convey in a photo.

It is strange to think that Anne's flight left Lourdes 8 hours after I did and arrived in the UK two hours later at a latitude that will take me six weeks to cycle to. However, all the sights and experiences I will have on my journey will be far more fulfilling.

Daily Blog: A day of variety. May 5th

It looked very much like today was going to be a repeat of yesterday, pleasant, but uninspiring. Woke early after a sound sleep. Skies leaden with solid cloud and chilly with a slight headwind and that is the way it remained until after a late lunch.

Forests, thousands of hectares of conifers all in regimented lines, all brashed to ensure maximum vertical growth and minimal knots in the finished timber. The D834 was a busy road, but faultless, smooth, not a pothole for 60 km. Now where in the UK can you find that?

Isn't it fantastic that we do not know what lays ahead of us? My handlebar mirror told me several times that I was about to die. It was wrong, although on two occasions I did see a terrified face, like the one I see in a mirror when shaving, glaring back at me for a millisecond, from the nearside wing mirror of a passing car. Some drivers do not know the width of their vehicles. Several European countries have road signs reminding drivers to give cyclists a 1.5 m space as they pass.

The day had started in an unremarkable way and subsequently provided considerable variety.

The mind of a long-distance cyclist meanders if the owner of that mind is not disciplined. Yes, singing songs at the top of your voice is a luxury that you cannot indulge in many places other than on a deserted road, but when the repertoire is exhausted, what next? Moaning about roadside litter ejected from vehicles was not on the agenda, there was none! Remarkable!

Soon after setting off a police car passed me going in the opposite direction. Twenty minutes later he returned on blue lights and siren and at a roundabout, stopped. Both officers looking up the adjoining dual carriageway drew their guns. Not surprisingly their overt presence prompted the oncoming vehicle they were interested in to do a U-turn, resulting in the pursued and pursuers heading up the dual carriageway in the wrong direction. Excitement presents itself often without an announcement.

House studying: there may now be a degree in this subject. The variety of different types of dwellings seen today was remarkable. Single storey, pantiles, half-timbered buildings, circa 1700. Flint buildings like those found in Norfolk, in the UK. Large stand-alone three-storey French châteaux. Single storey terrace homes, like those in Scotland, and all looking impressive in their own way.

I arrived in the town of Mont de Marsan. Initially, nothing made Mont de Marsan any more remarkable than the previous or next town. However, when crossing the wide bridge over the river Midou, surfaced with cobble setts that extend either side of the bridge and form patterns across the large town hall courtyard, your attention is grasped. There is also an apparent infatuation for life-sized bronze statues of naked women. Five in various poses are positioned on the bridge, with others on the approach road to the bridge. A further bronze statue is suspended by his feet as he dives, yes that is right! naked into the river beneath, obviously never quite making the water.

Lunchtime approached, as did the village of Sabres. A seemingly appropriate restaurant presented itself. I parked the bike in the empty and ample courtyard only to be told in an indignant manner that bikes are to be left outside the premises. Yes, understandable if there were no large empty spaces and there were some customers. In my most off-hand French, I made it known that this was the height of 'cycle victimization', and left. I am so pleased I did because hidden away down a side street was a fantastic restaurant called Au Petit Resto, where I had an excellent lunch. What is more, emerging well fed, that grey sky was now blue with a few fluffy clouds. And the sun was warm on my back. Not even the increasing headwind could dampen my enjoyment.

Lunch at Au Petit Resto.

The next unexpected event was cycling into Trensacq where an 'all things gardening' show had taken over this small village. The 'show' surrounded the church, an unusual building. The west wall, where the tower usually is, was just a wall extending as a single wall high above the church's west door. Furthermore, out of sight of each other and as if cantilevered, there were a pair of ancient timber Juliet balconies. These structures were roofed and looked in good repair. With no access apparent, how did Juliet get there for Romeo? A mystery.

Leaving Trensacq, having eaten a delicious warm croissant, I cycled on to Pissos where two sapeurs pompiers were getting into a fire appliance, blue lights already on. With two massive hose reels mounted on the rear of the appliance, I thought they were off to a bush fire. Two km down the road both they and other fire appliances and several police vehicles were managing a road traffic collision, although only one car was visible, a black Audi. The driver had decided to check *out the road-holding capacity of his vehicle's roof. This he had seemingly done for some distance and to see what benefits kerb-side soil has in providing additional adhesion, had spread a quantity over the tarmac. It was this that the firefighters were returning to the verge. As for the driver, who knows, he could have been sitting on one of those fluffy white clouds in the sky. One of the guys directing the traffic told me that there was a cycle path coming up. What a relief not to be constantly drawn to my mirror to see what was bearing down on me. The path was equally as smooth as the road and ran parallel with it for a while, then an increasing distance separated us. Sadly, the path ended after a few km and an 800 m ride took me back onto the busy D834.*

Fire appliances.

Variety it has been, right to the end of the day. I am in my tent behind a graveyard. The D834 is still busy at 11 pm. Having done my evening shop, I treated myself to a large beer in a bar before heading off to find a place to camp. This was expected to be easy with so much woodland around. On this perfectly straight road, where the vanishing point never does vanish, there was for the first time an endless fence that kept me out of the woods. Wide open fields were to the left and the headwind had again increased. Time to stop, but where? Eventually, the fence ended. I took off down a track. Found an ideal site and started to put the tent up when a swarm of mosquitoes arrived. Big and aggressive and determined to remove as much blood from me as possible. I retreated rapidly back to the road and tried to outpace them.

Having cycled 150 km today, and with the light fading, I wanted to eat and rest. I chose a grassy area behind a graveyard but again the mosquitoes arrived. I do not think I have pitched a tent and dived into one as fast. For a while even after I got in you could hear them hitting the tent material, trying to break in to feed on me. Packing up in the morning may be interesting. Let us hope these mozzies are not the Tiger mosquitoes recently identified as being responsible for the transmission of a host of nasty diseases including Zika virus.

It is well past eleven now and I need to sleep.

CHAPTER EIGHT
David Joins me

'There is no passion to be found in settling for a life that is less than the one you are capable of living.' Nelson Mandela

David had arrived in Royan and taken the ferry across the Gironde to meet me. We enjoyed a beer in the afternoon sun before catching the ferry across to Royan. David is a quiet, courteous person who expresses his views, but is always open to listening to others. It is a pleasure to be with him. Our apartment is on an upper floor of a multi-storey building overlooking parts of the town. Whilst in America Andy and I had become adept at getting our bikes into hotel lifts. This usually involved rearing them up on their hind wheels and jamming the front wheel into the opposite corner of the lift at head height. This technique has served me well. The large sun-drenched apartment enabled our cycling clothes to dry quickly whilst we rode into the town centre for an evening meal of fish and chips! During our meal, David made a few suggestions about amending our proposed route. We intended to cycle together for six days northeast to Fontainebleau. He had not un-naturally studied the route. On reaching Nordkapp I would have spent around 80 days in the saddle. I was more than happy to 'follow my leader' for a fraction of that time. Ahead of us lay some very enjoyable cycling and an education into French history and culture.

David had joined me to cycle from Royan to Fontainebleau where I would continue in a generally northeast direction and he would head to Paris. Unlike me, who was riding a Trek hybrid cycle with double panniers and carrying sufficient for my survival for a few months, David was 'going' ultra-lightweight. Over the years I have worked hard at perfecting the art of having everything I need on an expedition, whilst minimising the bulk and weight. So, it was with admiration that I surveyed the slick tyres on his road cycle that carried a pair of large but seemingly bottomless saddlebags. They were the Doctor Who's Tardis of cycle panniers, containing not only a tent, sleeping bag and mat, but also a toothbrush.

Although each were of minimum construction, the achievement still engaged my mind as to what I could jettison. These thoughts usually occurred when cycling up steep hills, although it must be said the warmth and deep comfort gained from a 'heavier' sleeping system and the benefits of undisturbed nightly sleep balances the issue.

Unbeknown to us a week of excellent cycling lay ahead. We were to see some of the best French architecture in the world and enjoy some beautiful weather (and some terrible weather too). David was to wild camp for the first time in his life and prove rather good at it. In particular, finding an enormous disused barn where we spent the night and dried out after a drenching. Much of our route hugged the banks of the river Loire. To have great company, good weather and be cycling through countryside that is a feast for the eyes, whilst being lean and fit through cycling the Alps, is a dream.

Having escaped the suburbs of Royan the following morning, we rode a quiet lane that ran parallel with the D728 turning north to the fine historic city of Brouage. Cycling through flat marshlands we arrived at Soubise on the south bank of the river Charente where a small ferry would have taken us across and then into Rochefort. Although the ferry was there, no ferryman was to be seen. We found out that a ferry further upstream was operating. This was to work in our favour. Cycling under the modern road bridge that took the D733, we came across a unique piece of history.

Whilst David and I waited for the ferry to cross from the other side of the Charente, a lady also waiting for the ferry engaged us in conversation. Immaculately dresses and manicured, Georgette asked the usual questions but in a manner that attracted our full attention. Obviously cultured, she had lived in Paris for many years and had chosen to move to the 'belle ville historique de Rochefort'. Although of similar age to ourselves, the years had been kind to her, exceedingly kind. She accompanied us across the river and walked with us into the city, showing and explaining the historic sites. Thanking her for her time, we parted at the old dock entrance to the city.

FACT FACTORY: Royan displays few signs of its extensive history. Sitting on the north bank of the Gironde estuary over the centuries its strategic importance has been immense. From the Vikings and before, to the Nazis during the Second World War, primarily as U-boat stock pens to permit easier access to the Allied Atlantic convoys, Royan has been of strategic military importance. Allied planes set about flattening the city between September 1944 and April 1945. It was known that 5,500 Nazis were holed up in the city with 3,000 trapped civilians. Efforts had been made to advise the French Resistance of these forthcoming attacks to minimise civilian casualties. Allied command was aware that this information had not been received; however, bombing commenced resulting in 1,500 civilian deaths and many being wounded. Napalm was used on April 15th 1945 to 'fire' the city, which later became known as the 'Martyred City'. Rebuilt in the 1950s the city is a Modernist architectural mecca and a tourist and cultural centre.

The Rochefort-Martrou Transporter Bridge is a rare type of bridge. Only eight of the eighteen transporter bridges built around the world remain standing. When cycling across America, Andy and I were fortunate to have seen another of these rare bridges in Duluth, Minnesota, although that was an aerial lift bridge that raises to permit shipping to go beneath and not a section of a gondola that is transported from one bank to the other. The Rochefort bridge only operated for two years from 1898 to 1900. It spans the river at 175.5 m. The concept and engineering were the work of the French engineer Ferdinand Amodin. It was abandoned in 1967 for a vertical lift bridge, which itself was demolished in 1991 after the opening of the dual carriageway road bridge. When David and I saw this fascinating piece of history it was sadly not in use and still under major renovation. Scheduled for completion in April 2020, the Covid-19 pandemic has stopped all work. Once completed pedestrians and cyclists will be able to use it.

Daily Blog: David joins me for a great day cycling. May 7th
David arrived by train in Royan the evening of the 5th and yesterday, whilst I cycled up from Maubuisson, he cycled the east side of the peninsula to St-Yzans-de-

Medoc. It would have been good if we had had the time to visit some of the famous châteaux, such as Margaux and Cap Léon Veyrin that are further to the south nearer to Bordeaux.

We both caught the 5.30 pm ferry from Fort du Verdon into Royan. An uneventful 30 minutes where we joined many other cyclists.

Today we rode north from Royan, a town that was levelled during the Second World War by the allies. Sadly, there were far more civilian casualties than Nazi soldiers. The town has rejuvenated and is now a popular holiday destination.

We had a few small difficulties orientating our way away from the town but did find the minor roads we were seeking to visit the walled town of Brouage. In Louis XIV days this wonderfully preserved piece of history was lapped by the sea. Through land reclamation, the sea is now not within eyesight from the ramparts. It remains surrounded by fortifying walls. There is also a cycle museum – which was closed!

Brouage, once surrounded by the sea.

David within the walled town of Brouage.

*Rochefort Transporter Bridge. Currently undergoing a three-year restoration. When completed
it will be the only working bridge of its type in the world.*

*When we were waiting for the ferry to arrive, Georgette introduced herself. She had
recently moved to Rochefort having lived in Paris and Berlin. She crossed the river with
us and told us many interesting things about the transporter bridge, French history, and
Rochefort. She also kindly showed us a picturesque route into the city centre.*

CHAPTER NINE
Castles, Beautiful Towns & Nuclear Power Stations

'The journey, not the arrival, matters.' T. S. Eliot

This morning we rode the 30 km from Secondigny north to Bressuire. It was a beautiful time of day with the early morning mist hugging the tranquil river. The willow trees leaning over the opposite bank as if drinking the water, appeared, and then disappeared in the rolling mist. A small herd of cows could be heard pulling the grass as they strolled aimlessly in a meadow. A heron, petrified, waited for breakfast to swim past. The occasional dog with owner in tow walked the riverbank. David, cycling ahead at a leisurely pace, was also absorbed in the serenity of the moment. How things were to change.

Later that day, after the heat had risen considerably, we found the town square in Bressuire with an open-air café. A 'larger than life' Canadian cyclist on a thoroughbred road cycle started chatting. He had cycled from Glasgow in Scotland and was heading to Santiago. We presumed Santiago de Compostela in northern Spain. With full panniers mounted on a carbon frame and 22 mm tyres, I wondered how many wheels, tyres and spokes he would be replacing.

As with every day of our lives, we are incapable of knowing how each of them will end. It is this knowledge, that you cannot know, that adds to the excitement. We can predict and apply logic, but the element of surprise remains.

David and I predicted that it was going to rain – sometime soon, but when and for how long and how heavy? A launderette that happened to be open provided refuge from the first downpour, it did not for the second! We left Bressuire under the misguided belief that no further rain could follow such a deluge. Cycling along the perfectly straight (and narrow) busy D748 the rain returned, with a vengeance that cried out, 'So you thought you had escaped me!' Heads down, rain piercing squinting eyes, sunglasses useless, we pedalled on trusting that motorists would refrain from texting on their phones and ploughing into us.

Now the desire to reach our destination was the sole objective. That destination only had to meet one criterion, to be dry!

I failed to see it, or perhaps I did not. A collection of buildings to our left, farm buildings, and a house. Farmyards are not the best places to wild camp. They usually have their own occupancies, wild dogs, wild cats, and rats, not to say cattle. All of whom have their agendas. Farm dogs usually want to either just kill you or to gnaw your leg or bum, cats and cattle want to feed and make it known loudly, and rats, well rats are just nasty and take delight in running across your chest seconds before you wake up in a cold sweat. Stealth is essential for undisturbed wild camping. However, David's brain was not as addled as mine. Having almost missed the overgrown entrance, we circled and rode into a dilapidated courtyard. There were numerous buildings in various states of decay. However, there was one dominating large stone-built barn that offered shelter. David's opportunisms had provided us a perfect place to stay. Only the inner tents were pitched to deter any marauding rats and unlike later in my journey, no one woke us pointing a rifle. For those interested these buildings can easily be seen on aerial maps south of Argenton-Château on the D748 near Baron Ludovic.

FACT FACTORY: Saumur, overlooking the confluence of the rivers Loire and Thouet, this stunningly beautiful example of a medieval town with the Château de Saumur dominating the town, is a feast for the eyes. Built as a castle in the 10th century by Theobald I, it has been developed into a palatial château. Saumur is the home of Le Cadre Noir, the French national horse-riding school. There is also an incredible museum of tanks and of course the Musée du Champignon.

Daily Blog: Rolling hills in the sunshine. May 8th

Today consisted of rolling hills, the downs were short, the ups longer. For a while, we cycled along a quiet lane beside a sedate river. Fishermen, some joined by their wives, sat beside rods. Some were content with a single rod, whilst others had several. The early morning light gave the view an ethereal feel. With the riverbank cottages and tiny timber jetties, the scene could only be in rural France.

In Secondigny we had a fantastic lunch at the Traiteur. This meal was one of the best I have had since leaving Tarifa. The three-course meal, preceded by a glass of excellent white wine, was suggested by David, and willingly agreed to by Tim.

David and Tim with the owner of the Restaurant Traiteur outside his restaurant after a great three-course meal.

The church at a little village called Bertignolles.

Having ridden around an EDF nuclear power plant and onto Ussé, later we arrived in Bressuire, where we had a welcome drink of fresh orange and met a large Canadian who was cycling from Glasgow to Santiago on a carbon bike fitted with panniers. It was in this town that we were fortunate.

As we left, the sky turned blackish. It had been a hot and muggy day and a serious storm was imminent with thunder rolling around. We decided to return the short distance to the town and, having bought our evening meal, took advantage of an open launderette. As the rain bounced down the road, turning it into a river, we and our bikes stayed dry.

The laundry provided refuge.

The first we escaped, the second we did not.

However, later we did get soaked en route for Argenton-les-Vallées. Two km before we arrived in the town, David saw a collection of disused farm buildings, in which we are now camped.

The barn from where I am writing this. Our clothes are drying, and we have eaten well.

Daily Blog: Castles, beautiful towns, and nuclear power stations. *May 9th*

After our night in a disused barn, where we were able to dry out from the previous evening's impressive storm, we were refreshed. An early start at 7 am quickly saw us in the first open cafe consuming two cups of strong coffee, before heading off to meet up with the Loire river for the first time. Our initial introduction to an ornate and impressive château was at Montreuil-Bellay as we crossed the Thouet river.

David and I enjoyed our second cafe visit at the L'escalier St Pierre creperie in Montreuil-Bellay after covering a quick 30 km.

From Saumur we followed the south bank of the Loire, along the D947 then the D751 stopping to eat at Le P'tit bar near to Port du Château de Montsoreau. This area was particularly pleasant. Riding on, we crossed over the river Vienne as it converged on the Loire. Saumur was a busy town with some impressive architecture.

Finally crossing the river to its northern bank and arriving here in Langeais, where a well-earned beer was enjoyed at La Conciergerie.

David and I both needed a shave and brush up and charge our phones, Garmin, power packs, and cameras, so have booked into an excellent gite, the Gite Le Clos du Paradis. What a contrast to the two previous nights.

The Château de Langeais medieval castle.

Images of Langeais.

Our accommodation for this evening. Gite Le Clos du Paradis. It certainly was bordering on paradise and a million miles from 'wild camping'.

CHAPTER TEN
Fontainebleau Calls

'Cyclists see considerably more of this world than any other class of citizens. A good bicycle, well applied, will cure most ills this flesh is heir to.' Dr. K K Doty

Our journey continued to follow the river Loire in an east north-east direction. The luxury of indulging in sleeping in a proper bed that was raised off the floor without the necessity of laying down to haul damp lycra cycling shorts up your legs whilst laying half in a sleeping bag was appreciated.

We had arrived too early to check in so enjoyed a cool beer sitting in the cleanest of town squares with its white stone buildings. Our room at Le Clos du Paradis Langeais boasted a high ceiling and shuttered windows, which when swung open provided a view across to the Château de Langeais medieval castle across the river Roumer. The house was large and imposing with a wide gravelled driveway leading to an impressive entrance hall. We later walked around the town and found a pizzeria. Having showered and shaved the night before, we had slept soundly and enjoyed an excellent breakfast before heading off towards Tours. This was to be a quintessential 'French' indulgent day riding beside the river Loire into Tours, which needs no description from me, save to say that it is beautiful, busy, and is impossible to do justice to in the time these two long-distance cyclists had to spare. Although the largest city in the Centre-Val de Loire region, Orleans is the regional capital. However, Tours exudes historic magic. Having left Tours behind us we cycled along the bank of the Cher. With perfect weather, we were at peace with the world. How could the day get any better? As lunchtime approached so an open-air restaurant, well not exactly a restaurant, more a garden with quirky art and unusual 'things' scattered around, popped up. With the river a metre on our right and the garden to our left, we sat and ate a healthy lunch before continuing.

Following the river Cher, we headed to Chenonceau and the magnificent château that straddles the river Cher. As I mentioned in the Blog, David was enthusiastic to see this French masterpiece of architecture. So, unfortunately, (but quite understandably) were hundreds of other visitors. Whilst cycles allow their riders to move around congested towns without parking difficulties and can usually be smuggled into hotel bedrooms without parking charges, in other situations security can be an issue, particularly if losing your worldly possessions would scupper the rest of your adventure. Given that where there are tourists there are usually thieves, I suggested that David went into the château and I remained with the bikes. He would have none of it, so we hatched a plan. A mile or so on the D40 past La Chevalerie we turned down the Rue de la Gare and cycled over the river bridge and along a well-trodden footpath through a beech wood and were rewarded with some splendid views of the château. Although we did not enter the château the views we gained from across the river were marvellous.

We continued, passing the caves at Monmousseau, and headed to the 16th century privately owned Château de Villesavin and were treated to seeing a convoy of vintage cars passing us. These pleasing sights were sadly balanced by coming across two donkeys that had not been cared for. With long coats that nearly touched the ground and were totally matted, this was unnecessary cruelty. Deep woods surrounded us and provided an easy place to camp for the night. On balance, most nights spent wild camping are enjoyable for a variety of reasons. This particular night we put our tents up before the mosquitoes arrived, of which there were not so many. As we ate our evening meal musing over how enjoyable the day had been, we both felt satisfied. The ground was soft with a deep layer of dry leaf mould beneath our sleeping bags and as the light faded, so the bird song became less until there was absolute silence.

The morning of May 11th saw us up early. Already within the 13,000 acre walled grounds of 17th century Château de Chambord, it took only a short while until we arrived at this Renaissance masterpiece. A mix of Gothic and Renaissance, this stunning piece of architecture, commissioned by King Francis I between 1515 and 1547, so obviously inspired by Leonard Di Vinci and probably designed by Domenico du Cortona, cannot fail to impress. The magnificent structure stands in splendid isolation on low marshland. It is the largest castle of its kind in the world and was only completed during King Louis XIV reign. David and I rode towards it unable to look away. We were completely on our own. We crossed a small bridge near where a few rowing boats were moored. As the last of the morning mist lifted from the water two swans glided past. The sun shone on the castle with light being reflected from glazed windows. To have this iconic château to ourselves was a real treat. As we left, I had a feeling of emptiness. I love touring but sometimes regret the necessity to move on. One of the benefits of cycling is that you see so much more as you travel through a country, you can stop more easily than in a car. However, more time is needed to progress a journey, to move along on occasions means you cannot do justice to a particular place. I would have liked to have spent the day at Chambord, even though within a few hours hundreds of tourists would be sharing the experience.

Daily Blog: Cake and château. May 10th

We left Langeais after a good breakfast provided by our wonderful hostess at Le Clos du Paradis Langeais, which included homemade jams and yogurt. We returned to the south bank of the Loire to Azay-le-Rideau, which involved an immediate hill climb. On to Montbazon, a fast 35 km for refreshments.

A sample of patisserie delights.

This fisher-lady was just leaving.

Suitably 'caked up' from the Artisan *boulangerie et patisserie*, we headed for Chenonceaux using the quiet D17 and D45. We found a couple of excellent riverside cycleways and, on the bank of the river Cher, came across a wacky outdoor restaurant, where we had a snack lunch of pate, bread and carrot, and some excellent fresh apple juice.

Both David and I had wanted to see Chenonceau, this wonderful and famous château, but the crowds were huge and my aversion to so many people changed the emphasis. David was brilliant and although I said I was happy to wait with the bikes whilst he looked around, we both agreed to seek out the iconic view from the other side of the river. We were not disappointed!

We then struck a north-east direction heading to Sambin, on to Cheverny and a beer at Arian at 5 pm in glorious sunshine. Throughout the day the sun has shone, but as soon as we started cycling the air was cooler.

We visited a couple of other châteaux, Château de Fougères-sur-Bièvre and Château de Villesavin, where we would have been charged six euros to take a photo. It was here that we found a couple of donkeys, their coats were long and matted; what a state they were in. There was also a classic car rally, led by a Triumph TR4.

We are now camped in the forest a few kilometres north of Villesavin, near to what may be a badger set. As I finish writing this, a cuckoo can be heard. A distant woodpecker is giving itself a headache, collar doves and small birds are singing as dusk arrives. It is all very tranquil as the bird song slowly subsides as the light fades.

A good day today with 118 km covered and 4,000 calories consumed. This was the eighth consecutive day I have covered over 100 km. I am feeling strong, but wary not to push too much each day to avoid long-term fatigue. There are still many more weeks of cycling.

We arrived in Orleans having taken the riverside path from Cléry-Saint-André and briefly cycled around the city before having a coffee and an ice cream. During the weeks I was on the road I rarely ate ice cream. It is not that I do not like it, it's just that it is so unhealthy, yet why should I be bothered, I'm burning thousands of calories each day. So, on the occasions I do have one, they are eaten at a speed that balances the 'melt rate' against the clock. The warmer the day and the softer the ice cream the fewer the moments of pleasure. The colder the day and harder the ice cream, the longer the pleasure.

Our trip together was coming to an end. A week ago, I had known David as a 'friend of a friend'. Now I considered him my friend. He had done something he had always wanted to and that was not only to cycle across France but to go wild camping, to go 'off grid'. I had thoroughly enjoyed his company and the rest it had given me in navigating the lesser-ridden routes across the country. For me, there was a realisation that I was about to re-immerse in total obscurity. Conversation would be limited to passing greetings and functional chat with shop assistants.

We took the road to Neuville-aux-Bois where we had lunch and arrived in Pithiviers late afternoon before going on to Farault and admiring several smaller châteaux. Our last wild camp was set on raised ground looking over fields of cereal crops towards the setting sun. Nature had balanced itself this evening by providing sharp thorns in the soil that could easily tear the tent groundsheet or worst, puncture our air mats. However, she had provided a strain of mosquito that both flew slowly and walked around their 'dinner plate' before stabbing its proboscis into their meal. Killing anything should not be condoned, except for one creature. Over the course of 8,000 km, I had and would without consent donate several pints of my blood to mosquitoes. Killing a few of them did not lay heavily on my conscience.

Arriving in sunny Fontainebleau the following morning we had a look around the incredible château. Unlike Chambord, that has never had permanent royal residency, Fontainebleau has been occupied for eight centuries. Unfortunately, after a week of having no time constraints, David was back on a schedule and had to depart for Paris, but not before an alfresco coffee looking towards the château from the Café du Château, of course. David headed north to Paris and I headed down the Avenue des Cascades and east towards Provins.

I had enjoyed his company and hoped that he had enjoyed mine. We had lived a week of our lives together and shared some good experiences. Although different from high altitude climbing, where your friendship with your tent 'buddy' is intensely important and can become the difference between surviving or dying, our relaxed companionship had rejuvenated me. I was ready for the next chapter of my journey to the northernmost point of mainland Europe.

FACT FACTORY: Born in 1412, Joan of Arc, who was to become known as The Maid of Orleans, was destined to be immortalised. Reluctant to accept a divine calling and having overcome The Dauphin's initial scepticism, at the age of seventeen she was given command of the French army.

In 1328 France had no king. The French royal house of Valois and the English house of Plantagenet fought bitterly for the prize. This was to become known as the Lancastrian phase of The Hundred Years War. The French were still reeling from losing at Agincourt in 1415. Joan's first task was to relieve Orleans, besieged by the English. If Orleans were to fall, France would fall to the English. With utter belief beyond all odds, she commanded the French army by example and forced the English to abandon their siege on Orleans. This she did having been previously wounded by an arrow.

The Dauphin Charles (to become Charles VII) was up against Henry V in his ascendancy. The Scottish were no friends of the English and on Easter Sunday in 1421, 6,000 of them routed the English at Baugé in the Loire, leaving Henry V's brother, Thomas Duke of Clarence dead on the field of battle. The Scottish commander, the Earl of Buchan, was now given command of the French army by the Dauphin, who had already established a personal bodyguard solely of Scots, the Garde Ecossaise.

On May 30th 1431 the English, having captured Joan of Arc, burnt her at the stake for heresy in Rouen in English-occupied Normandy. She died of smoke inhalation at the age of nineteen. The real reason the English murdered Joan was political. A young woman had successfully led the French army against the English, she had humiliated and embarrassed them and with her death, the morale of the French would fail and hence any further French military success would be compromised. They were to be proven very wrong. The French had satisfied themselves that she was not a witch, but it was a convenient charge for the English to level. Bishop Pierre Cauchon, who headed the farcical trial, even declined a soldier's offer to strangle her as a

'merciful' gesture, instead of burning. Cauchon announced, as a heretic she was to suffer as much as possible before dying, and ordered her to be burned.

Daily Blog: Fontainebleau calls. May 11th

As David said today, there is something satisfying about cycling across a map in a day and today was one of those days.

I was awoken this morning by what was probably a deer stumbling on two tents and bikes blocking its regular path through the forest. We packed up bone-dry tents and headed off on a path through the forest. It was cold. Shards of early morning sunlight penetrated through the trees. We arrived at our first impressive château (Chambord) before any other visitors. A photographer's dream, as the morning mist lifted from the water gardens, the low multi-arched stone bridge was perfectly reflected in the water beneath and the sun displayed the ornate architecture of the château to its best; a sense of being in a fairyland was easy to imagine.

We continued our ride through acres of forest before emerging on the D95, where at Cléry-Saint-André, we took the excellent riverside cycle path into Orleans. What a great city this is! Yes, it has its history concerning a determined and persuasive young lady bent on raising an army to fight the English and subsequently being betrayed and burnt as a witch, which she certainly was not. However, there is so much more to this city than just the history of Joan of Arc.

David and I enjoyed both a coffee and an ice cream in Orleans before cycling to Pithiviers using the less used picturesque country lanes. The forests that have stood since long before the kings of France used them for hunting deer and game were replaced by largely flat arable land. However, there were still surprises, such as this small private and immaculate château at Farault.

The private château at Farault.

We had no problem finding our campsite for tonight. Some 50 m from a minor road, it looks to an impressive setting sun over hundreds of acres of cereal crops. The mosquitoes are large and slow and not too many, even fewer now that we have culled any that landed on us, bar one on my hand, that left a substantial gift.

Tomorrow David will leave me at Fontainebleau and head into central Paris to catch his train home and I will begin the next leg of my journey, this time towards Luxembourg.

It has been great to have had David ride with me. We have enjoyed some brilliant wild camping nights and the weather, apart from one especially heavy storm, has been near perfect. It has also been good to have a few days off from orienteering, as David has done a remarkable job of route finding and taken us to some great locations. My sincere thanks, David.

The quirky riverside café.

Château de Chenonceau on the river Cher.

Château de Chambord.

David and I camp near Chambord.

A Life Appreciated

Visually stunning.

Orleans, as impressive as the description.

Château de Villesavin.

David and I enjoy our last camp facing west, absorbing the setting sun.

Daily Blog: Château de Fontainebleau. May 12th

Firstly, I must again give my apologies. I have just loaded two blog entries with selected photos and again been unable to publish them. It is more than a little disappointing! I feel as though a lot of effort at the end of a hard day is being wasted. Anyway, here is hoping this entry will be trouble-free. I will also attempt to load up the photos that did not previously load. If this problem continues, I will put all the photos on my website soon after getting to Nordkapp.

Château de Fontainebleau.

Fontainebleau is the only royal residency that has housed royalty for more than eight centuries, from Louis VII to Napoleon III. It started its life as a medieval castle in 1137 and soon became a hunting lodge. Thomas Becket consecrated the chapel for Louis VII in 1169. Today it is a national museum and a UNESCO heritage site. Unfortunately, David and I could do little justice to this magnificent site, having time only for a brief glimpse.

We enjoyed a last coffee together before he headed to Paris and I to Montereau-Fault-Yonne. This town has two bridges, one each straddling both the Yonne which ends here and joins the existing Seine. It is the point of confluence of the rivers. However, does the Seine run into the Yonne or vice versa? What cannot be disputed is

that many battles have been fought at this location, such as the Battle of Montereau on February 18th 1814. Napoleon personally became involved with the fighting against the Austrians, famously saying, 'Do not fear, my friends. The cannonball that should kill me has not even been made.' This was his last decisive victory.

Images of Napoleon.

The rain, as forecasted, arrived with gusty winds and the ability to drench in moments, and is set to continue tomorrow. I have taken refuge in the Chambre du Toucan, in a small village called Misy-sur-Yonne, not surprisingly a stone's throw from this impressive river that supports enormous barges, that in addition to their cargo often have the crew's commuting vehicle, such as an SUV, parked on the deck. The owner of my bed and breakfast is in the process of renovating the property. He has finished the guest room, which is splendid, with exposed stone walls and reclaimed timber. The bathroom is set in the bedroom with no dividing partitions and the whole large area is lit by roof lights. High quality, with the signature of a craftsman.

I am preparing for a wet day tomorrow. First to Nogent-sur-Seine, then on to Châlons-en-Champagne.

FACT FACTORY: Fontainebleau, only 3 km from the banks of the River Seine and 65 km south-east of Paris, this large and beautiful forest is the playground for Parisians and has been (for the rich) since the 12th century. The kings of

France have used the Château de Fontainebleau since there was a fortified castle there in 1137 as a base to hunt the abundant game in the extensive forests. Kings who used the palace were Louis VII, Philip II and Louis IX (who was later canonised, Saint Louis).

In the 16th century King François I transformed the palace to make it into a 'new Rome'. The château is the epitome of opulence and the surrounding grounds, with many statues and fountains, including (weirdly) four seated hunting dogs all peeing into a fountain, with Diana, the Roman goddess of hunting as a centrepiece, give an insight into how French aristocracy lived. It is no wonder the peasants revolted on learning of these cruel divides.

To dispel the belief that Marie-Antoinette, wife of King Louis XVI, on hearing that the poor had no bread, replied by saying, 'Qu'ils mangent de la brioche' (Let them eat cake), is a fact. This is, in fact, not a fact. Having been inaccurately attributed to her, it galvanised the populace's hatred towards her and the whole monarchy and fuelled the revolution and the subsequent loss of her head via the guillotine. The biographer, Lady Antonia Fraser, believes such sentiment and words would have been out of character. She was a highly intelligent and sensitive lady who previously had often made generous donations to the poor. The story was not new; King Louis XIV's queen, the Spanish princess Marie-Therese, had said: 'la croute de pâté' (the crust of pâté). Several others were also attributed to have said similar callous remarks. So 'fake news' has been around long before the 45th President of America. Sadly, the guillotine has been retired.

CHAPTER ELEVEN
Goodbye France

**'Do not be angry with the rain, it simply does not know how to fall upwards'.
Vladimir Nabokov**

With fading images of statues of serenely smooth, curvaceous, and beautiful women and perfectly muscled men, I turned my back on historical opulence and returned to the world of cycling. I am comfortable with my own company. There are times I loathe myself, am full of self-doubt, and think myself plain stupid. However, for whatever reason I seem to be blessed with a fair degree of common sense, an abundance of determination, usually sanguine, and an aversion to failure – or is that an attraction to success? The sense of loneliness passed within a few hours. I say loneliness, more perhaps losing the ability to share immediate experiences with someone else.

Although David and I had wild camped for most of our week, we had enjoyed a couple of classic French 'Chambres d'hôtes', which had been most agreeable. Perhaps I was becoming soft but camping that night did not appeal. In the small village of Misy-sur-Yonne, I found an unassuming lodging. An ordinary door opening directly onto the street hid behind it, a fascinating home. With old beams, flagged floors, and history oozing from all corners, my first floor pitched roofed room was massive and included a roll-top cast iron bath in the bedroom. The village was that small I had to cycle to the next to what I had been promised was a good restaurant. A proper bed, bath, and food tonight, only that there was no restaurant. I later ate the food (bread, cheese, yogurt, and fruit) bought from the corner shop, sitting on a bench overlooking the river as it began to rain. Had there been a restaurant I would have been soaked on my return. After an excellent petit déjeuner, which was anything but small, I headed off to and around Nogent-sur-Seine and to Anglure in the rain. Hoping for a good meal at Fère-Champenoise, I found the place void of life. With limited food and the rain now heavier, I hit the D5 and headed for Châlons-en-Champagne. This fast and straight road took lorries towards the A4-E50 and they were in a hurry to get onto it. The rain lashed down. With rear-approaching and oncoming lorries seemingly indifferent to the dangers they posed of passing by when parallel with a cyclist, it put the fear of God into this cyclist. With less than a metre off my left arm passing at 70 km/h. With the wind turbulence and heavy rain, this was challenging. My life totally in the hands of the competency of strangers, this was the most frightening experience of the whole trip. The 13th of May was a Sunday; what would the road have been like during weekdays?

I needed to survive, I needed to find a safe place to camp for the night. To the right of the road was a dense conifer plantation. I found a convenient ride between the trees and pushed the bike 100 m from the road. Soaked to the skin and shivering I pitched the tent, climbed in, stripped off, and dried myself. I would be warm in the morning when I put the still wet clothes back on and with the sun on my back, the clothes would soon dry. A smile returned to my face as my body warmed and the comfort of a mattress of deep leaf mould promised a good night's sleep. I was not disappointed. Refreshed and with renewed enthusiasm I thought of Robert Falcon Scott as I emerged from the warmth of my sleeping bag and dressed in wet lycra, my warmth evaporating within seconds. I pedalled like a lunatic to get warm before arriving in Châlons-en-Champagne for a calorie-loading breakfast.

Daily Blog: Wet, oh, so wet! May 13th

A journey, like most other things, needs to have contrast to enable better times to be appreciated. Well, at this precise moment I am very much appreciating the better times.

I am cold, wet through, been attacked by mosquitoes that are either wearing wetsuits or are impervious to this torrential rain. The tent is up, I am inside it and can only partially dry my clothes with body heat by continuing to wear them.

So today has not been a good one. In marked contrast with the last week, today has seen me cycle beside endless enormous flat featureless fields on a road hardly wide enough for two lorries to pass. Sucked along by an extraordinary number overtaking me, some so uncomfortably close so as to avoid collisions with oncoming traffic.

However, there were a few humorous moments, including a porta-loo heavily secured with locks in splendid isolation in the middle of a deserted field. My addled brain ran to thoughts of how valuable the contents must be.

Yesterday, in anticipation of forecasted heavy rain, Anne kindly arranged a B and B in a little village called Misy-sur-Yonne. I mentioned it in my last blog and need to add a footnote. What a wonderful couple the owners are. Both artists and interesting. I was also given an excellent breakfast of muesli, orange, coffee, scrambled egg, bread, and homemade jams. As things turned out, it was just as well! I have cycled over 100 km mainly in the pouring rain on that breakfast and a cup of black coffee.

Where do the French go on Sundays? Or, for that matter, most of the remaining week? Their gardens, in the main, are well tended and they certainly grow far more vegetables in them than most English people. The houses are well maintained and in good repair. So, when does all the work get done? Village after village I have ridden through, I see not a soul, they appear to be lifeless. Today was a prime example, even in the sizeable town of Fere-Champenoise, where I had banked on getting a proper restaurant meal, there was nothing open except, fortunately, a small grocery. I had not expected anything between Nogent-sur-Seine through the lanes to Anglure, but this town was a reasonable size. So, my late lunch and evening meal consisted of biscuits, (I have never eaten a whole packet in one go before, so that is another first – not to be repeated), cooked chicken, sardines, pate de champagne (had to really) an apple and a banana. Oh, and a beer.

Where I am camped tonight epitomizes today. I am in a wood next to Châlons-en-Champagne's effluent treatment plant, opposite an extensive wind farm, (some would draw a correlation there). The rain is hammering down on the tent and the traffic on a wet road surface is very audible, but I can still hear the turbines. Camping is peaceful? Mmm!

And to the positives, the tent is totally waterproof. It cannot rain forever. Yes, my clothes will be wet and cold when I get dressed tomorrow morning, but if I cycle fast, I will soon warm up. The sun might shine as well.

Determined not to repeat the experiences of yesterday, I turned off the busy D3 as soon as possible and taking the peaceful D65 cycled through continuing rolling fields of arable land. Less than 200 m above sea level the landscape reminded me of the Fens in England. Occasionally there were large concrete grain silos. One, about 20 m high with nine silos, was being painted or cleaned by a tiny solitary figure halfway up, suspended on a platform he was hauling upwards. He may well still be there now.

The rain had not given up. The previous day's deluge had carried into the night and today had remained wet. It dawned on me that perhaps David had taken the sun and predominately good weather we had enjoyed whilst we were together, back to England. Although not as heavy as yesterday, it was persistent, and the enjoyment of cycling was ebbing. It did not take too much persuasion to opt for a dry and warm place to stay for the night. That small voice whispering, 'You're getting soft, Ralph,' was drowned out by a louder voice saying, 'You are supposed to be enjoying this experience, think of that hot shower, a cold beer, and dry clothes to put on in the morning.' So that is how I arrived at the Red Horse in Sainte-Menehould, a traditional hotel/pub that would not have been out of place in an English country town. Anne had booked it for me and although certainly not cheap it was a welcome break from the incessant rain that continued throughout the night. The meal at Le Cheval Rouge lacked quantity; yes, tasty, but a 'machine' requires more sustenance. Breakfast redressed the balance and I again headed off under leaden skies.

Daily Blog: Awoke to the sound of rain. May 14th

It is late! 7.30 am as I lay in my tent listening to the rainfall. I should be on the road cycling by now. The rain drowns the sound of both the traffic and wind turbines. Save for a short respite yesterday around mid-day, it has rained incessantly for 36 hours.

All my gear is nearly as wet as it was last night. I have decided to stay in a hotel tonight in Sainte-Menehould. This has necessitated a change of route, as the plan was to head NE on country lanes for 140 km up to Stenay. I will still be doing around 60 km and will be looking forward to a hot shower at Le Cheval Rouge, that Anne has kindly booked for me. It is unlikely there will be many photos today.

Now shaved and showered and having just used every conceivable space in my room to hang a wet tent, wet Thermo-Rest, damp sleeping bag, and all my washed cycling clothes, I have had a call from the hotel manager. He said that I am in the wrong room and would I please move. If he could only see the room.

Domestics in the Red Horse.

My powers of persuasion worked – fortunately! And I remained in the same room.

I only had 14 km to cycle into Châlons-en-Champagne this morning, but on the N5. I just could not get any wetter. I was past caring – but the lorries! So many, and on numerous occasions oncoming lorries would pass exactly at the same time as one was overtaking me, leaving the closest of margins for error.

Châlons, I am sure, is a great city. Its cathedral is very impressive, even in the gloom. I sort of warmed up over a coffee and bought supplies for lunch and got into a conversation with a couple from Baldock in Hertfordshire, a town not far from the first Fire Station I served at, Stevenage, in the mid-seventies.

Back on the N5, I again ran the gauntlet with wagons passing close to my left elbow, till Basilique de l'Épine, where I cycled south of the N5 to Sainte. Menehould, through tiny villages surrounded by undulating hills with an occasional line of poplar trees on the distant horizon. Doing a 360-degree turn showed just how open this countryside is. To every surrounding horizon, there was not a single building to be seen, not a hedge, a few small woods. No 'small time' French farmers here, everything is big. Fields of peas, wheat, barley, rape.

The less exciting is also needed.

The rain did stop when I reached Dampierre. It had started a few hours after David left on Saturday and has continued until Monday afternoon, with one or two hours' rest yesterday lunchtime. I also hear that the weather in England is very pleasant.

On a lighter note, I saw this mailbox outside a house today. What detail!

Immaculately kept homes.

And if you ever think a job is too big for one person to do, have a look at this daunting and boring task.

He is either painting or sandblasting the whole building (and will be for some time yet).

Today has been sort of a rest day with only 65 km cycled. The hotel has enabled me to do all the necessary domestics and as I have not had a rest day since April 9th, apart from the time with Anne in Lourdes, I certainly do not feel guilty. Again, depending on the weather tomorrow, I could be leaving French soil. I am planning either to camp near Stenay, which is still in France, or go on to Florenville in Belgium. It depends on what there is to see en route.

May 15th and I took a north-east route through Varennes where King Louis XVI and Marie-Antoinette were arrested. Today was to be my last in France and it was to be a sombre day. The last few days had been testing, most of the time I had been cold and wet, and although the countryside around had a definite character it had not been dramatic. My mood was slightly depressed and now I had arrived in the part of the world where tens of thousands of soldiers had sacrificed their lives for their countries. I should let the blog do the 'talking' here. We can blithely moan about our hardships today, some of which are profound, but the horror and suffering of these soldiers is hard to surpass.

I arrived in Stenay and left via the D13, too quickly. Throughout the ride up from Tarifa I had checked both beforehand and during the ride for any places of interest that were en route. Leaving Stenay without knowing of or visiting the Museum of Beer was a regretful mistake. The weather had improved, the landscape was more interesting with rolling hills, with the occasional short steep one. In a reflective and appreciative mood, I found a beautiful place to pitch my tent just south of Mogues, the last settlement in France I would cycle through. The Belgian border was a few hundred metres up the hill in the field where I enjoyed a couple of beers and an evening meal, sitting comfortably on my cleverly designed space-saving seat from under which so many disturbed and hungry ticks were awakened to come for their meal of blood, but not tonight.

I was leaving France tomorrow. It was a beautiful evening with the sun shining and a visual warmth on the surrounding countryside. A gentle breeze ran across the tall grass making it look like water. I fell asleep a happy man.

Daily Blog: Goodbye France. May 15th
What a brilliant day this last day in France has been. I shall miss seeing Mairie in every town I pass through.

This particularly beautiful town hall was in the little village of Wiseppe.

The rain returned with a vengeance during the night. However, it was of little consequence, laid in clean white linen and not in a tent.

Breakfast at the Red Horse Hotel, Le Cheval Rouge, was excellent, which in part made up for the evening meal. Whilst taste is vital, quantity surely also plays a part. As advertised both in French and English on the menu, the 'slab' of roast salmon must have been mistaken for a stickleback or minnow, 20 euros please! Dessert was a digestive biscuit with tinned tangerines arranged on top and covered with cream from a tin, 6 euros! So, I do not feel any guilt in admitting I had a substantial lunch today that was very 'similar' to breakfast; strange, that!

Lest we forget.

As I left the hotel in Sainte Menehould the sky was in a sullen mood and ready to rain again. My mood stayed sombre too as I left the town and visited the first of several World War One cemeteries.

After a few hills, all in an upwards direction, the sun suddenly broke through. Oh, so good to see and feel. I turned onto the D67 and rode steadily uphill, through the Forêt Domaniale. Shafts of sunlight penetrated through the canopy. The leaves were still wet from the night's rain, this further accentuated the light. In small, wooded glades the morning mist hung in the air as the light gave it a mystical appearance. A stream meandered, twisting slowly down through the wood. The sunlight rippled on the water's surface. And in the denser woodland, where the sun could not reach, it was impossible not to look for that elusive fully grown stag. Although with the bird song, the picture was perfect without any mystical beast.

I rode on at a leisurely pace, not wanting this part to end. There were constant reminders of the loss and suffering caused by the 'War to end all wars'. I passed cemeteries with thousands buried and yet I saw a small, isolated memorial with a soldier's battered helmet placed on it tucked away in a quiet corner.

I arrived in Varennes-en-Argonne, the town where Louis XVI and Marie-Antoinette were arrested. Louis was subsequently judged by the Republican Convention for treason (a king being accused of treason), found guilty, and executed on January 21st 1793 at the age of 39. Marie-Antoinette stood proud throughout her trial but was executed on October 16th the same year.

The scenery was varied. First the woods, then open grass fields with buttercups, cow parsley, thistledown, and ox-eye daisies, surrounded by hawthorn trees heavily laden with blossom. Then rolling hills to be replaced by mixed animal and arable land and numerous small woods and everywhere, reminders of the Great War, lest we forget, and rightfully so. We must never forget.

This evening I had wanted to camp straddling the French-Belgian border. The nearest I could manage is in a grass field in France looking up to a terraced mound about 800 m away which is in Belgium. I am just east of Auflance, up a rough track from the D417. The view is wonderful, and the location must be the best yet. No mozzies, thorns, people or buildings, total peace save for the skylarks.

- BELGIUM & LUXEMBOURG -

CHAPTER TWELVE
Hello Belgium

'Life is like riding a bicycle. In order to keep your balance, you must keep moving.' Albert Einstein

Having crossed the border into Belgium, Florenville was the first town I arrived in. Neat, functional, and with no street litter. I took the quiet roads to Chiny and onto Suxy, enjoying the cool air of the morning knowing that the day would be a warm, laid-back affair. Agriculture was everywhere. Away from the towns, the way of the land prevails. My first job, even before leaving school, had been working on a farm in Hertfordshire in England. On leaving school I was milking cows in a building known as an abreast parlour. The cows were brought in from the fields, sometimes with a friendly but productive Hereford bull. Each cow would enter the parlour and step up onto a raised platform where a milking cluster was attached to her udder and the milk collected in a bulk tank in the neighbouring room. On occasions that bull also walked in with his harem to watch the process and to get in my way. He was big – and friendly. All this happened in the early 70s. Imagine my surprise to see in 2018 a herd of cows being milked in a field by machinery attached to a tractor and trailer. Belgium in many regards remains almost historically rural and appears proud to be so.

As I write this book now over a year since the trip, I am trying to keep the blog I wrote whilst cycling, a separate entity: the blog reflecting my thoughts and experiences at the time they occurred, with these writings having a more measured reflective view. Sometimes an experience, whilst dramatic, exciting, or devastating, may not be a lasting memory. I think it goes without saying that the longer the experience, the more impactive on the memory it remains, unless that event is so explosive. This is certainly the case for the cycle ride across America, Spain to Norway, and the 7,000 m and 8,000 m mountain climbing expeditions.

These memories are punctuated by specific incidents, whether it is a negative, such as a crash, falling through a crevasse on a mountain, surviving an avalanche or a positive, summiting a mountain whether on two wheels or crampons, a beautiful sunset or in a rain-drenched bus shelter in Belgium.

My blog of May 16th is worth a second mention. It was scything with rain again and I had taken refuge in a bus shelter when a bus pulled up and the driver brought a wheelchair to the pavement, returned to the bus, and carried a young lady down the steps and put her onto the already soaked seat of the chair. She spoke excellent English and as neither of us were going anywhere in the deluge, the conversation continued. She was interested to know about the countries I was cycling through and shared her knowledge of them. As so many English people do, I brought the weather into the conversation, moaning about how wet it was. This she thought was funny as she had just heard that I live in Yorkshire near the Pennines in the UK, not a place renowned for having low annual rainfall. What she said next hit me between the eyes. "I so wish I could cycle; I would love to see different countries on a bike". She was young, intelligent, in her prime with her life ahead of her, but with no legs. In the short time we had met it was obvious that she was a determined person. How she had lost her legs did not matter, how she was coping, did. My admiration for that young lady was immediate and lasting, even now I rightfully feel belittled by her courage. If she were able, she would have willingly cycled in the pouring rain and a headwind. I do hope her life is a fulfilling one, I think it probably will be. She was not to be the only person on this trip who took my breath away with admiration.

Arriving in the busy town of Bastogne I was amused to see rocks arranged in wire cage work in the shapes of animals, a full-size boar, and others. There was also an ape and a bull made from vehicle engine parts, I think some would call it Junk Art, but highly effective, and a Second World War tank to commemorate those who had died fighting for Belgium. A disconnected mix of art and memorabilia.

Although I have been to Luxembourg before, the temptation to add another country to those visited on this trip was strong. It was certainly a 'tick in the box' visit. Arriving from Belgium I camped one night and passed through the village of Troine before returning to Belgium and Houffalize, where I was to meet up with Andy Hill who, you will remember, was the guy who introduced me to rock climbing during the 'Middle Ages' and subsequently dragged me 'kicking and screaming' across America on our Bianchi cycles. Andy had planned a trip that for much of the route disassociated itself from a quickest straight line whilst still complying with a tight schedule of forty days. We travelled 4,000 miles in those 40 days and had a fantastic time experiencing the true north of North America. I am indebted to him for asking me to share such a brilliant adventure.

Daily Blog: Hello Belgium. May 16th

The silence during the night was total. So rare these days. No rain during the night, but the sky was far too dark to promise a dry day. This prompted an early pack up. I had multiple visitors all over the tent, slugs, all shapes and sizes, each had to be flicked off the tent to avoid a squishy mess tonight. Similarly, the bike had enough riders on for a Tour de France peloton on a single bike. The campsite was so good, it is worthy of another photo.

The beauty of Belgium.

With several passengers, I headed off into Belgium:

A leech.

A wood ant.

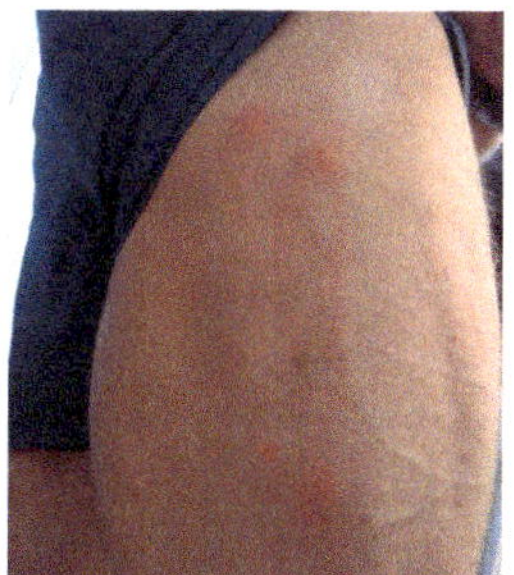

The buffet bar.

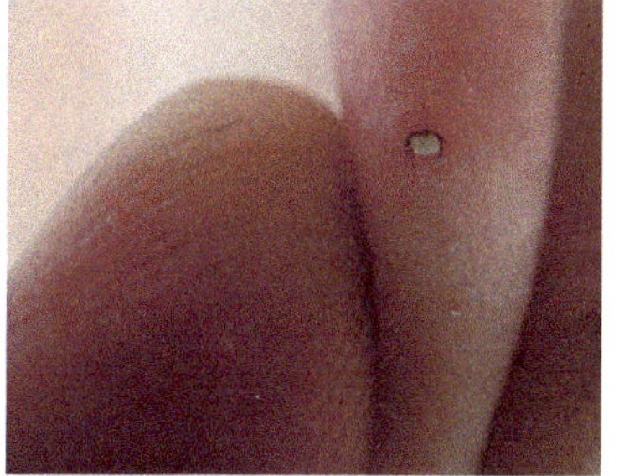

A tick takes a meal.

The first town I arrived in, Florenville, was different from the recently passed-through French towns. Mainly the buildings were modern, using breezeblocks, slate, metals, and flint. This was to be the norm through Chiny and Suxy.

Now, some of you will know that many decades ago I was a herdsman for a while, milking cows on a few farms before joining the Fire Service. However, I have never seen or heard of taking the milking parlour to the cows in the field. So, this was a first for me.

Yes, that is a milking machine running off the PTO (Power Take-Off) on the tractor.

I also experienced a belittling moment today. The prevailing wind has not been prevailing for at least a week. Even before David left in Fontainebleau it was coming from a northerly direction. Over the last few days, it has increased and is carrying heavy, short downpours of rain. A little like Andy, Luke, and my Scottish trip from the west coast to the east coast, when the wind had come from the east and not, as expected, from the west. I had taken a break from one of these short downpours in a bus shelter. When a bus arrived, the driver carried a young lady in her twenties down the steps and put her into her wheelchair. She joined me in the shelter. In our small talk, I bemoaned the weather. She had already seen that I was on a long *ride and simply said, 'I do wish I could cycle, I would love to see different countries on a bike.' She had no legs. Having said our goodbyes, the wind and showers went un-noticed.*

I am in a bar in Houffalize, that celebrates everything about the 101st Airborne Division of the American air force, sheltering from the wet stuff from above with some hot wet stuff for within. Looking across the town square there are various artistic structures.

An American tank and rampant bull.

I amended my route after a chat with a couple in a cafe to miss out on Arlon in Luxembourg, and now intend to dip my pedal into this small country and hopefully wild camp somewhere near Troine before meeting up with Andy tomorrow.

Daily Blog: Goodbye Belgium, hello Luxembourg, and hello again Belgium. May 17th.

Sitting in the sun with a cooling north breeze in the chic little town of Houffalize back in Belgium and enjoying my second strong black coffee, listening to Elton John sing 'Rocket Man'.

My brief visit into Luxembourg was an enjoyable one and was probably more to do with ticking boxes of countries visited on this epic ride. My campsite for the night was different from the previous night. Thankfully still void of mozzies.

Shortly after zipping up for the night, that 'zip' in the sky was again opened with a grand prelude of rolling thunder. There was a two-minute delay before the rain fully penetrated the trees, then the tent was hit as if it were a target for numerous water hoses. The sound was amazing, more thunder immediately above, now accompanied by a light show of lightning that lit the inside of the tent as if in direct sunlight. My Jack Wolfskin tent did not let a drop of water in. After an hour, the rain stopped, and peace returned even more silent than before, and I slept soundly.

I am waiting here in Houffalize to meet Andy Hill, who has been cycling in the area. Andy planned our incredible cycle ride across America from Seattle to Boston a couple of years ago. He and I are going to ride together for a few days. The intention is to include two short, but steep climbs often included in the professional cycling races. The Mur de Huy, with a maximum gradient of 26%, and La Redoute, with a 17% gradient.

As I was about to leave Houffalize a group of Harley Davidson motorcycles parked up. Now I am also fortunate enough to own a Harley. Perhaps, just perhaps, I brought the wrong pair of wheels for this trip. No! Definitely not! Motorcycles have their own attributes, but this trip was designed for pedals to gain satisfaction. By the way, yes, there was a dog inside the mini caravan.

The Harleys, one with a mini caravan for a 'not so' mini dog.

Andy and I met as scheduled and rode to Mormont to our B and B. Benoit and Isabelle welcomed us to their beautiful home, Cert'Titude, a truly rural and eco-friendly home.

With homemade beer as well. All is good!

It had again rained during the night. It had not lasted long and was accompanied by a spectacular show of thunder and lightning. My only night in Luxembourg was a memorable one. Arriving in Houffalize, a clean, pretty town in cool but delightful sunshine I enjoyed a beer and watched a group of Harley Davidson motorcycle riders arrive, two with miniature caravans in tow, one of which carried a dog. This town, like so many others in the area, was devastated during both the World Wars. Nowadays there are few obvious signs of that devastation.

Andy and two other friends had been cycling some of the First World War cemetery and monument routes. I met him on the roadside on the N30 north of the town as he was dropped off from their support vehicle. We headed to Manhay. When Andy and I had cycled across America we averaged 100 miles a day and were on Italian Bianchi road bikes. With just a change of clothes and the absolute essentials, we had reduced our carrying loads to as little as possible, choosing to 'credit card' the trip, no tent, no sleeping bags, mats or cooking facilities. Fast, light, and expensive, but high on octane, adrenaline, and enjoyment. For these few days in Belgium, Andy was again in that same mode of fast and light and on his faithful Bianchi thoroughbred, whereas I was on my faithful, yet slower hybrid Trek. Images of Don Quixote and Sancho's mounts are relevant here. I perhaps have said before how I enjoy wild camping but the attraction of the finer forms of living are not lost on me. Andy had booked our accommodation for the next two nights and they were to be palatial. The first, a country residence of near opulence, was just outside the town of Mormont and was entered via an archway contained within a period residential building leading onto an expansive courtyard and gardens surrounded on three sides by beautifully maintained stone residents with a lawn to the left dropping away into the walled vegetable garden. It appeared we were the only guests. I felt a little uneasy, as film sets of a few movies came to mind. We should not have been concerned, both the evening meal and the breakfast reflected the impeccable standards of this almost monastery-like hotel.

We cycled the 45 km to Huy in the morning sun, chatting and enjoying each other's company. Andy and I have known each other for many years. We used to babysit each other's children. They are now in their thirties and most now have children of their own! Arriving in the large, cobbled town square of Huy, we sat at one of the many alfresco tables and ordered a beer and omelette and considered our climb of the afternoon, the Mur de Huy, known as The Wall of Huy. At an elevation of 204 m, how hard could this climb be? Certainly not as hard as the Col du Tourmalet or the Kitzbüheler Horn, so why did Laurent Jalabert call it 'essentially a staircase' and Christian Prudhomme call it 'the longest kilometre of the racing season, a mountaineering competition'? The Mur de Huy has a maximum gradient of 26%, with an average of 9.9% over 1.7 km. Even as a cyclist when I see other cyclists struggling on hills as I drive past, it is easy to view that climb in isolation. That struggling cyclist could have covered 160 km and climbed 2,000 m before I saw him. They had a right to be struggling. I am in awe of the professional cyclists, their ability to cycle so hard for so long, and then to perform at the end of a long race to win by a split second is near superhuman.

In turn, Andy and I left all possible weight at the bottom of the climb and each sped up the N66 and turned right onto the real climb, fuelled by relatively fresh legs, a rapidly digesting lunch, and a pint of Dutch courage. Andy first arrived back down with a beaming smile. Similarly, I thoroughly enjoyed the climb, descending more slowly to take photographs. We cycled along the river

Meuse for a while before heading NW to the lanes around Oteppe and our next bed and breakfast indulgence. A little elusive, we eventually found our beautiful country retreat. On occasions, we have found ourselves in accommodation that does not provide an evening meal and is miles from anywhere that does. After a day in the saddle, this can be frustrating. There is often an expectation that guests will be arriving in cars. However, our hosts were pleased to offer us a pleasant evening meal accompanied by a few of their own brewed beers. In the morning we returned to Huy and travelled via the N66 to Sougne-Remouchamps, where we climbed La Redoute. With a maximum gradient of only 17% and an average of 9.5%, this has a 292 m elevation gain. The climb is legendary, being on the route of so many of the Liege-Bastogne-Liege classic one day events. The climb was first included in 1974 and has since rightfully achieved iconic status. The Liege-Bastogne-Liege was first held in 1892 and at the time was considered to be the world championship. Many stories can be told of 'The Fort'. In 1980 the race was held with snow falling. Bernard Hinault was victorious, but his hands were badly frostbitten, and he permanently lost all feeling in two fingers. Andy and I had no snow to contend with and again thoroughly enjoyed the experience of the historic climb. As David Cronk had done previously, Andy and I parted company and he headed NW for his ferry back to the UK, whilst I headed E then N on country roads. As I was thinking just how enjoyable the last few days had been, I cycled past a bar that attracted me. A cool beer would add to that enjoyment. So, in Aubel I had my last refreshment before leaving Belgium and entering the Netherlands.

Daily Blog: Mur de Huy. May 18th

Andy and I enjoyed an excellent breakfast before heading off from Mormont across country to Huy to cycle up the Mur de Huy. With beautiful weather, still a cool northerly wind, we thoroughly enjoyed our short day's ride here, arriving in the town square and eating a healthy omelette before heading off to the start of the climb.

The notorious chicane on The Mur de Huy, at 20%, Laurent Jalabert called it a staircase.

These photos were taken on my descent run.

Although the climb is 26% at its steepest, it is relatively short at 1.3 km and was not as testing as some of the Yorkshire hills. However, it should not be forgotten that the professionals have raced for miles before reaching this hill and then race up it. We took turns in looking after all non-essential luggage whilst the other did the climb.

Tonight, we are staying in a château, which is beautiful. Extensive and perfectly maintained grounds. Stunning oak wood has been used in our three-roomed suite, set on two levels. A real treat.

Daily Blog: La Redoute with Andy. May 19th

Sitting in the evening sun with a beer in front of me listening to Nora Jones sing 'Come away with me', in the Netherlands, I am reflecting on another enjoyable day that will be remembered for many years.

Riding with Andy was great, both yesterday and today were perfect. Thank you, my good friend.

After our night in a château, which had the flavour of how the rich and famous live, culminating with a superb breakfast, we cycled back down into Huy, then back up the N66 hill (too early for such a protracted lung burster). We took a different return route to Sougne-Remouchamps to cycle up La Redoute. There must have been an event on, given the number of cyclists. However, there was only one old git on a hybrid cycle.

We kept to the same format as yesterday, stripping all unnecessary weight from the bikes. I enjoyed the climb and being amongst younger cyclists who were also putting in a lot of effort. Here are a few photos of this 1.7 km climb, average gradient is 9.5%, with a max. of 17%, so a little longer than the Mur de Huy yesterday, but not the 26% max. gradient.

La Redoute climb, at 'only' 292 m of elevation, this punchy hill can open the lungs.

Never mind who 'Alice' was, who was Phil? Painted a hundred times on the road, he had to be someone important. Well, he certainly was in the cycling world, particularly in this area, as he was a local lad. Phil Gilbert was the cycling world champion for several years and the locals had every right to be proud of their son's achievements.

A particularly enjoyable night.

Having left the inn where I had a wee drink in the smart village of Aubel, it was time to find somewhere to sleep. 10 km on and I was still looking. I even thought of going into a 'proper' campsite that I passed, swimming pool, shops, adventure play area, people (lots of), children, mostly all shouting (lots of), so I cycled on and on until I found a hilltop ridge looking down on five villages, each with its church spire. A hot air balloon has just floated across the setting sun. People are around and can see my tent, but I do not think anyone will object to my presence. With over 110 km cycled and 1,600 m climbed, I would not want to have to start looking for an alternative site this late in the day.

Once into the Netherlands, an immediate change is apparent. Belgium is beautiful, every private home seems to be unique in its design. There is no street litter, people are polite, it is a country I would like to get to know better. Now the Netherlands (and yes, I have only been in the country a few hours) has, it appeared, taken these principles several steps further. The villages and towns are immaculate, and even Aubel, which is only just in Belgium, presents itself with pride. Restaurants are not places just to eat, they are places of beauty. There is a relaxed atmosphere, people smile. I accidentally left my cycling glove on my pannier. Of course, it was going to blow off, and it did. A lady called to me as I continued to shoot down the hill. A car driver stopped, collected the glove from the lady, and brought it to me. Now that would put a smile on anyone's face: it did mine.

This area is well known for its cycling. The roads have designated shoulders in different coloured tarmac and people of all ages are out cycling. I have never seen so many couples and families on two wheels. There are also many statues and sculptures of cyclists.

One of many cycling sculptures in Belgium.

- NETHERLANDS & GERMANY-
CHAPTER THIRTEEN

Behind the Stern of a Tornado

**'The world is big, and I want to have a good look at it before it gets dark.'
John Muir**

This was May 19th and I camped on a gently sloping hill overlooking several towns between Aachen in Germany and Maastricht in the Netherlands, neither of which could be seen or heard. I had been cycling all day, covering over 100 km and climbing 1,500 m. It had been a good day. A sense of peace and contentment accompanied me into a deep sleep.

In this area of Europe the international borders are close, making leaving Belgium, entering the Netherlands at its most southerly point, skipping through the most westerly point of Germany, and back into the Netherlands in thirty-six hours an easy achievement on leg-powered two wheels. The German town of Saeffelen sits on a small land peninsula that nearly dissects Maastricht from the remainder of the Netherlands. This was the town where yet again I left Germany for a few kilometres before returning to try and breakfast in Heinsberg. I cycled through the deserted streets, a ghost town, the only thing missing was the tumbleweed. I stopped and asked a lady where a hungry cyclist could get some breakfast. She said that nothing was open. I tried to ask why, but the answer was lost in translation. Later I remembered that it was Whit Sunday. It reminded me of the UK in the late sixties when Sundays were a day of rest. The lady then offered to take me back to her apartment where she would cook me breakfast. As kind as the offer was, perhaps a positive response was not appropriate. She then told me that I could get some basic food from the railway station kiosk. My memories of Heinsberg are of a town that has shunned the 'coffee culture', and of thousands of bicycles racked in tiers in parking areas without a single rider to be seen.

Roermond was my next destination, with its impressive cathedral, and was the venue for a carbohydrate-loading lunch and onto Wankum. Almost certainly named without knowledge of language dynamics, the town sign is photographed by thousands of tourists, with an eye for amusement, whilst others ignore it with quiet disdain. The town's other claim is that it did have the most used petrol station in Germany. British troops serving in Germany used their fuel coupons there as they left the country.

Daily Blog: Behind the stern of a tornado. May 20th

How can it be 7 am five times in ten minutes? Those churches with the spires seem to each have a different take on time.

I did not close the tent last night and was rewarded this morning with a wonderful early view of a misty valley below with the poplar trees casting long shadows over the adjacent field. Small birds dive in and out of the poplars next to the tent, carrying insects back to their fledglings that I can hear as the parents arrive at the nest. The day has all the ingredients for a warm one. Time to pack up and start cycling.

Today has been interesting and at times frustrating. The concept of separating cyclists from other road users at every opportunity and the alien methodology of doing so has proved testing. It is me who is at fault, I know, but how are we to know having been cycling on the road for several kilometres that there is a cycle path on the other side of the road camouflaged by long grass? Cycleways stop abruptly, swap to the other side of the road without signage. Tree roots breaking out from beneath the tarmac are inextricably attracted to cycle paths, making them highly uncomfortable if taken by surprise. The effect of these roots caused sufficient vibration to dislodge a pannier. People walk on cycle paths; road maintenance teams use them to put their porta loos and office cabins on. It is not that I am not appreciative. When they run for kilometres without interruption, they are fantastic. However, it just is not possible to maintain a steady speed. Although these idiosyncratic features do not put off thousands of cyclists using them. Today was a holiday in Germany. Street carnivals and markets in many towns and hordes of cyclists, from children who may still not be able to walk, to the incredibly old, who may have lost the ability to do so, but can still cycle.

My first windmill before leaving the Netherlands.

The deserted city of Heinsberg. Nothing was open except the railway station café, to which I was directed by a lady out walking, the only person I saw for the first half-hour in the city. She offered to 'take me back to her flat and cook me breakfast'. Now, my mother said I should never ……

Roermond city centre and cathedral were impressive. Although the remainder of the city was dead, there were two restaurant areas open. I ate a very filling carbonara whilst listening to some fine musicians. This set me on for a good 50 km. As the day progressed it became apparent I would have to take what food presented itself, otherwise there would be no evening meal or breakfast. A pizza shop open on a Sunday holiday was not an opportunity to be missed; who knew what was up ahead? Squashed in its box in the panniers, it would taste delicious later.

Now the reference to a tornado. On a major road, cycling NE near Grefrath, the whole road was barricaded off, behind which a hydraulic platform enabled tree surgeons to dismantle a tree. Being impossible to pass, we, a group of cyclists, followed my map and did three sides of a square to get back en route. As we did, we saw scores of trees blown down, all facing the same direction. Some had destroyed garages, sheds, and conservatories. My remote support network back at Base Camp, Anne, says there was a big storm on May 6th, heavy rain, winds, and a tornado, *that had sadly killed a man in Hamburg and had blown five container ships from their moorings. Although some way SW of Hamburg, the damage was substantial.*

Again, difficulties were encountered in finding a wild campsite. Wood ants are not to be taken lightly. Fortune favours the long-distance cyclist. I arrived in the sleepy hamlet of Wankum to find a bar-restaurant open. Steak, chips and salad and a large beer. Life is good, but the pizza does not look so good now. Breakfast? maybe!

I left no evidence of having camped, except the horizontal indentation of a body shape in the leaves. A particularly good night's sleep. The pizza was breakfast. Separating the cardboard from the topping was entertaining.

Through the pretty town of Alpen and onto Haltern, cycling east from Wesel into a brisk wind which could not detract from the beauty of the area made even more surprising by its proximity to Essen, Duisburg, and Dortmund. Yesterday I was viewing the damage left by a tornado, today, mingling with festivities in Haltern. The experiences of a long-distance cyclist are varied. I camped on the edge of a field just outside the hamlet of Bulbern. Slept well as thunder and lightning were accompanied by rain. The noise of the hay baling machine that woke me in the morning was not about to envelop me in a hay bale, as my dream had threatened. It was cutting the grass on the other side of the hedge. From deep sleep to a defensive reaction in seconds, not a good way to wake up.

Daily Blog: In favour of cycle paths. May 21st.

I need to retract some of my criticism of cycle paths. Unlike many in other countries, these do not stop just outside the towns. They run for miles alongside major roads. This makes cycling these routes more enjoyable and safer, regardless of the damage caused to the cyclist's rump, (see tree root reference yesterday).

I approached the bridge over the Rhein to the west of Wesel, missing the cycle path approach that started a mile away on a disused road (no signs). Once committed to the bridge with regular traffic, there was a one-metre high barrier to protect cyclists, no way of getting to the other safer side. However, once on the bridge you could frustratingly see the cycle path approach route! The bridge is a beautiful piece of engineering.

A classic car passes through the neat little town of Alpen.

Embrace the wind! Today it has increased noticeably. Still no change in its general direction, into my face. Sometimes I feel as though I am pushing a London double-decker bus sideways into it. So today the headphones went in and Genesis filled my head and 100 km later I arrived in Haltern. Haltern is in a festive spirit. The town square filled with people enjoying the sun. It was here that a gentleman approached me and asked about my trip. He was a keen cyclist, having ridden the Tour de France a few years ago. He offered his age at 68 years young. His son and grandson looked in awe at him. It invited my comment that he was an inspiration to them. The response was three smiles of agreement.

Daily Blog: Thunder and lightning very, very frightening. May 22nd

Found a flat grassed headland to camp on last night and was entertained by the antics of half a dozen hares chasing each other in the grass as dusk arrived. Slept very well but was woken by a massive machine that I first thought was in my dream. It was a hay baler, and I was about to be chopped into segments and rolled into winter fodder. In reality, it was a grass verge cutter on the roadside of the hedge. Although I was not aware of this until I cycled past it later.

During the night, the thunder and lightning had again been spectacular.

Needless to say, I have a wet tent to dry out in my hotel this evening. Yes, it is that time again, three nights roughing it and I need to charge my devices and get a shower and shave. So here I am in the wonderful city of Munster. The ride in was a short one in the early morning sunshine. Here are a few photos: -

The double-layer cycle park at Munster railway station.

Traffic census on route to Munster, where the red carpet was waiting.

Shops on Prinzipalmarkt opposite St. Lamberti church square.

St. Paulus-Dom (cathedral).

I arrived in Munster on May 22nd. What a city; for all the crowds it was quiet and so clean.

I had camped for several nights now and my power pack was exhausted, my phone, Garmin, and lights all needed charging, and as adequate as 'tent washes' are, I needed a shave and decent shower. Tonight, I would sleep in a room with walls and a ceiling.

Today was going to be special. My stomach full, having eaten an enormous and delicious breakfast, I headed for the town of Tecklenburg in the district of Steinfurt. The town, having been built around a hilltop ruined castle, not surprisingly required a little effort to get to. The benefits of having cycled up those mountains in the Pyrenees having long since evaporated, I found the effort needed a little disconcerting. On arriving in the town, you cannot help but be in awe. What a wonderful place, cobbled streets and a town square, half-timbered white-painted buildings with a few ancient wattle and daub houses and fantastic cafés. One of my inspirations for doing this trip came from meeting Andrew Sykes, who had cycled from Tarifa to Nordkapp, albeit a different route, and had written a book about his exploits. It was at a talk in Halifax in West Yorkshire that I had met him, and it was from that seed my adventure had been germinated. Whilst my route had and would coincide in part with his, I had chosen to 'collect' as many classic cycling climbs as possible, with many lesser ones that could not be avoided, to access those classics, (not that I wanted to avoid them). In his book, Andrew had mentioned Tecklenburg as a 'must visit' place. I would concur with him.

The next couple of nights I camped in quite different places. The first initially unknowingly in a nature reserve, where I relocated my camp to a more appropriate place, and the second in a field in an isolated place where I was visited by some guys who had come to the field to frighten off the deer and fawns as the farmer was to cut the grass for hay early the following morning. The fawns would not have run away, preferring to hunker down, and would certainly have been killed. They were equally surprised to see me there as I was to see them. We chatted for a while and they advised that I should be gone before the farmer arrived in the morning. Passing through Steinfeld, Lohne, and Vechta, home of high-salaried Germans, I was enjoying what the country was showing me.

Having been asked to relocate, unaware I was in a nature reserve.

The lanes leading to Harpstedt were a pleasure to ride and with the sights of heron, deer, and fish leaping from a lake, fresh in my mind from the nature reserve, life for the nth time was good, as the famous and historic city of Bremen beckoned.

My blog covers the better-known aspects of this city, so a little on the accommodation. A large first-floor room with enormous windows, excellent considering the scorching weather. If only there was not the busy road below, which also had trams rattling along and a parallel railway line that carried more freight trains than passengers, with a frequency that would draw envy from the UK rail industry. This in no way detracted from the wonderful sights that I saw in Bremen, but I was pleased to return to the countryside and its tranquillity.

Daily Blog: Coffee and sightseeing. May 23rd

I like Germany. As cyclists we see more than most and although much of what we see is good, we also see the consequences of selfish drivers. What takes a second to throw out of a vehicle window remains on the roadside for a long time. The pizza boxes, the takeaway coffee and soft drinks cups and plastic bottles and broken glass, most are found at a calculable distance from where they were purchased. Let us see if we can apply a formula:

POP = Point of Purchase.

CPET = Car Park Exit Time.

ETD = Eating Travel Distance.

PHs = Progress Hindrances. i.e. traffic lights, roadworks, and cyclists.

ET of P = Ejection Time of Product, i.e. electric or manually operated windows and time to remove spilled produce from lap – without mowing down a cyclist.

So, to apply the formula let us say: -

POP+CPET+EDT- the total of all PHs+ETofP (with a loading value of 5:1 for manually operated windows or if hands are covered with ketchup). Once calculated, discarded 'take away' food WILL be found on the roadside verge as 'thrown away' rubbish.

But not in Germany. It is amazing. Yes, in Spain, to a lesser degree France and certainly the UK. From where I am sitting in a busy area having my third caffeine fix of the day, I cannot see a single piece of litter. Enough of this philosophical claptrap, but there is a point to be made.

Today has been laid-back, almost horizontal. I am a few days ahead of my schedule and at this rate will be arriving in Hamburg a couple of days before Anne is due to arrive. So, I am ambling along.

*The weather has been near-perfect, save for that strong NE wind. Before I convert you all to the attributes of travelling as a free agent and wild camping, one final mention of a less favourable aspect. Ticks. Yes, previously mentioned but I have acquired several more. These little critters usually are not large. These, however, were minute! Only having used the camera on macro setting and enlarged the image could you identify the little ****. They had buried their heads in my skin under my watch strap and on my chest. Not for the squeamish, but these seemingly innocuous parasites can carry some serious diseases. I have developed a method of minimising the chances the effect of their generously given, but unwanted fluids may have. I have a small Swiss army knife given to me on my retirement from the Fire Service by the then Officer in Charge of Summerbridge, Pete Somerville. The method: remove tick with tick remover (now found), insert the knife blade into the skin on site of where tick's head was submerged. Now the easy bit: get it to bleed.*

As I have no idea how long the tick has been feasting, the whole process is far from exact, but if what they have injected can be washed out, then perhaps some horrible disease has been averted. Finally, and importantly, sterilize the area.

The city of Munster is captivating, with a peaceful atmosphere, even though thousands of people are moving around. The cleanliness and order, and not forgetting the patience of everyone. It lacked that intense urgency that so many people who live and work in cities have.

Today the treats continued. After an enormous breakfast at the hotel Europa, I headed for Tecklenburg. This medieval hilltop town was certainly worth the hill climb

to its centre, where I was met by a portly and friendly police officer's smile. Sweating I may have been, but I am jolly sure it had been many years since he had cycled. Still cannot get used to them all wearing guns slung low on their hips as if in a Western movie. The character of Horse, from the TV movie 'Bonanza' came to mind.

The run down the hill from Tecklenburg was a delight, reaching terminal velocity on my 'rig' for the first time in many days.

The historic and beautiful town of Tecklenburg.

Not that I know much about the German people, but I would not have them down as being too much into quirky things, more practical and forthright. So, the edifice on this roundabout was a surprise.

And why not? A stack of teacups on a roundabout.

This evening I have found a great campsite near the small town of Lappenstuhl. There is a beautiful setting sun which is highlighting the silver birch and pine trees. A massive modern wind turbine is rotating slowly and, again, has the sun reflecting from it.

There is now only 200 km to cycle to Hamburg and seven days until Anne arrives. I am averaging around 90 to 100 km a day, so have decided to have some time in Bremen.

The next two weeks are going to be relaxing and as Hamburg marks the halfway point between Tarifa and Nordkapp, (excluding all the climbing in northern Spain and the Pyrenees), this break will be a good launching pad to continue through Germany into Denmark, Sweden and then the long trip north through Norway.

A footnote: Four gentlemen and two GSP dogs (German Short-haired Pointers) have just turned up. They were friendly and told me that the farmer is cutting the grass for silage early tomorrow and they have come to chase off the fawns that will not run away. They were very pleasant and interested in my ride. They have advised me to not be in the field when the farmer arrives in the morning.

A raised platform found in so many fields, from which the deer will be shot.

Daily Blog: They did not return with guns. May. 24th

With their reference to me being safe because they did not have their guns, a thought was sown and, in the depths of sleep, grew. They seemed nice enough, though.

I did not know how early the farmer would arrive to start silage making. Unlike hay, morning dew is no problem when making silage, so I was away by 6 am in anticipation of the farmer's arrival.

A beautiful, cool, sunny day, (still a brisk north east wind). In Vorden the bakery was open at 6.30 am. The lady serving spoke perfect English. When I asked her where she had learned, she shrugged her shoulders and said, 'School, many years ago.' I wish I had listened to my language teacher, Ms. Burgess, all 6 ft of her and size 11 shoes.

Damme, the next town, was still asleep, except for this character in the town square.

Each town in this area has a large, red-bricked church, all a regular shape and void of ornate architecture. Many of the streets are cobbled that form various patterns.

Arriving in Steinfeld you could be forgiven for thinking you were in racehorse country. Life-size statues of horses, many in the same pose, adorn the town and surrounding area.

The reference to Coventry on the horse's rump was lost to me.

It was here I had my second coffee, not two hours from the first: we are killing time – I have eight days to do 200 km.

Sitting having my coffee, a lady using a wheeled Zimmer frame came in. She parked the frame in a deliberate and precise manner, turning it to face the direction of her intended exit. Perhaps alcohol was to be consumed and the immediate support of the frame would be essential. The frame could not have been more central in the confined space but seemed a procedure well-practised. She sat at a round table laid for eight to eat. Then the waitress arrived with two enormous oval plates laden with food. A conversation between this lovely lady and me commenced. She was enthusiastically telling me everything about …… I have no idea and similarly, my responses were taken as if they were completely understood. The reality was that neither of us comprehended a word of what the other said. So how was it possible to have this ongoing dialogue? We both smiled and used expressions. Did it matter if we were none the wiser? It was an exchange of happiness!

In Steinfeld, there was a perfect example of a half-timbered barn seen so frequently in the region.

In Lohne there was another large, red-bricked church at its centre and a particularly good market where I bought smoked salmon and strawberries. A strange combination, but nice.

Just south of Lohne I happened to look to my left into a large window and caught sight of a fleet of classic cars and a few motorbikes. There was no signage to say why they were there. The collection included a 1940 Wanderer motorcycle, an Isabella coupe, a 220S Merc, and a Porsche Standard tractor. Yes, Porsche made tractors before they made cars.

I believe I have entered the German equivalent town of Cheltenham, Harrogate, or Bath in England. The ladies are dressed for luncheon as others would for an evening meal. Some men are wearing ties. Designer clothes outlets and jewellery shops abound. High-class cafés host well-heeled customers, me being the exception with no tie, unshaven, and looking as though I have been on the road for a few days. Not a single vehicle is over two years old and all spotlessly clean. What a difference a few kilometres make. I understand that Vechta is one of the homes to those who earn the highest salaries in Germany. The shops reflect this, Esprit, Marco Polo, Leos, and Weiss, with many facing me from across the street.

The well-heeled town of Vechta, excellent coffee and a full-bodied cheesecake.

Life is hard work sometimes. Since Tarifa, I have lost 7 kg. My arms are scrawny, and my legs reflect the work they have done over nearly two months. The problem will arise when the cycling stops. The determination to stop eating will have to be considerable.

Another fantastic camping spot for tonight, although it took some finding. Having chosen my site I sat for an hour, drank a beer, and noted that one cyclist and one tractor had passed in that time and if I stayed low in the tall grass, I was invisible. Time to pitch the tent, I stood up and looked straight into the faces of a couple walking their dog not ten metres away. 'OH!' I said; a pregnant pause followed. 'Good evening', said the sweat-stained cyclist, who hadn't yet washed, 'May I camp here?' It is all about timing. Their dog, a large one of an unknown breed, was enthusiastic about me. He smiled, showing a complete set of both top and bottom teeth. He was that enthusiastic about me that he was emitting a rumbling sound from deep inside his throat. Had he not been attached by a lead to his master, I am sure he would have now been attached to one of my legs. The gentleman was adamant, I could not stay there. However, after some persuading, he suggested I camped among the trees at the top of the hill. So here I am under a crab apple tree hunkered down in the cow parsley.

Daily Blog: What a wonderful part of Germany this is. May 25th

It is 6.30 am, I am looking from under my crab apple tree down the hill to a small pond surrounded by reeds. There are ducks on the water and from the water's edge, a small deer has fixed me with a frozen stare. The weather is perfect, still windy though. This is the life, only the sounds of nature and solitude. I pack up, check the bike, and see I have a puncture in my front tyre – When did that happen? – but could not care, life is good.

I cycled less than a mile and had to stop. I was surrounded by small managed lakes teeming with wildlife. Ducks of numerous varieties, swans, rabbits, hare, and more deer. No wonder the gentleman had wanted me to move up the hill into the trees to camp. I had no idea I was on the edge of what is probably a wildlife sanctuary.

I cycled through beautiful lanes to Harpstedt. Well-maintained and profitable farms abound. There is a fair amount of intensive pig rearing, going by the tell-tale odours. There is money in this area.

Would you want the bus to arrive with these facilities?

Every bus stop has a cycle stand adjacent to it, the process being that bus passengers cycle from home, park their bikes, have a picnic, and never get wet whilst waiting for a bus that always arrives within one minute of the timetable. German efficiency!

Similarly, there seems to be no expense spared even for the birds.

A massive pigeon loft.

Now in Harpstedt with its red brick church.

This town, with cobbled streets, with a place for everything, reminds me of the German town of Hahndorf, north of Adelaide in Australia, built by German immigrants to remind them of their fatherland.

All the traffic that had not been around this morning was now forming massive traffic jams through the suburbs of Bremen. Just to confirm that my initial reluctance to embrace the cycleways of Germany is now history. I have cycled only for a few kilometres actually on a road with other vehicles and whenever, which is frequently, a cycle path crosses adjacent roads, all motorised vehicles give way unless traffic lights say otherwise, or you are the young driver three days ago coming up a slip road off the motorway looking in the wrong direction. Your face was a study in horror, as you thought you were about to exterminate an old English cycling git. The cycle paths are wonderful, but progress is considerably slower, although so much safer, (when drivers are vigilant). This means that none of the traffic congestion affects cyclists; this, in turn, encourages more to cycle. Hence the thousands of cycles.

I am now in a hostel for a few nights and have swapped the sounds of nature and solitude for the sounds of trams, trains, buses, cars, and aircraft. The positives are: no ticks and no dogs that eat cyclists.

CHAPTER FOURTEEN
An Introduction to Bremen

'Nothing compares to the simple pleasure of a bike ride.' John F. Kennedy

Knowing that the outskirts of most cities are not a reflection of what usually lays within the centre, I was not too perturbed as I cycled into Bremen. I had expectations of seeing some outstanding architecture and learning more about the town's history. Arriving early on May 26th I took advantage of the deserted town centre to explore before the inevitable wave of tourists arrived, after having eaten hotel breakfasts. I would also have all the following day to 'dig' deeper into this interesting city. It was a beautiful morning, the air cool and refreshing with a promise of a hot day ahead. This time of day was good for pushing the laden bike around to the various points of interest. By mid-afternoon, the city was crowded and the temperature nearing 30 degrees. I found my lodgings, a first-floor apartment above a busy main road behind which there was an equally busy railway line. With high ceilings and large windows, the spacious room and bathroom had seen better days but was functional and was only to be a base for two nights. Having showered I walked in the opposite direction to the city centre to find a supermarket, as I had not passed one on my way out. The nearest turned out to be a wholesale market, with multi-packs of everything. The second, some way on, ticked the boxes. Back in my room with the windows wide open, a damp towel draped over my shoulders, and drinking cold beer, sitting with my bare feet on the windowsill, the temperature started to fall. It was my eldest daughter's birthday. I would have liked to have been with her that day.

An early start again to capitalise on the cool morning air and the deserted streets. Today the bike was naked, no panniers, no tent, just a couple of water bottles.

I returned to the town square to again look at the Town Hall, or City Hall, as it is also called. Built-in 1410, this beautiful ancient brick structure had an incredible Renaissance façade added in 1612. I was unable to go inside to see the remarkable banqueting hall and the painting of the Judgement of Solomon. Not for the first time on this trip I was privileged to have visited another UNESCO World Heritage Site. Within the shadow of this remarkable building is the statue of the Bremen Town Musicians, which are the characters of the Brothers Grimm.

I wandered to the charming medieval district of Schnoor: once a poor area of the city, it now hosts artists and is a mecca for the creative. The Schlachte district on the east bank of the river Weser was also another beautiful place, all enjoyed in fine weather with excellent coffee on tap in the numerous well-presented cafes. As the streets became fuller, I retreated to the botanical gardens and enjoyed their tranquillity, before heading back to my lodgings.

Daily Blog: An Introduction to Bremen. May 26th·

The trams stopped running around 1 am and although the trains ran all night, they were not so bad. I cycled early into Bremen to take some photos before it became busy, and it certainly did. 7.30 am it was almost deserted, by 9.30 am I was in the way of someone wherever I stood. I am now having a coffee outside the Theaterbremen in a quieter part of the city.

Well, the Brothers Grimm, Jacob and Wilhelm, have certainly ensured that a rooster, cat, dog, and a donkey continue to bring prosperity to Bremen. The story is of a motley menagerie of animals who have all been mistreated throughout their lives and want to become musicians in Bremen. This story has become one of the mainstays of tourism in the city. It is somewhat ironic that in the story these animals never arrived in Bremen, succeeding in tricking some thieves and moving into their home. However, Bremen's history and architecture are equally deserving of attention. If I were not to show some photos it would be remiss of me and perhaps your appetite would remain 'unwhetted'.

The Town Musicians of Bremen.

The second greatest attraction seems to be the Bremen Roland. Erected in 1404 to replace a timber one burnt down by the Bishops, I had to wait until the sun cleared the twin spires of the Dom before Roland received the light needed to show him in all his splendour. He was the paladin of the first Holy Roman Emperor, Charlemagne, and is an emblem of city liberties that protect the city, even to this day in some regards.

The Statue of Roland.

Knight and bike.

Similarly, two statues of knights mounted on their horses looked more appealing in the morning sun than shade. My 'horse' looked less impressive in comparison.

My first port of call was to Böttcherstrasse. This 100 m-long street, purported to be so narrow, is amazing, although far wider and longer than some UK streets such as Whip-ma-Whop-ma-Gate in York. This collection of buildings is stunning, but the motivation behind their existence is disturbing. Ludwig Roselius commissioned their build in the Impressionist style. Also sympathetic to National Socialism he thought Hitler's ideas to be the way forward and from this incentive, the Böttcherstrasse was created. During the build between 1922 and 1931, he applied to join the Nazi party but was twice turned down. Hitler thought the Böttcherstrasse a reflection of a degenerate and, fortunately for us, decided not to knock it down but to put a preservation order on it, to display something wholly 'unacceptable'.

The city square.

Bronze statues seem now to be in many cities around the world, whether they are taking up half the room on a market square bench, as Blind Jack is in Knaresborough in the UK, or one of the presidents of America that stand on many of the street intersections in Rapid City, not far from Mount Rushmore. Bremen has practised this indulgence for longer than most cities. The emphasis is on nakedness. It is strange, but not surprising, that certain parts of both male and female anatomy remain remarkably shiny.

What well-dressed touring cyclists wear when sightseeing, even in 30 degrees of heat.

FACT FACTORY: Bremen is a quintessential medieval Germanic town, with an impressively large cobbled central square criss-crossed with tram lines and bounded with beautifully ornate historic buildings. Within the square stands the statue of Roland. Leaving the open space of the square there is any number of narrow cobbled streets with ancient half-timbered and wattle and daub cantilevered buildings housing expensive tourist-driven wares.

Most people remember the famous Brothers Grimm (born in Bremen) and their tale of the Town Musicians of Bremen, the fun-loving animals, and the young troubadour. The tale's protagonists have become the symbols of this city.

The bronze statue of the Town Musicians is the work of Gerhard Marcks and was erected in 1953, whereas the town's protector, Roland, was erected in 1404. His Durendal (sword) is unsheathed and ready to defend the town's people.

Bremen is the capital of Germany's smallest federal state bearing the same name, which consists of only two cities. Regardless of its size, however, it has the largest population of all German states and a record number of millionaires.

The city's most famous 100 m street, called Böttcherstrasse, has only seven buildings, among which are the houses and fountains of Robinson Crusoe, Atlantis, and the Seven Lazy Brothers.

Robinson Crusoe's house was built by the coffee merchant Ludwig Roselius, whose ideas and finance made the Böttcherstrasse possible. In Defoe's novel, Crusoe had been the son of a Bremen merchant who settled in York, England. Roselius saw in himself a connection with Crusoe's father. At 100 m, Böttcherstrasse, like Whip-Ma-Whop-Ma Gate near The Shambles in the city of York, is a small street filled with architecture that delights the eyes.

Robinson Crusoe is a novel by Daniel Defoe, first published on April 25th 1719 and thought to be the second most translated book in the world after the Bible. The first edition credited the work's protagonist Robinson Crusoe as its author, leading many readers to believe he was a real person, and the book a travelogue of true incidents. Born in London in 1660, Daniel Foe later changed his name to Defoe to sound more gentlemanly. Although largely remembered only for his writings about Robinson Crusoe, he was a prolific writer, writing over 300 works. He was a well-travelled trader and pamphleteer, and thought the city of York pleasing and beautiful. He was temporarily imprisoned for his thoughts but also consulted by politicians. He died in his seventieth year.

Robinson Crusoe's house was destroyed by bombing in 1944 and rebuilt in 1954. All the original internal décor has gone and been replaced with scenes from Crusoe's story.

The night was to prove anything but tranquil. The rain arrived when I was in Munster, (not to be confused with the larger city of Munster north of Dortmund that I had visited a few days earlier), having a coffee and then yet another. On entering the town there was a statue of a young couple portraying deep love and with the man in uniform they are saying their farewells. Munster felt strangely familiar with its high military presence. It reminded me of Ripon in North Yorkshire. With Claro Barracks just outside the city, soldiers were seen daily. I had not originally intended to come as far south to Munster, aiming to go to Hamburg to meet Anne, who was again flying out to spend a few days with me, but as in Lourdes, where we had last met up, I had gained a few days on my schedule. She was due to arrive late on June 1st, in five days.

After the rain had cleared, I headed south towards Bergen. Although not relishing the thought, to be this near to the infamous Bergen-Belsen Nazi Second World War concentration camp and not visit would not sit well on my conscience. I cycled further than planned, passing through Muden and Baven before happening on a picturesque, wooded parking area with a log cabin café that was closed. Cycling beyond the area now off the road on sand tracks with pine trees all around, I had found an ideal place for the night. It was to be a noisy one with rifle fire from hunters until the sky was pitch black.

Daily Blog: The tranquillity of the woods. May 28th

This afternoon the clouds unzipped, and an absolute deluge fell from them. As the initial half-inch diameter drops bounced, I moved undercover in the café. The rain had arrived at a convenient time. I was even able to get the bike undercover. The only 'down' side was I felt obliged to augment my finished coffee with a mixed fruit crepe and another coffee. This was not as difficult as I thought it might be.

I had cycled about 100 km east-south-east across to Munster. In some ways, this town felt a little like Ripon in North Yorkshire used to, with the number of young soldiers in town, most of whom had arrived at the supermarket checkout minutes before me. A large area to the west of the town is a military training ground, which I had just cycled around.

The day was largely uneventful, although I did see the best example of a working windmill to date.

A fully operative mill.

Having stopped for lunch at the Netto supermarket, I was checking my map when an exceedingly helpful German gentleman asked where I was going and did I know how to get there. Or he may have said that he and his wife of fifty years had just won the Euro Jackpot. Only he knows, because I hadn't a clue what he was saying and politely said so – several times, to which on each occasion he raised his voice a quarter of an octave. After all, it is a fact that when speaking a language not understood by the other person, by raising your voice and repeating the same sentence, the listener will immediately comprehend what is being said. He, having taken the map from my hands and unfolded it, enthusiastically spoke at length on the various ways of getting to Munster, I think. Anyway, the rain arrived when I was in Munster, drenching a statue of a couple who symbolise how war separates loved ones.

Off to war and so young. The sunshine was short-lived.

I found the German Tank Museum in Munster, which I intend to visit tomorrow on my return from what will probably be a very moving visit to the concentration camp at Belsen.

I am now wild camping on the edge of a wood.

What was thought to be an ideal pitch.

The farmers were hunting earlier, they have stopped now that it is dark. They are after deer which they shoot from raised seated platforms. I have included a photo of one in a previous blog. It is silent now except for a few animals moving around, but no trams, trains, or traffic as in Bremen. Maybe I should not have titled this blog 'The tranquillity of the woods'. The hunters had only stopped shooting temporarily, perhaps they went home for supper. The shooting went on until 1 am, rifles, not shotguns and it seemed to a sleep drunk cyclist they were repositioning and driving the deer in my direction. This appeared to be the case when some deer passed the tent.

CHAPTER FIFTEEN
Bergen-Belsen. How Could This Have Happened

'The use of travelling is to regulate imagination by reality, and instead of thinking how things may be, to see them as they are.' Samuel Johnson

As we get older, it would be unusual for us not to have accumulated experiences, both enjoyable and distressing. My career in the UK fire service had provided many, some good, although some upsetting and disturbing, with a few having lasting effects. What I was to see on May 29th 2018 will remain with me perhaps for the rest of my life. Some do not agree with immortalising such abhorrent events. We as a race continue to have short memories and repeatedly commit atrocities against each other time and time again. How much easier would it be to wipe all reminders from our memories if the 'Bergen-Belsens' did not exist as a testament to our cruelty to each other. Having just watched two mares in a field with their playful foals, my mind was not ready to see the deserted large expanse of concrete and the platforms that had been the railway station used to receive the arrivals contained in the cattle trucks. They were not cattle, they were humans, brought in their thousands to their deaths. I say in the blog that to state facts and figures would only in part convey the extent of the brutality. Raw figures can hardly transmit the extent of individual suffering and loss. However, not using these figures opens the mind to persuasion that perhaps it was not as bad as history recalls.

I wrote the following additional blog shortly before my visit:

That night I found a great camping place tucked away beside deep pine woods in the corner of a small field. I could look down an incline and over the gently rolling hills and forested landscape. The hunters were out, and regular rifle shots were heard. Some I thought were too near, but as dusk gave way to blackness the shooting stopped. It was about two in the morning when the tent moved. From deep sleep to absolute alertness, I listened in silence to what was outside the tent. Were we playing a listening game here? Who would crack first? Was it an angry hunter or an animal? The tent moved again and this time there was a definite snotty exhalation of breath as a deer walked off. This had been unusual as the deer previously had barked to each other, giving their positions away. Maybe the hunters had caused them to wisely move around silently.

The following morning was beautiful. The rain had cleared the air, the mugginess had gone, and life was good. Back on the road, I slowed to look at two mares with their suckling foals. Then past an army barracks. On reflection, this was the mental turning point. We all know what horrors happened at Belsen. Did I want to go and see in detail just how abhorrent it had been? If I turned and cycled back north, I do not think I would have forgiven myself. Throughout history, barbaric acts have been committed. Some say it is important that we remember them, to lessen the chances of future genocides and ethnic cleansings. It is one of the reasons why school children visit war graves in Flanders and countries have annual Remembrance Days, but still, the atrocities occur. How many more would there be if we obliterated the previous from our history books? Human kindness knows no bounds, but tragically, so does human cruelty.

Belsen covered an enormous area; this is just one small corner.

As I pushed my bike towards the entrance of the museum a gentleman approached me and could not have been more polite in advising me that cycles were not permitted. I was invited to secure the bike outside the entrance, but he insisted that I brought all my gear into the entrance foyer, where he helped me load it into a locker. The next few hours of my life will be remembered for the rest of my life. It is difficult to comprehend the scale of human suffering and the barbaric cruelty. Walking around the site where thirteen thousand rotting corpses had lain when Lt. John Randall and the small band of SAS soldiers had arrived under operation Tombola on April 15th 1945 was beyond sobering.

Daily Blog: *Bergen-Belsen. How could this have happened?!! May 29th*
The rifles stopped at 1 am. I was awake again by 5.30 am. Not a good night's sleep, but a fantastic location.

Continued my ride to Belsen, past the enormous modern barracks. I was expecting Belsen to be busy, a hundred or so of youngsters were there. Even later when I left there were only about six coaches and thirty cars.

I know that what I have read, watched, and experienced today will remain with me forever. We all know to a point what happened here, but to walk the ground where these atrocities occurred is another dimension. To state facts and figures would only in part do it justice but it is impossible to convey the extent of human suffering caused by a ruling force so institutionalised as to accept systematic barbaric cruelty as normal human behaviour. We most certainly need to remember how easy it is for humans to become void of humanity.

I make no apologies for including this in the blog. From the outset, it was going to be a sobering blog. I think it vital we never forget.

A monument near the railway sidings where the prisoners were marched to the concentration camp.

It would not be appropriate to show some of the more gruesome photos on display at the museum, but we should all see them at some time to remind us of what horrors the human race is capable of.

Indoctrination.

Terror.

Before the mass-murdering and surgical experimentation began.

When I arrived, I had failed to see a 'no cyclist' notice. A kind gentleman politely approached me and explained where to put my bike and assisted with putting my gear into a locker. We saw each other several times during my visit and when I left, he was at pains to again assist me. It was very remiss of me not to ask his name. If that gentleman reads this blog, please accept my thanks for your help, you are an excellent ambassador.

Having arrived back in Munster and knowing where a bike shop was, I called in to ask whether they could give the bike the 'once over'. It was not as if I could not do the job myself. To be honest, I needed some normality. It was 3.45 pm, short notice, and I did not expect a yes. Thirty minutes later Rolf Drewes of Farbenhaus Drewes cycles in Munster rolled the bike back into the shop from the works bay. Job done, and I did not have to remove all my bags. Thanks so much, great job! The gears have taken some punishment over the last two months and 4,000 km and the brakes too, with all the descents.

I cycled up to a German tank museum just out of town. Suddenly seeing the few on display before you go through to see, presumably many more describing in detail (maybe not in English) how they were designed to cause as much destruction as possible, I decided I had seen enough human cruelty for one day. The tanks would have held my interest had I not had five hours at Belsen.

A millpond adjacent to a working water wheel in Munster.

One in a collection of reconstructed medieval buildings.

Having bought my evening meal from a supermarket, I was having a drink from a plastic bottle and noticed two men checking the litter bins as they came up the street, one on each side. They were removing all tin and plastic containers. I have seen many people returning them to supermarkets. So, there must be a return on them. One of these gentlemen explained that he had been in the army but was now extremely poor. He spoke with limited English, so a degree of guesswork was involved in what he was saying. He sat beside me and waited for me to finish my drink, I gave him the bottle and a little money.

It is almost dark. Over the weeks I have become reasonably acquainted with the local wildlife. This evening was special, though. Sitting in my 90-degree pop-up seat with a can of beer to my lips, I caught sight of a head above the bushes about 20 m away. I froze, as did the fox looking directly back at me. For a full minute, neither of us moved. It was pointless reaching for the camera. Then he was gone, only to return with curiosity. I am utterly silent as he edges nearer to the tent. He has just shaken himself and, with a last look at the tent, trotted off.

FACT FACTORY: BERGEN-BELSEN.

On April 15th 1945 Lieutenant John Randall, a highly experienced SAS officer, and his small covert command of SAS soldiers stumbled on two Nazi officers who offered no resistance. The stench of rotting flesh was pungent as the SAS group realised; they had entered a concentration camp. As if to show the English around a country estate, the two Nazi officers offered to take them on a tour of the camp.

By 1945 Belsen had two camps with a total of 60,000 prisoners, most of whom had died of starvation, overwork, or brutal and sadistic medical experiments. In 1940 it had been a prisoner of war camp, Wehrmacht. Initially, prisoners had no shelter so scraped dugouts in the soil to afford minimum protection from the weather that could be scorching hot, to freezing cold and wet. By 1943 it was a concentration camp and although there were no gas chambers, within a year, conditions deteriorated to unfathomable deprivation. Randall walked amongst thousands of starving people and 13,000 rotting corpses. Arriving at Belsen was not the end of the SAS's operation called 'Tombola', so Randall and his command left within hours. John Randall was the first allied soldier to discover the truth of Belsen. However, a doctor, Llewellyn Glyn Hughes, who arrived shortly after Randall, started the process of treating the survivors.

Each person of the thousands who died is as important as the others. Memories of such events are usually held through the eyes of the few who gained the attention of the world. For Belsen, it is Annelies Marie Frank (Anne Frank). Her diary, *The Diary of a Young Girl,* written when hiding between 1942 and 1944, has immortalised her. Captured in 1944, she died of typhus in Belsen in March 1945, a month before it was liberated.

Between 1941 and 1945, more than 70,000 people died. Many were buried in mass graves found after the liberation in April 1945. There are to this day 13 mass graves and 15 individual graves. Nearly 20,000 victims are buried in the Horsten cemetery some 600 m from the former camp.

The barbaric medical experiments were condoned and overseen by its camp commander, Josef Kramer (known as The Beast of Belsen). Formerly in charge of Auschwitz, he and Irma Grese, who was a warden in the women's section, murdered and ill-treated thousands. Both were hung after their trial at Luneburg in December 1945. Grese, at 22 years of age, was the youngest woman to be hung under British law in the 20th century. Anne Frank was 15 years old when she died. Two young women born into this world as equals. Worth perhaps a moment of thought.

I will remember my few hours at Bergen-Belsen on May 29th 2018 with a profound mixture of feelings. Feelings of utter disdain and disbelief at the ability of humanity to normalise such barbarism. Yet history is so frequently punctuated with such atrocities. No other animal that shares the same planet has the capacity for such cruelty. My optimism for humanity has been affected. The likelihood of us, as the most advanced species on planet Earth, creating our own extinction is beyond probable.

In a reflective mood, I retraced my route north passing the tubular iron memorial structure near the railway station where the prisoners arrived in cattle trucks. The mares and foals were no longer in view. The museum had been designed and presented thoughtfully, factual, and without judgement. Any human being with a modicum of humility would be moved. School children were seen reading solemnly, a few crying, none of the usual jovial behaviour reserved for school outings here.

Returning to Munster and having had my bike kindly checked by Rolf

Drewes at his cycle shop, I headed to the tank museum, where I opted not to enter. With plenty of time on my hands, I went for a 'mooch' around the city, visiting the massive white balls near the Aasee lake, reminding me of the 1967 TV cult programme, *The Prisoner*, with Patrick McGoohan trying to escape from Sir Clough Williams-Ellis's wonderfully designed village of Portmeirion in Wales. Other places that caught the attention were the Prinzipalmarkt, St Paulus-Dom, the historic town hall, and the Schloss residence. With my thoughts now diverted I headed to Steinbeck and onto a peaceful camp behind a graveyard and a chance meeting with a young fox.

The encounter with the fox had lightened my mood further and, in the morning, I set off in high spirits. Not even the rain that arrived, as I passed a large communal covered barbeque, dampened them. An hour later I emerged from the covered barbeque having been entertained by children's chatter, as they were taken by parents to their school that was next door. Arriving in Luneburg was a joy. This historic town, with its architectural variety of buildings with steep, pitched, red-tiled roofs and stepped gable ends, grabs the eye. Over 70,000 people live in this calm, quiet town. Much of its development was due to salt production. Nowadays it is the arts that provide the town's prosperity.

I was enjoying this amble around the north-east of Lower Saxony. Another night was spent under canvas, although these days tents are not made of canvas. Neither do they want to be, when the emphasis is so frequently on reducing weight. My two 'person' Jack Wolfskin at just 2 kg had been worth its (small) weight in gold. It was certainly going to earn its keep that night. I camped just outside Jesteburg on the edge of a cornfield, hugging what grass there was on the headland, although inevitably some of the tent was pitched on the soil. It was as if a dark grey curtain was being drawn over the sky and as it was, thunder exploded above, multiple times as forked lightning lit the ever-darkening sky. The wind increased to shake the surrounding trees. Then, as if a massive tap had been turned on, a deluge of water arrived. It had a leading-edge, a vertical tsunami. The thunder did not let up, cracking overhead it smothered all other sounds. Within minutes the field turned to mud, the crop was bent double as it was pounded. And not one drop of water entered the tent.

I still had a day before meeting Anne in Hamburg so had decided to head to Stade, some 70 km west of Hamburg. Another ancient town that was first mentioned in records in 934. In the midst of my mind, I recalled that this town was captivating, quaint, with history seeping from its buildings. The fish market, the cobbled streets with brick and timber buildings, some leaning precariously and seemingly defying gravity. The attraction of Stade is that it is uniquely original. There is no need for the eye to block out modern buildings, there are none.

Daily Blog: *Thunder and good fortune. May 30th*

A second night with no need for a sleeping bag, it is very warm and muggy. Through the night I was being crawled over by small ants. I wondered how they had got into the tent. Over the years I must have spent hundreds of nights in tents. This one opens on both sides and I usually use the left side. Last night, due to where it was pitched, I used the right. I had failed to fully close the tent side that morning and scores of little ants had come searching, inquisitive little creatures. My fault, silly mistake, coinciding with there being ants around. This prompted an early breakfast and pack- up. The clouds built rapidly, looking very ominous. A bus shelter would be handy. Sometimes fortune does favour. Not 3 km down the road in the little village of Oldendorf there was more than a bus shelter. A four-metre wide hexagonal-covered barbeque area with lighting and power was waiting. Within minutes the rain arrived, accompanied by thunder building to a crescendo. If the ants had not invaded, prompting me to get moving earlier, then everything would have got very wet.

On the ride onto Luneburg, I travelled on a concrete road with expansion joints, but this one is in Germany, not America, where there are so many concrete roads with expansion joints. This one was smooth and not an invitation for Mr and Mrs Boil and the baby Boils to start travelling with me again. (In my blog of 'Seattle to Boston in 40 days', I had affectionately created a fictitious family named Boil, who rode with me across some of America, attached to a certain part of my anatomy.) I stopped on this road to put sun cream on. My casual glance at a lorry driver as he passed had me instantly angry; he was turning the page of the book he was reading, that was placed on the steering wheel. Estimated vehicle speed, about 65 km/h, chances of survival of a cyclist if rear-ended- NIL. You must wonder how many others are doing the same.

Minutes before the storm in Oldendorf.

Luneburg is an impressive town, from its cobbled streets to an amazing array of different building styles. Not only did the designers achieve individuality with the angles and shapes that form the skyline, but they also used brick, stone, and timber to make the whole external appearance as ornate as possible. Several horse-drawn carriages pulled by pairs of Belgian horses take tourists around the old parts of this quaint town.

A taste of Luneburg.

After a very pleasant few hours in Luneburg, made just that bit better with an excellent ice cream, for one Euro!, I did my evening shop early and headed NW for Luhdorf, passing a massive Amazon warehouse, and on to Pattensen. A suitable camping spot could not be found. En-route I visited the woods, as nature called, only to have it confirmed that the mosquitoes are both starving and exist not as individuals but one homogeneous cloud of bloodsuckers, with the sole intention of draining me of mine. Sitting on the saddle for the next few kilometres was not a pleasant experience. I cycled on through Thieshope, Brackel, Asendorf, and into the upmarket town of Jesteburg, where a little later I found a lane that looked promising. The tent was pitched on the edge of a wheat field behind a hedgerow.

The clouds had been building rapidly. No sooner had I got the tent up when a repeat of this morning's storm occurred. Preceded with long, loud rumbles of thunder, there was the 'mother' crack of thunder almost above, spontaneously followed by a sustained flash of lightning. The wind came from nowhere, blowing the trees and hedgerow, and then a curtain of rain swept across the sky, and within a few seconds it had travelled across the field I am in. To increase the drama further, the thunder was continuous for twenty minutes, there was never a quiet moment. Always rolling, frequently crashing, it was quite a show. I cannot recall having ever experienced such a storm before. Now, the birds are singing, everything is dripping wet and still, the thunder can be heard rolling away in the distance.

Storm imminent.

Storm front arrives.

The day started with a storm and closed with a spectacular one, and the 'old git' did not get wet. Now, that makes a change.

Daily Blog: Day three of four sightseeing. May 31st

The storm cleared the humidity for the night and with the sun again warming the air at 6 am, it promises to be a hot day.

After the storm, the night was beautifully silent until aggressive dogs started barking at 2 am. Previously I had put this sound down to Roe deer, as foxes are far less common and make a different sound. Cornfields are also less favoured by deer than wood and grassland. Chatting with Anne this morning I mentioned it. She did an online search and as a result, we have learned something. Germany has a raccoon problem, a 'one million' problem. Although they cull 60,000 a year, they are still a growing problem and a menace. First introduced from America before WW2 they were farmed for their pelts. During the war, a stray bomb landed on one of these farms allowing around 24 to escape. Now, Germans love their hunting, hence why most fields have a raised timber stand where the riflemen shoot from. To improve the variety of prey, more raccoons were released. A similar story to the twenty-four rabbits released in Australia by Thomas Austin in October 1859, originally again to provide sport shooting. That also went a little off track. Raccoons make a variety of sounds including chittering and growling, so it is unlikely the barking can be attributed to them. I also now know traps baited with chocolate are used, and care needs to be taken when walking through undergrowth. Raccoons carry disease and are not shy. They have been known to get on a train. Presumably by accident, or have they taken to commuting?

Today's sightseeing involved visiting some beautiful towns via country roads, all except one having cycleways.

The day started with a ride through woods on a dirt track and finished sitting on the bank of the river Elbe.

Arriving in the town of Buchholz at 7.30 am, nothing was open except for one coffee shop – fortunately! By 8.30 there were many cafés open and hundreds of people around. Wenzendorf was nice and the larger town of Buxtehude was special. However, the prize, should one be needed, should go to Stade.

From Stade it is only about 50 km into Hamburg. I was tempted to use a proper campsite this evening, anticipating back-to-back industry along the Elbe south bank. What a lovely surprise, having gone up a flight of steps that took you over a high flood embankment, there was the river, maybe half a mile across. I saw a container ship that was going into Hamburg using the northern channel behind an island, and not ten minutes ago two emergency services speed boats skimmed the water going flat out on blue lights. The whole bank is still rural. Now, so peaceful!

Tomorrow I will ride into the home city of Angela Merkel, the German Chancellor. I would like to use the Elbtunnel, the historic tunnel that goes under the river.

A beautiful functional water mill.

The historic centre of Buxtehude.

The captivating centre of Stade.

Container ship heading upstream to Hamburg.

Wild camp beside the Elbe. Last for a while. An apartment awaits in Hamburg.

FACT FINDER: Located lower downstream to the mighty port of Hamburg, just off the southern bank of the river Elbe, Stade has been inhabited since 30,000 BC. In the 1,100s Stade was ruled from Bremen by the Prince-Archbishops but in 1208 King Valdemar II of Denmark conquered it. Later in the 13th century, Stade became a prominent member of the Hanseatic League. This league was a commercial and defensive confederation of merchant guilds and towns throughout northwest and central Europe. The Hanseatic League dominated the Baltic maritime trade for three centuries. Fortunately, Stade has long since been bypassed for Hamburg, which has resulted in a time warp being preserved.

From Stade I cycled east to the mighty river Elbe. Having pushed the bike up the substantial southern bank flood defence wall, the river presented itself. That night I camped quite openly in meadowland beside the river's edge. Beyond the island of Lühesand, ocean-going ships appeared to be sailing across dryland, headed into the mighty port of Hamburg as ships before them had done since 1189 when Frederick I had expanded the port. The following morning, a cooler sunny day, saw an easy ride through the massive dockyards to the Elbtunnel. Although not that old, this tunnel was built to ease the travel between the city on the north side of the river and the docks on the south side, and has some quaint decorative features depicting aquatic life in polished tiles along the subterranean route. Having surfaced from the tunnel I was in the centre of the city within minutes. No camping tonight. Anne and I had opted to stay for a few days in some luxury, an apartment north of the centre. The keyholder had arranged a time when we would meet at the accommodation. The building was Georgian era and I imagined what it was going to be like inside. High ceilings, large rooms, and a bath that a dirty, smelly cyclist could swim around in after five nights of roughing it. An hour or so later, with no one having met me, I was not so happy. At last, my phone call was answered. After profound apologies, the front door opened, and I was invited into the office behind it. I had waited two hours, not two metres from the person who had arranged to meet me on the pavement. He had been there since 9 am that morning. Much can get lost in translation. Comfortingly, the rooms lived up to expectation and a taxi arrived shortly after with my wife. We had last seen each other in Lourdes, and it was a joy to be together for the next five days. I had cleaned the bike, cleaned myself, shaved, and washed my limited wardrobe. So apart from being rather thin and having the tell-tale sun-tanned legs, arms, and backs of hands and panda eyes of a long-distance cyclist, who would have guessed we were not a normal couple? Anne completed the normalisation process by giving me a haircut.

During our stay, we visited the Miniature museum, the Maritime museum, the Speicherstadt warehouse district, and St Nikolai church. A taxi had brought Anne and now one collected her to take her to the airport. Our next planned get-together was in Tromsø, northern Norway. An hour later I left and headed north to the border town of Flensburg via Borgdorf-Seedorf. Two days would see me in Denmark.

Daily Blog: The second half starts. June 7th

This morning the whistle blew for the start of the final 4,000 km of my journey to Nordkapp.

Anne and I had a great time discovering Hamburg. Its industrial and maritime history, the Speicherstadt Museum, the incredible Miniatur Wunder museum, the water and light show to music, and the St Pauli tunnel, among others. We had a beautiful apartment that was so peaceful, given it was in the city. With the windows wide open throughout the night, there was silence, broken only by an enthusiastic blackbird at first light who sang with gusto from the same place on the roof of the opposite house every morning.

With additional clothing and replenished stocks of energy additives and toiletries and warmer clothing, including cycling shoes, my load is heavier than previously, and trying not to increase the overall volume was difficult.

The weather has been perfect for days now and is set to stay warm for a few more.

Miniatur Wunder Museum

So realistic.

The Rialto Bridge, St Mark's Square and Campanile in Venice.

The International Maritime Museum.

Water and light performance.

I write this on the headland of a cornfield, where the tent is pitched on the soil. No rain is forecasted, let us hope it is accurate otherwise it is going to get messy. The temperature hit 31 degrees today. However, this is a shady spot with a cooling breeze.

I have decided to try and reduce the daily distances back to my original targets. Having arrived several days too early in the Hamburg area, it was good to spend time going off route for some sightseeing, but this was not the intention. I am in danger of doing the same both for Gothenburg and Oslo, where three days have already been allocated for each city. The main reason for this is the surfacing of an old injury. Several years ago, I sustained a severe knee injury in a climbing accident whilst descending one of the Russian Snow Leopard mountains in poor conditions. The accident could have been far worse for the three of us, but it has left me with a permanently weakened right knee. Riding every day is testing it, particularly the constant stopping and starting at side roads and transferring body weight to the front wheel to reduce the shock loading to just the pannier weight on the rear wheel when going up and down curbs. Cycle paths have their merits but require more vigilance than when riding on the main carriageway and it is not possible to maintain a constant speed for more than a few minutes. If I do not exceed the intended daily distances the knee should hold out, otherwise, it is a cocktail of pain killing drugs.

St. Pauli tunnel.

FACT FACTORY: The Elbe tunnel or St Pauli Elbtunnel was opened in 1911 and was heralded as a technical sensation. Accessed via four enormous lifts on either bank, the two 426 m long tunnels lie 26 m below the river and have a diameter of 6 m. The tunnel enabled thousands of workers to commute from the city of Hamburg more easily to the shipyards and docks. More bridges now span the Elbe, so fewer vehicles now use the tunnels, although the novelty factor is high. It remains a great means of transport for both pedestrians and cyclists.

Miniatur Wunderland is a replica of the city of Hamburg covering 200 square metres. Within it is the largest model railway system in the world with over 190 trains pulling 1,800 wagons over 2,600 m of rail track. Yet this is only one statistic of this amazing achievement. This multi-storey building in the Speicherstadt warehouse district also contains miniature versions of parts of Germany, Austria, France, Italy, and America. There are a thousand buildings, 50,000 people, and 1,300 vehicles including an airport. There is everything from a zoo to an opera house to garden allotments. Humour is never far away, with hidden adult playfulness to be seen by the observant eye. Two brothers, Frederik and Gerrit Braun, set about building the largest model railway system in the world in 2000 and from there grew what is now a phenomenally impressive exhibition that continues to expand and encompass all aspects of human life.

The International Maritime Museum is the story of Peter Tamm (1928-2016). Peter's obsession with all things nautical was probably started by his mother who, whenever he was ill as a child, gave him a present of a miniature ship. Now contained in a building with nine floors in the HafenCity, there are 38,000 miniature ships together with over a million pictures, 100,000 books as well as countless other nautical items ranging from oil paintings, uniforms, maps, and instruments. The collection is that diverse it is impossible to indicate its breadth. Perhaps a teaser would be to say, within in it there are over forty original letters written by Lord Nelson.

Hamburg has rightly been likened to Venice, it has more bridges, over two thousand of them, such as the wonderfully named and so frequently photographed Poggenmuhlenbrucke, and canals are everywhere. Deich

(Dike) Street is the oldest remaining street in the city. First mentioned in 1304, it is near the Speicherstadt with its restored 17th and 18th century buildings. As with so many cities around the world, a devastating fire destroyed much of the city centre in 1842, starting at 42 Deich Street. Fortunately, some of this area was spared, including the Speicherstadt warehouse district. This area is another UNESCO World Heritage Site.

CHAPTER SIXTEEN
Back to Basics

'Travel is fatal to prejudice, bigotry, and narrow-mindedness.' Mark Twain

Anne and I left Hamburg on June 7th; she is heading back to Yorkshire, I am heading north to Borgdorf-Seedorf. At Bad Bramstedt I entered the country lanes and enjoyed the afternoon sun. The following day I arrived in Rendsburg early on a bright sunny morning. I cycled under an elevated steel structure that carried railway rolling stock yet looked too frail for its task. It was more akin to a Meccano construction. I later found out that this 2,500 m bridge stood over 40 m high and was built in 1913, so could not be that frail. It took the Neumunster-Flensburg railway over the Kiel canal and is the longest (only) railway bridge in Europe. It gains height by using a loop that trains travel 360 degrees to gain the required elevation. Suspended beneath the bridge is a transporter bridge, one of only twenty built in the world and of a similar type as the Rochefort-Martrou transporter bridge that David and I saw in France. Unfortunately, in January 2016 a cargo ship, the Evert Prahm, accidentally rammed the aerial transfer platform. A subsequent collision also occurred and since that time the transporter part of the bridge has been out of action. It would have been good had both a train been passing over the bridge and a ship sailing beneath. Fussganger has several claims to notoriety, not least the importance of having the longest bench in the world, this 501 m (do not forget that vital metre) sits alongside the Kiel canal. Ideal for Covid social distancing for 250 people, minus spaces for two lunchboxes. I had a little difficulty in finding the descent entrance to the Fussganger pedestrian tunnel that goes under the canal, but once found it provided a perfect entrance to the city on the northside.

The Neumunster-Flensburg railway bridge.

The Fussganger tunnel.

I continued to the picturesque town of Schleswig with its pretty, small single-storey cottages radiating from a small immaculate church with a similarly immaculate graveyard, where a gardener busied himself cutting the grass edges. I say in the blog that I cycled around slowly. The truth was that I was desperate for a pee and urgently needed to find a convenient place. There were none, the village was pristine, not a single thing out of place. Resorting to desperate measures, I adopted the professional cyclist's approach.

So many European border crossings have massive, tarmacked areas, many are now deserted such as those between Hungary, Slovakia, and Poland, that Luke and Andy and I cycled through several years ago. These are eerie places often with deserted buildings and some with sentry towers. The border at Flensburg had the familiar vast area of tarmac but it was manned with police emerging from large, tented structures. The experience of leaving Germany and entering Denmark was a pleasant one. An inquisitive, smiling officer asked my reasons for wanting to go into Denmark. Dressed in lycra with a loaded cycle between my legs, a sarcastic reply was tempting but would not be wise. He wished me well and I was off into yet another country. Andy, who I had cycled across America with a few years earlier (and a few other places), had sung the praises of Denmark. His daughter and her Danish husband had lived here. As the width of the tarmac shrunk to 50 m I looked across to a few shops. Confirmation that Denmark was a free-living liberal country that liked pizzas was confirmed, as the retail outlets presented themselves in an equal ratio of sex shops and fast-food outlets. As I left Germany this time, not to return as I had done when first arriving, a reoccurring thought crossed my mind. It had been over two months since I had cycled away from Tarifa. In some ways, it seemed an age ago, in others surprisingly short. It was becoming hard to mentally hold together a linear memory of all the different places visited. Did that happen before that, did I see that before that, where was it that that happened? I am a great believer in the idea that we as humans never forget anything, it is just the recall of that memory or fact that escapes us. How is it that without prompting or any identifiable trigger we suddenly remember (or recall) an event? I consider myself to be fortunate to have experienced so much in my life. Some experiences, like so many people, I would have preferred not to have had, but the vast majority have been enjoyable and enlightening. Given some rare peace and solitude, our minds can meander through our memories and hit on obscure long-lost experiences. If asked where I met Joanne Newman or Ryan Sykes or Aldo Rock or numerous others on this trip, I would be hard-pressed to recall where I met all of them, but I can remember their faces and our conversations. The sheer volume of places seen on a trip like this clouds the brain's recall mechanism.

I climbed Carstensz Pyramid, possibly the most exotic mountain in the world, now known as Puncak Jaya in Western Papua, with a friend who was a GP, a lovely guy, intelligent, witty, curious, and humble. Like me, he loves adventure and travel. He sadly had a brain haemorrhage. Being a medical doctor, he recognised the signs and was able to call his wife, who is a surgeon. Fortunately, he was at home and was rapidly hospitalised and subsequently recovered. Apprehensive of a further haemorrhage and the effects it may have on his memory, he decided to write about his climbing and motorcycle experiences, so in the unfortunate event of losing his memory, he could read about these achievements. The book has since been published and he continues to have no use of the book for the original reason of writing it.

One common motivator for travellers and adventurers is living the experience, achieving something that is personally extraordinary, being fulfilled, feeling the adrenaline fill your body, playing with, and weighing up the risk. As we get older our memory files become larger than our 'still must do' or 'still would like to do – but can't do' files and whilst we continue to indulge, we also gain satisfaction from what has been achieved. To lose that ability to reflect (not to dwell) is a loss hard to contemplate. So perhaps the benefits of writing are twofold. We, as the long-distance cyclists, climbers and adventurers do want to share and encourage others to enter the world we enjoy, to leave the security of modern living, but we also never wish to have our experiences wiped from our own memories.

Not once had this journey of mine prompted me to think of not finishing, of not arriving in Nordkapp. It had been and would continue to be challenging, infuriating, frustrating, elating, and just plain fantastic.

I was looking forward to discovering Denmark, my next country.

Daily Blog: *Back to basics. June 8th*

The town clocks are striking 9 am in Rendsburg and already I have seen some diverse sights. A warm day lies ahead, which sits nicely with my intention to have a short one and stay at an official campsite on the banks of a lake or fjord near the busy, but picturesque town of Schleswig. The old part of this town is very appealing with immaculately maintained, beautiful cottages, (even the climbing roses have their individual paling fences half mooned around them). The streets are narrow and cobbled, radiating from a small central church, whose unusual circular graveyard is void of a single weed, as a gardener surveyed his handy work having cut the lawns.

The picturesque village of Schleswig.

Could not resist this one, walking on water has also moved with the times.

I had slept well and again did not need the sleeping bag. When I emerged from the tent at 5.30 am, there was a dense early morning mist laying over the field. This evaporated quickly, and the sun shone through.

The railway line ran parallel to the road behind the hedge where I had pitched the tent. This morning I again followed it until it became elevated on an extended steel structure that eventually bridged the river. The minimal supporting structure seemed incapable of carrying the weight of any train, let alone long freight trains.

It was not immediately apparent how to cross the river into Rensburg. The road I had intended taking, most definitely did not entertain cycles. There had to be another way over, other than a ferry or another bridge that was some distance to the east. The Fussganger tunnel, not as grand as that under the Elbe but equally convenient, provided the solution.

What a pleasant town Rendsburg is, with its brick and cobble sett streets, old buildings, and enormous cobbled square. There is a relaxed tranquillity about the whole town. The modern buildings have been blended well with the old, save perhaps for H&M and C&A. The brick-built church surrounded by sycamore trees, under which the smooth brick path runs, caused me concern. My bike had developed an immediate fault and was about to fall apart, such was the noise from both wheels. The bike being ridden beside me was also about to fall apart, as were all the bikes around me. The noise was being produced by the sticky sycamore tree deposits on the smooth surface. This was acting like a suction between the tyres and bricks that made the strange sound.

One of the pleasures of cycling.

As I write and drink coffee here in Rendsburg, I have a character sharing my table in the town square. He has an incredibly long moustache, ponytail, an ornate ring for each of his fingers, and a different country's flag painted on each of his fingernails, and not the first person to have an inability to recognise that I am unable to understand what he is saying. He is probably a remarkably interesting person, but I have no way of telling.

It is 9.30 am, I have little idea what lays ahead today, or tomorrow, or any other day until Nordkapp and that is what makes this journey so enjoyable. So best fill the water bottles and get moving.

I did not find the campsite beside the fjord. Well I did, but the wrong sort, it was only for camper vans and utility vehicles, some housing motorbikes in their rear compartments! So, I have headed north through a weird area of a square mile, east of Schleswig, consisting of numerous large buildings all boarded up. It looked like an old army barracks, but with a renovated windmill in the middle.

My last night in Germany, only 17 km to Flensburg and then about 12 km to the border with Denmark. I am camped not in an official campsite, but a field of long grass, listening to the evening bird song and a cuckoo and drinking the finest German beer I could find. Life is good, but back to basics after the pleasures of Hamburg.

- DENMARK -
CHAPTER SEVENTEEN

Great Expectations

'We travel not to escape life, but for life not to escape us'. Unknown

My first night in Denmark was the night of June 9th opposite the small island of Barso, near Genner Strand. The following day was a wet one. Travelling in rain north on the 170 to Kolding I picked up three punctures, all on the rear wheel and all requiring the removal of the panniers. On one occasion I took the liberty of using the shelter provided by an open garage after having first tried to raise the owners. I arrived in Kolding wet through and determined to replace my not-so-worn tyres with heavier Kevlar puncture-protected tyres. I stayed in a warm bed and breakfast overlooking the working harbour and, in the morning, having paid a very un-Yorkshire price for two new tyres, headed up the hill out of Kolding.

The next port of call was the Viking burial site at Jelling. I cycled north on quiet roads to Vejle before turning northwest to Jelling. This important Viking village became a UNESCO World Heritage Site in 1994. I talk about this in the blog.

Quiet cross-country lanes took me northeast towards Arrhus. I had enjoyed both the cycling and the cultural experience of Jelling. Feeling content, I found a field with oilseed rape growing to a height well above my small tent, so pitched it a few metres into the field where the farmer had missed with the sower and had left the soil barren.

Aarhus is Denmark's second largest and fastest growing city. I arrived early in the morning before most had woken up. Although large and predominantly of new structures, there are areas where old buildings dominate; these are of red brick and half-timber, mixed with white half-timbered properties. A canal meanders through the town with pavement cafés and restaurants on either side. Back streets and waterways are boarded by ochre and other mellow-coloured houses with many flowers and small trees adding a rural atmosphere. By contrast, the harbourside is a large expanse of a paved area. So far, the Denmark I had seen was clean, with no street litter and no chewing gum on the sidewalks. Aarhus was no exception. It is a cultural centre, long known for its musical traditions covering all genres. There are many festivals and a popular theatre-going culture.

One of the benefits of cycling in Denmark, or indeed hiking or any other activity that lends itself to overnight camping, is the national provision of camping facilities provided by the Danish Nature Agency. There are four levels of provision ranging from being able to sleep on the forest floor or in a hammock without the use of a tent, to Stor leirplads (large campsites). There are also several hundred basic timber shelters. These structures are raised off the ground, roofed with one side open. They are warm and comfortable, the only downside being the lack of mosquito protection, although campfires (balplads) are permitted outside the shelters, the smoke from which keeps the blighters away.

From Aarhus I again wandered from the direct route north and headed towards Ronde and southeast to Ebeltoft. The plan had never been to go east to Copenhagen, rather to go north to Frederikshavn and catch the ferry to Sweden and Gothenburg. I wanted to see the less trodden parts of Denmark; I was not to be disappointed. Cycling around Kalo Vig on minor roads in warm sunny weather was a delight. I was in my own world when a car sounded its horn immediately behind me. Turning around I saw a lady driver waving frantically at me. Could this be another incredible coincidence of a chance meeting of a distant friend or a work colleague of twenty years ago? Such things happen to me with unexplainable frequency.

To dive off at a tangent, these coincidences are regular and sometimes verge on the frequent. Such as meeting a friend, Lance, in a French motorway service station in the middle of the night when returning from climbing in Italy. Bumping into an Austrian friend, Helmut, in Punta Arenas in Chile and subsequently climbing with him in the Antarctic. These are highly improbable meetings, but the following are even more so. After I finished my ride to Nordkapp I took the Hurtigruten ferry from Honningsvag down to Tromsø, where Anne met me in full daylight at midnight. A few days later we travelled to Bergen on another

Hurtigruten ferry and whilst having our first dinner on board we met Doreen and Malcolm, a lovely Scottish couple from Inverness. I happened to mention my brother-in-law's name, an unusual one, and Doreen and Malcolm looked at each other and said they had friends in Cape Town with the same surname. Turns out they had had dinner with my sister, her husband, and his son and wife when they were visiting a few months previously. There are many more examples. In Moscow, heading to the Caucasus mountains to climb Elbrus, Liselle and Mark joined me as the other two climbers. All three of us lived within a mile of each other in North Yorkshire and had not known each other before. In 2012, I was in the Dhaulagiri area of Nepal with a trekking group, a great bunch of people, and as we got to know each other, a couple from New Zealand, Wendy and Russell talked about Wendy's job as a celebrant in Tauranga. It turned out that she had recently held a marriage ceremony for Mike, who I had climbed Everest with two years before. Perhaps the last coincidence for now was when I was climbing for the first time on Khan Tengri in the Tian Shan in Kyrgyzstan, one of the five mountains known as the Russian Snow Leopards. My tent buddy, Jon, an Australian, went to school with my cousin Dave in Adelaide and has remained friends ever since. So, the six degrees of separation for me is eminently tangible.

Back to the storyline. The car overtook and stopped in front of me, the lady jumped out, waving. No six degrees of separation here, a total stranger. In near-perfect English, she told me that the road ahead became very narrow, and vehicles travelled fast, and had recently killed several cyclists. She said that there was a partially hidden entrance to a cycle track back along the road and advised that I took it. The kindness of that lady may have been a lifesaver.

Rolling over pleasant hills with perfect weather and a sense of the sea ever present made the afternoon a memorable one, one that would be enhanced by an ice cream. A small village shop had what was needed and a healthier evening meal, oh and two cans of beer. Arriving at the deserted pebbled beach through sparsely forested pines and sand dunes with the setting sun on my back would put a smile on anyone's face. That evening I swam in the sea and ate my evening meal looking towards Sweden. The euphoria continued into the following morning as the rising sun reflected off the calm sea and, apart from the quiet lapping of the small waves, only silence could be heard. Most of the wild campsites that I had found since leaving Spain had been more than adequate and some had been outstanding. This was an outstanding one, with favourable weather, swimming in the sea as the sun set and opening the tent to a rising sun in the morning with a refreshing wake-up swim, this was hard to top.

Pointing the bike NNW, I headed across country to again meet up with the coast at the tiny little hamlet of Lystrup Strand. To its west was a military firing range that was in full use, with rapid fire emitting from behind high wire fencing and a particular road sign that caught my eye: 'LAV FART' - probably the best place for them. I caught the small ferry that took me across the Randers fjord into the immaculately kept village of Udbyhoj Vasehuse. Not long after I found a place in a young fir tree plantation to camp and enjoyed a restful night.

I arrived in Aalborg on June 14th having crossed the flatlands from Hadsund. Whilst critical of the high chimneys that emitted pollutants into the atmosphere and the quayside industrial oil storage tanks, industry is an integral part of modern life and over recent years the Danish government has been at pains to embrace environmental issues. One of the more recent pieces of legislation has been the Environment and Climate Laws and Regulations 2020. The shipyards were first established in 1912 by the Stuhr brothers. Over the years Aalborg has become known for its industry and university, and with a population of 130,000 it is by far the largest most northern city in Denmark. Adding to its importance is the Transport wing of the Royal Danish Air Force at Vadum, which is just outside the city.

Away from the industry of the docks, there are small sailing boats moored at the quay adjacent to alfresco cafés and restaurants beneath period terraced houses. The mix of old architecture and new, so often at odds with each other, seems somehow to blend. Although it is Denmark's fourth largest city, in parts it retains a character belonging to a past era. This thousand-year-old city spawned by the Vikings boasts an astonishing array of restaurants. Yet I could only eat at one.

The Vikings were the first to recognise the strategic importance of the city, sheltered from the sea and with water access both to the west and east, and used it to launch raids on the English east coast. But let us not forget that the

Vikings were not just consummate sailors and efficient warriors. Not tainted by the mighty Roman empire, their culture was a pure ancient one born of family and community values and a belief that bravery and valour were rewarded in the next life. Reg, in the Monty Python sketch known as *What did the Romans ever do for us?*, got it very wrong and was reminded of roads, aqueducts, education, and wine. The belief that the Vikings were savages who were marauders, raiders, rapists, and murderers is far from the truth. Like the Romans they eventually benefited other cultures too. Initially, in AD 793 the first raids were violent affairs. Drawn by the exceptional wealth of Lindisfarne Priory and its isolated location, opportunities like these would be seen as a way to a better living, and within a few years the Vikings were settling to cultivate English soil and contribute to a post-Roman world.

Daily Blog: Auf Wiedersehen im echten Norden. June 9th

My last night in Germany was peaceful, just the sounds of nature, including the barking of a deer some way off. Surrounded by tall grass with no buildings in sight, this was the most isolated site since some in Spain.

After a leisurely start, a ride of 28 km had me in Flensburg by 8.30 am and drinking a coffee in the town square where the Saturday market was in full swing.

I am hoping to find Sankt-Jürgen-Strasse where there are some historic, albeit now upmarket, fishermen's cottages.

I found the cottages, not in a location expected such as a wharf or a harbour, but behind more modern buildings remote from the harbour. I also found the rain, or it found me. It is steady and heavy.

The rain eased and I continued to explore the town. Old buildings, a trumpet being played beautifully from high up in an ancient house, drew a small crowd beneath the window. On the finish of a particularly rousing piece, there was spontaneous clapping. The performer never showed themself.

The 'Angels' were in town. About thirty, leather-clad, sitting astride their Harley Davidson motorcycles. It hurts me to say that these bikers did not show as much interest in my bike as I did in theirs.

On the gentle hill up to the last German supermarket before the run down to the country border, I passed two cyclists. The lady's load must have lacked for nothing. I asked whether they were going to Nordkapp. They said that they were 'nearly' going there. I asked no more and said enthusiastically, but with little belief, that we may see each other again.

My coffee (plus) in Flensburg.

Note the age of the men and the stilettoed heels.

On the Border (Chris Rea)

Once this border was policed heavily and had a nervous atmosphere about it. Now there is a relaxed procedure. Two police officers occasionally and at random check a vehicle's contents from under a temporary tent structure and drink coffee from an urn in the rear of a transit van. There are no buildings.

So, what changes once you have crossed the border? For the cyclist, there is an immediate change. No more weaving around pedestrians or stopping at every minor road when cycling the major road. In Denmark, the cyclist is not usually separated from other vehicles but has a dedicated strip of road on both sides. No swapping from one side of the road to the other and playing 'chicken' with oncoming cyclists or tree roots that break up the tarmac and, if not vigilant, provide a 'crushing' experience for the rider. Put simply, in Denmark a rider can remain in the saddle for more than ten minutes.

I was not expecting such a dramatic change in the local wildlife or an even more relaxed attitude towards some subjects.

Seen in a garden centre.

First shop across the national border.

Denmark welcomes.

Genna Strand.

I was aiming to find a suitable camping spot with a sea view and stumbled on Genna Strand. With its quaint marina, white painted fishermen's cottages, and a circular walk around a small peninsula where you can find a Viking longship at anchor, it is a gem of a location.

There are so many official campsites in the area. There is the noisy young person's campsite, the 'I've been thrown off Ryanair and EasyJet flights, men will be idiots' site, the 'all campers like loud music on Saturday nights' site, or if you are fortunate, there is the field with the cuckoo and babbling stream.

Daily Blog: Day two in Denmark – a wet one! June 10th

Woke at 4 am with sleepiness and lethargy deciding that rain would not arrive for a few hours. Woke again at six and immediately changed that decision. I packed up camp fast to avoid a soaking. However, good fortune was again with me as I arrived in Haderslev just as the rain did, and I dived into a supermarket café. Unknowingly, I had already had the best part of the day.

The western coastline of Lille-baelt is charming, with rolling hills, lakes, and long views east across the water. I hung onto those thoughts throughout the day.

There is not too much to say about today. On leaving the supermarket café the rain returned as I cycled to Kolding. The camera remained in its pocket. I got drenched. I also got three punctures, all in the rear tyre and all within 4 km. My thanks to the owners of the open-sided garage for lending me the dry space to repair the first puncture. I did ring your doorbell several times before taking the liberty. There was no shelter for the second puncture nor for the third. Benjamin and the family who he has just started working for, assisted in getting me back on the road.

The plus side of the day? (because there always is), there was no wind, and the cycleway was smooth and fast.

Anne, my established travel agent, general manager, and tour operator, booked me into a bed and breakfast in Kolding that boasted a sea view, where I am now showered, shaved and the gear is drying out and the punctures repaired, although I have failed to locate the sea from my room but found the provided earplugs for the traffic noise useful.

Tomorrow will be a better day. That said, the rain and the punctures were not that irksome.

To finish, the only photo taken today was in Haderslev minutes before I dived under a pub parasol.

Daily Blog: Great expectations. June 11th

Kolding has its attributes. There is Modavi, a vineyard that prides itself on producing modern Danish wines. Although it looks like a newer town, it has existed for 750 years and there is also a sizeable port. First records mention Kolding in 1231 in King Valdemar's book of land taxation. With a castle being built in the 13th century came status and trading power.

Koldinghus Castle was a favourite with the Danish royalty for centuries.

In more recent history, the royals moved to the capital and in 1807 a fire destroyed most of the building whilst soldiers who were normally billeted there during the war against England and Sweden were absent. Having been restored, today it is a museum which also hosts fine arts exhibitions.

Borch's house was built in 1595 and is one of the grandest examples of renaissance townhouses in Denmark.

Helligkorsgade 18, built in 1589.

I have decided that although the tyres on the bike are not too worn, (I replaced the rear one not so long ago), doing so would reduce the chances of getting further punctures. Waiting for the shop to open and then fitting the tyres resulted in a late getaway from Kolding. Breakfast was an excellent coffee in Greg Steen's cafe and bakery. Had I known the coffee came with biscuits I would not have had the pastry – honestly!

There has not been too much cycling today. This morning 35 km to Vejle, finishing with an exhilarating downhill ride into town, before the climb up to Jelling, where I spent the best part of the day.

The second ride of the day was around 65 km and was particularly enjoyable as a strong tailwind blew me along. 42 km/h on the flat has a certain feel-good factor on a loaded touring bike. Although caution is needed, as drivers do not judge cyclists' speeds accurately and suddenly realise they need more distance to overtake you, causing oncoming traffic to brake to avoid a collision. I should have explained that today there were very few cycle lanes, so I had no option. I bought my evening meal and breakfast for the following day in Horsens and then retired to a field of rapeseed, where I am camped.

Hidden away in rapeseed.

Images of Jelling.

The main event of the day must be a visit to Jelling. As one of about a thousand UNESCO World Heritage Sites, this is a special place. I spent several hours walking around both the site and the engaging hi-tech museum. I was fascinated by a piece of history I had previously been ignorant about. There is so much to say, but I am aware it would be easy to write reams and perhaps such things do not float everyone's boat. So here is just a taster. The site centres around two enormous burial mounds, two Rune stones, (on one of which the word Denmark was first mentioned), and a stone ship. All this was contained within a 1.5 km palisade made of oak timber to a height of 3 m to keep out invaders. The monuments are around 1,000 years old. King Harald Bluetooth built the palisade in the 960s. The south mound is the biggest ever found from the Viking age, although curiously no burial chamber was placed in it. Unlike the north mound, where precious artefacts were found in 1820 and where probably the body of King Gorm the Old was laid before being moved to under the wooden church that preceded the existing stone church built in the 1,000s. Lastly, the stone ship was massive, 350 m long. Norse mythology said that the dead could sail in the ship to the gods in Valhalla.

Contrary to popular belief the Vikings were not just into plunder, rape, and pillaging. They were explorers, farmers and inventors, living in a complex structured society where worship of their gods was paramount. Belief in their gods demanded that human sacrifice was necessary, with the most precious, handsome, or beautiful in their community being those best to sacrifice to and appease the gods.

Daily Blog: Four pounds 50p for a small cup of coffee. June 12th

We jest about Scotsmen being prudent with their money and Yorkshiremen being like Scotsmen, but with the generosity removed. I am neither. Anyway, I do not believe this trait is accurate, I know many generous Yorkshiremen and a few Scots. And the reason for mentioning this is…? I have no objection to paying for anything provided it reflects the quality of the product or service. So, a small coffee, served beside a stagnant stream, in the middle of town is not worth five pounds. Rant over! A prologue – the next coffee was three pounds and twice the size. 'Enough said, you old git.'

Anyway, what does it matter after such a fantastic afternoon? This morning was another quick 35 km, this time into Aarhus, a large town, clean, modern, with fewer older buildings than others, but a fine period church and an exceptionally fine Town Hall.

Aarhus fine period church.

Aarhus town hall.

The first part of this afternoon's ride was alongside busy roads. Then having turned onto the quieter Ronde road after the climb up to Hornslet, I again missed the sign for the start of a cycleway. Due partly because of conditioning and there being no forward advisory signs, so if you are cycling at a reasonable speed, it can be easy to miss the start of them and then frequently have to jump a ditch or climb a bank to gain access. I had just missed the start of the cycle path after the Ronde junction when a lady pulled into the lay-by. She sounded her horn and called me over. She politely told me that there was a cycle path, and I should be on it as the stretch of road was dangerous. Jane, thank you for putting me right. It was good to meet you, albeit briefly. The cycle path you directed me onto was excellent. It was from this point that the remainder of the 70 km ride became pure joy. Beautiful sea views, classic sports cars, and petit timber homes.

I was south of the National Park Mols Bjerge, heading SE to Ebeltoft. Here there is the Fregatten Jylland, an impressive three-mast frigate.

The cycle path towards Ebeltoft.

Although certainly not on a northerly route, I had wanted to visit this area, which is renowned for its outstanding beauty. It is difficult to say what makes it so appealing, no one particular thing that jumps out, it just all fits together to create *a quiet serenity. I cycled around the whole peninsula, past boatyards, and marinas that reminded me of my uncle's town of Goolwa in South Australia. Then there were many small, perfectly kept wooden houses tucked away down grass tracks that reminded me of childhood memories of my great grandparents' home in Bembridge on the Isle of Wight in the UK.*

Isolated homesteads near Odden.

After a few directional difficulties involving no through roads, I found Boeslum Strand. And what a find! Yet another fantastic wild campsite. There was an excellent shelter, but it had two sleeping bags in it, giving the impression it was going to be occupied for the night.

The occupied night shelter.

I pitched the tent 20 m from the beach and, sitting at the provided table, had an evening meal looking out to sea with the warm evening sun on my back. Having also swum, life was near to perfection.

Daily Blog: *There was a smile on my face before my eyes were open. June 13th*
What a setting. The sea rippled onto the sand, skylarks flew above, and the sun shone. After another swim, breakfast was served at the same table as dinner. This time I looked out to sea with the sun on my face.

After 40 km of riding, I was looking forward to a coffee and perhaps a few calories. Ryomgard, a reasonably sized town, was dead, apart from the school children playing in the playground, (who were very much alive) and the gentleman who told me that the pub opened at 10 am and the landlord would rustle up a coffee for me. Disappointing, especially as this café I photographed looked good, but did not open until 2 pm! every day of the week. We need caffeine in the morning.

No one minds being awake at 4 am with a sunrise like this morning.

Ryomgard, a deserted town.

Netto came to the rescue with the calories, but I was coffee starved. I walked into a bar in Auning where six men were sitting. All eyeballed me, (had they never seen an unshaven middle-aged man in lycra before?). I turned and left, letting the saloon doors swing shut as my spurs spun on the heels of my cycle shoes. Mounting my bike, I rode off down the sleepy street, aware that curtains were twitching. My trigger finger stayed close to my bicycle pump.

The west end of Auning town was different, modern shops, like …. Netto, (every town has one!), clothes and art shops and just the best cafe I have been in for ages. Excellent coffee, quality food, great music, great atmosphere. I stayed for over two hours!

The objective for today was to try and get back to the sea to repeat last night's enjoyment. I cycled to Hevring; it was not suitable. The firing range is next door and given the rapid fire that could be heard, they were spending a lot of taxpayer's money.

This sign made me smile. I thought triangular road signs were warnings, not orders.

Looking for a place to camp for the night, a calculated guess had me heading down a long and rough road to the sea at Havno. However, the whole area had small timber houses dotted throughout the woodland with a high wired fence at the end. So, I retraced my 'tyre' prints and continued to find a suitable camp location. I have cycled 98 km today, the last 25 in search of a site. I am back in a wood that is miraculously free of mozzies.

The bike and rider got a bit blown this afternoon heading uphill into a stiff headwind. The whole ride was exhilarating but hard work. The wind was strong enough to create a nasal vortex. 'Outdoorsy' people know about this phenomenon. Whether you are a hiker, runner, mountaineer, cyclist, or anyone who has experienced strong winds in your face, the wind negates the need for a tissue. This was the strength of the wind this afternoon. Weirdly it was quite enjoyable – the wind, not the nasal vortex effect.

Over the many weeks of cycling, not un-naturally my body had become lean and cycle fit. I carried little body fat. Although I had climbed many mountains since leaving Tarifa in Spain, that fitness had declined as I cycled through less arduous terrain. However, there were many shorter, punchier hills, and the constant daily cycling maintained a good level of fitness. It was this conditioning that made the Danish countryside an easy ride and consequently, yet again I found myself ahead of schedule. The idea was to have a few days of sightseeing in Oslo. The planned few days could now be extended to five, making it worthwhile for Anne to fly over from the UK and join me. Still with plenty of time to spare and knowing Frederikshavn, from which the ferry to Gothenburg sails, was so near, I decided to visit the relatively new fishing harbour and the small town of Hirtshals at the northern end of the Jutland peninsula. A dilemma presented itself. One of the criteria of this trip was to visit as many European countries as possible. I had never been to Sweden before and although the proposed visit was only to be from Gothenburg north to the Norwegian border, it would, for now, tick the box and enable me to see the historic maritime city of Gothenburg and the Swedish coastline north towards Oslo. I had every intention to return to Sweden. Alternatively, I could go straight to Norway by taking the ferry from

A Life Appreciated

Hirtshals across to either Kristiansand or Larvik and approach Oslo from the southwest.

Hirtshals town on the Skagerrak coast was born from a modern fishing harbour that is now also a small ferry port. I was fortunate to have been bathed in warm sunshine as it is exposed to the mercy of weather blown from the sea from nearly all directions. The greatest attraction is the 35 m lighthouse located a short way southwest of the town. Built in 1863 it has a range of 25 sea miles. First lit on January 1st 1863 and electrified (that was the translation) in 1939. Certainly, worth an hour of anyone's time.

Although there was a crosswind at times, the weather was bright and sunny and the 'feel-good' factor was high, enhanced further by a brief and pleasant visit to an immaculately kept church with seashell paths at Tornby Bjerg.

The lighthouse at Hirtshals, worth the climb to the top.

I cycled via Uggerby and Tversted along flat and deserted country lanes towards Frederikshavn. The decision to go to Gothenburg across the Kattegat had been made. Unconsciously the draw of Sweden had won over an early arrival in

Norway. With the sun shining and a now gentle cooling breeze, I was at peace with the world. My phone rang: this sound had not been heard for days and took me by surprise, even more so when the voice at the other end was my bank manager. Somehow either my wife or I (or, heaven forbid, someone else) had used our credit card to buy foreign currency and the account had racked up considerable interest. A shock and a costly incident, but it had little impact on that wonderful afternoon.

Daily Blog: (Day off) The one and only 'No Blog Day'. Wild camped north of Aalborg. June 14th

Daily Blog: Danish pastries in Jutland. June 15th

Not to have at least one pastry a day whilst passing through Denmark would be a missed opportunity. I am in Bronderslev, watching people come and go in a bakery. They are all so happy. Many workmen in company branded protective clothing. The sun is shining and the wind blowing hard from the west. Whilst cycling my clothes have dried on me from last night's rain.

I leave Bronderslev and go to Hjorring and onto Hirtshals, passing through Tornby Bjerg with its beautiful church.

Tornby Bjerg church with its meticulously raked paths.

I have mentioned before how well maintained churchyards are. Even the gravel is raked into shell-like patterns. I have also seen farmers harrowing their stone yards and drives to keep them looking neat. Not something you would see in the UK.

Now we all know the Danes have a history of being tough and used to the elements. Perhaps that is why this structure is considered as protection against those elements.

Weather protection?

Cycling before lycra

For a small part of the ride today I rode with Amerly. He is cycling from Paris to Nordkapp, and it was his first long solo trip. He had left Paris three weeks ago, which is impressive progress. He intended catching the ferry direct to Norway from Hirtshals to Kristiansand and going over the mountains to Bergen, then up the coast. We may meet up again north of Viggja; stranger things have happened.

I could not help but take a photo of this cycle sign, reminiscent of days when cyclists were not twisted into contorted shapes and did not wear strange clothing.

I had a great ride east, with the wind behind me through country lanes towards Frederikshavn. I started to look for a place to sleep as the sky rapidly turned to grey. Rain is forecast for tomorrow, so best to be near Frederikshavn. It was a gamble as to how near to the town I came. Strangers in tents in back gardens are pushing it a little. Then an ideal field presented itself. I rode straight through a tree archway into a hay-cut field.

I think we both saw each other at the same time. A German Shepherd dog can certainly outrun an old git on a bike, especially black, mean-looking ones (dogs, not gits, although, after five days of only tent washing, I could be cleaner)! As much as he would have liked to have savaged me, he was an obedient creature and responded to his owner's command of 'Leave!'. I left that field a little quicker than I entered. The search for a place to rest continued.

I have found another hay-cut field about a mile from town. It is massive and has solved the mystery that existed for me in Germany: whether the rapid barking sounds heard in the evening and during the night were raccoons or deer. Three deer have just been spooked by my tent and stampeded away. I got out of the tent to see them standing 200 m away, still making their noise. For such elegant creatures that pure aggressive sound seems alien.

I fell off my bike today. My fault. I had missed the start of a cycle path and with feet still clipped in, decided that it was possible to cycle through the grass from the road onto the path. It was not! There was an unseen ditch. Bent my glasses that were in my pocket, but that was not the worst. I had my usual evening meal and beer on board. Not until I unpacked for the night did I see that the bottom of a pannier was a darker colour than usual. I can confirm that the panniers are very water/beer-proof. Inside, my spare clothes had received an unscheduled wash. The tin had punctured, at its base of course. And the positive – not a single biscuit was broken, and the yogurt remained in its pot.

The harbour at Hirtshals.

Expressions, it is the same the world over. This was in Hjorring, an entrance to a public building.

A pig town.

The quality of air is usually excellent. However, this in Denmark and apart from Vikings, mink farming and pastries, and a few other items, pigs prevail! Their unique odour drifts across the landscape. The above photo is of a large pig complex. These 'Pig Towns' cater for everything any pig could wish for, but nowhere is the word 'bacon' mentioned. Links with Boxer, the old horse in

George Orwell's 'Animal Farm' come to mind. The irony is that Napoleon was a pig ruling over the other animals. Enjoy your bacon the next time you have bacon sandwiches.

CHAPTER EIGHTEEN
A Rude Awakening

'The problem is not the availability of guns, it is the availability of morons'
Antonio Meloni

Today had been another enjoyable ride. The people I had met had been happy. My journey to the northernmost part of Jutland had been an 'add-on' to the trip and one I had thoroughly enjoyed. Denmark would become a special memory. As I approached Frederikshavn on the eve of June 15th the aim was to get as near to the town as possible to minimise the effects of the anticipated downpour and to allow time the following day to either spend sightseeing or, if the ferry times were good, to get across to Gothenburg. Coming out of the quiet lanes onto the main road into the city I was fast running out of time to find a suitable place to camp. This was my fifth consecutive night camping, and it crossed my mind to go into the city and find lodging to clean up. Suitable wild camping locations near towns can be difficult to find. The first I abandoned because of an enthusiastic dog. The second would have been good had there not been a gardener attending his allotment. I cycled off-road into a wood with well-trodden paths and came out in a field where the crop had been harvested around small islands of trees. It was unusual to see these small coppices as they would have made field management more difficult. I pitched my tent against one of these 'islands' looking towards the outer industrial area of Frederikshavn. Whilst I ate and drank the habitual beer from a can, (bottles are not good news if the bike falls over) I not only heard deer barking but saw them this evening. Life again was good. Although I cover what happened next in the blog, the experience was profound.

I slept well. That was until a dream started, a dream that was not a dream. Being woken by someone shouting at you is never the best way to end a night's sleep. I was being ordered to leave in no uncertain terms and as I unzipped the tent to see an angry man holding a rifle in his hands, it was a sobering wake-up call. What made it even more surprising was that I could not for the life of me think how my presence was being so offensive. In Germany, where hunting occupies a parallel with religion, it would be more understandable. Then the penny dropped. Those deer the previous night may well have been disturbed by my being there and the contents of the aggressive man's rifle destined for those deer would not result in venison. The angry man gave me thirty minutes to GO!! Saying he would be back, and I would not like that. All the many mornings spent breaking camp over the past months and fine tuning the packing helped me 'disappear' mighty quickly – that and a good dose of adrenaline.

Daily Blog: A rude awakening. June 16th

'Hey! You in there, you need to go! Now!' I was fast asleep; was it a dream? The aggressive demand was repeated. I unzipped the tent to face a man holding a gun. The anger on the man's face was all too apparent. Somehow, me being in this enormous field, interfering with nobody, and leaving only an indentation in the grass, annoyed him to the extreme. He said that he would be returning, and I would not like that. 'I'll be gone in 30 minutes,' I said. He turned and walked off. This was the first time since starting this trip two and a half months ago, and having wild camped 90% of that time, I have been challenged. The guys in Belgium checking the field for fawns before the silage harvest were surprised but they could not have been nicer.

Although all the signs and forecast said the rain would be here today, fortunately, it has not arrived otherwise packing up would have taken longer and Mr Angry may have become terribly angry.

In anticipation of the rain and having been kicked off Mr Angry's field (I presume it was his), I have arrived in Frederikshavn by 7.30 am. Anne has booked me into a hotel for two nights before getting the ferry over to Gothenburg on Monday afternoon. My right knee remains the same, so although it is tempting to do a ride today, I think a few days off the bike would be advisable.

With my bent glasses now 'unbent' by a kind optician and having booked my passage across to Gothenburg, (many thanks to the Stena Line girl who helped with the easy to use, complex, self-help, suicide-provoking ticket machine), I am sitting on Palm Beach with an ice cream, only the third since starting this trip, I believe.

The palms may be viewed with good binoculars to the right of the notice

I have included this photo taken from the elevated walkway to Stena Line's booking office, not because it is any good, it's not, but because these vehicles are unregistered new Volvos in Denmark waiting to be shipped to Sweden. Mmm.

I arrived in Frederikshavn before most people were awake. I had a weird feeling running around my head, feeling detached from the world and a little unnerved. I sat for a while on a bench near the elevated gangway to the ferry before pulling myself together and heading around the corner into the high street and a very pleasant café where I spent a few hours charging my powerpack and phone. The day was first spent meandering around the town then visiting a botanical garden and a deer park.

The rain whilst in the botanical garden this afternoon had been a prelude to the evening's downpour. It ran in torrents down the streets as I sat in a cosy restaurant and ate an excellent chilli, washed down with several beers. The price was staggeringly expensive. The city of Frederikshavn's population of some 25,000 is supported by one-day shopping tourists from Norway and Sweden, shipbuilding, fishing and engineering. Earlier that afternoon I had explored the town and found myself on a palm beach. Many promotional photos show this 'beach'. As I licked on only my casually recalled third ice cream of my trip, or perhaps was it the fourth since leaving England weeks ago, I mused that the camera could lie after all. Palm trees deserve better.

I had purchased my Stena Line ferry ticket for Gothenburg before the rain arrived and was grateful that Anne had booked me into a hotel, knowing the forecast was sure of heavy rain. These occasions also served as good opportunities to give the bike and my gear a thorough clean. After all, we were heading to one of the cleanest countries on the planet and a smelly, dirty 'old git' on a cycle would not attract positive attention.

Daily Blog: A day around Frederikshavn. June 17th·

Slept late then enjoyed an excellent breakfast. No man with a gun this morning. Contacted daughters, grandchildren, and supportive wife. I left the hotel late morning to visit several local sights and am now sheltering from a deluge.

The sky minutes before the rain arrived.

Had a quick look around the botanical gardens before dashing for shelter. The roses in the Rosenhaven were particularly impressive. The quirky were also present with several unusual carvings.

Weird tree man near the Byens hyggeligste restaurant and troglodytes emerging from the ground.

Last night, having borrowed an umbrella from the receptionist as protection against a downpour, I had enjoyed a good meal and beer. I am pleased I enjoyed it. The chilli and beer cost 35 pounds (the beer was 8 pounds).

Today, having sheltered with others in a park amphitheatre, the sun returned after an hour and I returned to the Bangsbo museum and botanical gardens. The sun was catching the light in the water that still fell from the beech trees. There were surprises around each corner, such as Johannes Boolsen's collection of stones, including 1,000 carved stones from 3,000 BC.

Johannes Boolsen

A deer park with two of the four species found in Denmark, red and fallow, the other two being sika and roe.

The museum is housed in this remarkable building.

Back in Frederikshavn I saw the Martello Tower. Historically this building stored gunpowder. Built in 1686 to 1690, the first floor is a cannon deck whilst the ground floor is now a museum. It was strategically important for the Danes during the war against Britain from 1807 to 14.

The Martello Tower that used to house gunpowder.

Having a few days off from cycling seems strange, almost alien. Once I have seen the sights, I am at a loss what to do. I will be in Sweden for about a week. Then Norway! So far, rough calculations say I have ridden 6,500 km, with another 2,000 km to complete.

- SWEDEN -

CHAPTER NINETEEN
Wet and Windy Sweden

'Travel makes you modest, you see what a tiny place you occupy in the world.'
Gustave Flaubert

The following morning, I pushed the bike to the allotted place for cyclists to wait to board the ferry. There was one other cyclist next to me. Touring, as I was, we fell into conversation. Yoya Braams was cycling around the North Sea, a route that takes in all the countries that border that sea. From the Netherlands, she was a keen cyclist. We chatted while we waited to board and having secured our bikes on the ship, spent the crossing of four hours talking. There are some people that you naturally warm to, and Yoya was one such person. Tragically when young she had had an accident whilst on her cycle when a lorry had run over her foot. This had resulted in her leg being amputated below the knee. During the early years, she wore a skin-coloured prosthetic that endeavoured to minimise the visual impact. However, such is her character, in her own words she decided to 'go naked'. The workings of the prosthetic are on show for all to see. We said our goodbyes on reaching Gothenburg, not realising that our paths would cross again. As we go through our lives occasionally we are fortunate enough to meet inspirational people, people who have overcome personal difficulties, and whilst we may wonder how they achieved this, they see nothing out of the ordinary. This was a chance encounter that made me more appreciative of life. Thank you, Yoya.

I cannot recall much of the ferry crossing as Yoya and I had been deep in conversation throughout. We had said goodbye to each other, and I had headed off to find my lodging for the next two nights - a large, traditional timber-clad private house that was subdivided into bedsits. With plenty of room and cooking facilities, it was an ideal base from which to explore Gothenburg. Fran, the owner, told me there was an excellent supermarket just up the road. He was right.

Having first showered and dressed in ordinary clothes, i.e. not lycra, I arrived at something akin to Harrods Food Hall for the masses. The quality and variety of the food were beyond good, and I also managed to get some Piston Head beer called Flat Tire. On arriving at the checkout, I did a double take on the lady who was to pack my shopping. I can remember from an early age my mother teaching us kids not to stare. Now, I know beauty is in the eye of the beholder and what is beautiful to someone may not be so to another, but no one on this planet could deny the beauty of this 'late twenties' lady. She was stunning, the epitome of a Scandinavian woman. I cannot believe that she would not now have left that supermarket and be heading for a different life of modelling fame, or perhaps she was quite content to carry on meeting real people in the real world. Did I stare? I probably did!

Gothenburg was windy, very windy, the sun bright and I felt alive. I became an inconspicuous tourist for a couple of days. Cycling into the city centre, the bike without panniers felt light and responsive. The river Göte älv borders the north of the city and is the primary reason why the city is such an important seaport, providing easy access to the sea and sheltered mooring.

I walked along the quayside passing several navy ships including the HMS Smaland, which is now a war museum, on past the SS Marieholm, now a restaurant. With the opera house to my right and a ubiquitous bronze statue of which so many adorn prominent positions in cities around the world, I looked across the water to a four-mast tall ship, rigged with flags from the nautical alphabet. This was now a three-star hotel, The Barken Viking. Cabins are available at surprisingly low prices for sailors and landlubbers alike.

The fish market, Feskekôrka, was designed by Victor von Gegerfelt and, built in 1874, this church-like structure is by no means large. It is light and airy and worthy of a brief visit during which you should certainly purchase something from the tremendous array of seafood on sale.

The Oscar Fredrik church in the city centre, a late 19th century neo-Gothic church built in the European Gothic style rather than the Nordic style, cannot be missed. First opened on Easter Sunday in 1893, this red-bricked, multiple blue-spired building with decorated roof slates and steeple reaching for the heavens, is an impressive piece of architecture. Inside stained glass has only been used above the organ in the circular west window and above the high altar in the east window. A feeling of airiness is achieved with both the north and south sides having clear glazing and clean internal design lines running the eye up into high vaulted ceilings. There is nothing drab or melancholy about this place of worship.

The Trädgårdsföreningen is a wonderful garden, one of several parks within the city area, and one of the best 19th century horticultural gardens in Europe. Even for those without any interest in plants, this place has a tranquil atmosphere that is also pleasing to any eye.

Gothenburg is also the home of the Volvo museum, which is west of the city. I decided to stay more central and see a variety of interests rather than spend time on viewing cars, as iconic as they may be. Similarly, the Museum of World Culture could have so easily absorbed a day, having over 100,000 diverse objects from around the world encompassing archaeological, ethnographical and historical art. This did provide a dilemma, whether to spend time solely looking at one or two specific locations in the city or to roam more generally to absorb the atmosphere and get a feel for the whole city.

Daily Blog: Wet and windy Sweden. June 19th

The trees are dancing vigorously outside my bedroom window with the branches hitting the glass throughout the night. Depending on which weather forecast app I look at, there is a choice of weather ranging from 100% rain to 3% rain tomorrow. Going on the accuracy of today's forecast, which said no rain, as a tool for planning, these apps are limited.

So, the first time in Sweden for me. Given the wind I had anticipated the passage over from Denmark to have been a little rough; however, it was surprisingly smooth. Departing Frederikshavn at 2 pm we arrived in a dull and heavily overcast Gothenburg at 5.30 pm. The whole trip went largely unnoticed due to being in conversation with a remarkable lady.

Several cyclists had gathered in Lane One waiting to board the Stena Line ferry, a large ship that can carry many coaches, wagons, and all manner of vehicles. I fell into conversation with a solo lady cyclist. That conversation continued throughout

out the crossing. Yoya is a remarkable lady and after four hours of chatting, we both agreed it was as though we had known each other for much longer. She rides horses, sails, and cycles and has dealt with a life-changing event in a way that you can only be in awe of. Her current adventure is cycling around the North Sea. This involves following the coasts of Holland, Denmark, Sweden, Norway, across to the Orkney Isles then to Scotland, and down the east coast of England.

Yoya, it was great to meet you and I do hope we will be able to have that meal in York in September. You have my number and if there are any places in the UK you are in two minds whether to visit, do contact me.

As I write this, the heavy rain continues. I am about 7 km out of the city and would like to have a look around the sights. Could be wet.

Having returned from the city, dry, blown dry that is, I have had an enjoyable day. Initially, I was sceptical: any 'hop on-hop off' bus or boat tour that includes Starbucks and a Hard Rock cafe in its itinerary must be dredging what they can offer the tourist. However, I found some excellent places. Gothenburg has its own Covent Garden-style building, the Saluhallen, and a fish market, which certainly does not look like Billingsgate in London. Opened in 1874 the architect, Victor von Gegerfelt, designed a unique roof truss system to improve food hygiene standards by reducing horizontal surfaces that collect dirt.

I then found an excellent fleet of ships of all kinds moored on a quay. Included was a minelayer and other navy vessels and a lighthouse ship, together with a Gothenburg barge. At one time there were 1,600 of these barges working at unloading vessels until the 1960s. The motorised lifeboat, the 'Adolf Brett', slowly replaced the rowing lifeboats from 1935.

Other noteworthy places to visit are the Opera House and the gardens of The Garden Society of Gothenburg, one of the best preserved 19th century parks in Europe. Not one, but two multi-functional sports stadiums adjacent to each other, with this bronze (yes, more bronze) statue of Gunnar Gren, who played for IFK Gothenburg and AC Milan, later to become a coach.

The Feskekôrka market in Gothenburg.

Gunnar Gren.

An appropriate beer for a cyclist.

- CHAPTER TWENTY -
Bridges and Ferries

'Adventure is worthwhile in itself.' Amelia Earhart

With all my Flat Tire beer cans now empty and binned, I left Gothenburg on June 20th. The day was going to be a wet one. Michel, who I write about in the blog, rode with me for some hours during which the heavens opened. We chatted as we cycled, slowly the wet penetrated to our skin. Fortunately, a small bakery in a roadside hamlet was open. It was tiny inside. The two young ladies kindly gave us coffee and we ate their delicious cakes as we sort of warmed up before heading back out into the downpour. Anne had booked me into a bed and breakfast, and on arriving Michel continued cycling. On occasions, plans do go wrong. Cold and wet, I stood on the doorstep about five metres from a warm shower. The lady who answered surprised me by saying that she had no booking for me and that there was no room. Then again to my surprise, Yoya walked around the corner. Having not stopped in Gothenburg, she had arrived the day before and had set up her tent on the adjoining campsite. The owner was pleasant but insistent and gave directions to another place a few kilometres up the road. An hour later, colder, wetter – if that were possible, I was in some wood at the location given, where there was definitely no accommodation. Now fixated on a warm shower and a bed that had a mattress, I returned to the bed and breakfast site. The owner was no longer in. I decided to pitch my tent beside the campsite shower block. To be able to shower and sit in the site kitchen whilst the rain hammered on the roof was a plus. Yoya had kindly cooked last night's evening meal. To have hot food was a special occasion. To keep the weight to a minimum I had chosen not to carry cooking equipment on this trip. I can easily manage on cold food with the occasional hot meal that is appreciated even more because of its rarity. In the morning Yoya and I said our goodbyes and I headed in the fresh cool morning sunshine to an excellent cold breakfast in Grebbestad followed by a look around the numerous small yachts, a food shop for the day, and a public/cyclist convenience stop.

Now, we hear so much about marauding Vikings arriving on the coasts of England and Scotland, but not so much about the Scots reciprocating. Such a party attacked Grebbestad and paid the price. All were killed and buried there, their graves being marked by standing stones. Or is this folklore? With no written account, the verbal telling of these stories down the generations ensures that most are embellished. Why, given the opportunity to enhance the excitement of your audience, would you not, especially if they were paying for the privilege of listening? From King Arthur to Robin Hood and all the other characters the truth is so intertwined with wishful thinking, exaggeration, and distortion as to be a little untrustworthy, but they fulfil their aim, to entertain. That was until modern science arrived and is now able to a degree to 'separate the wheat from the chaff'. Sometimes it is best to leave a fairy tale, a piece of folklore or legend undissected. The legend of Greby Standing Stones is about a settlement called Tanum. Legend would have it that the dead Scots were cremated and 'potted', then a standing stone was placed over each of them. The settlement never recovered from the attack although all the Scots were killed. The quest to clarify came with the excavation of some of the hundred or more stones in the 19th century. No evidence of weapons or Scottish artefacts was found. Given that these would have been buried with the corpses for use in their afterlife, the legend becomes a little thin. But if all the Scots were killed in battle would their foes have buried them with such honours. Although history is dotted with examples of enemies honouring their dead foes in recognition of their bravery. Anyway, the fields of graves had been dated to the Iron Age, 5th and 6th century AD, the pre-Viking age known as the Vendel period. Accuracy prevails over entertainment.

One cannot help but think that if the Vikings raided the Scottish coast, which they certainly did, would the Scots not retaliate? Show me an occasion in history, where given the same circumstances the Scots have not. The Romans with their mighty First Reich failed to conquer the Vikings and the Scots. When we talk of Scots, we should also include the Picts. It is more likely that they were the ones who played the major role of repelling the Romans, refusing to fight in the way the Romans wanted to. Referring to Monty Python and the 'What did the Romans ever do for us…' sketch. Well, they wrote down much of what we know about history during their reign of the known world. Recognising that it can only be biased, there is still worth in it. Julius Caesar said of them (Picts), 'Our infantry were but poorly fitted for the enemy of this kind.' The Romans called them Picts, abbreviated from 'The Painted'. They fought naked, covered in blue dye and tattooed, shaved completely except for the head and upper lip, they were masters at hand-to-hand combat and battleground trickery. They knew the terrain and could vanish as quickly as they attacked and, although by Roman accounts ten thousand were killed in battle, they did not disappear as a race until the 10th century, the last Pictish king being murdered either by the Vikings or the Scots in 843 AD. A picture of how these races were intermingled emerges as one of a violent, short-lived life underpinned by established cultures and beliefs in an afterlife. Tanum is now a UNESCO World Heritage Site.

Cycling through beautiful hamlets and small towns such as Hambergsund, today was a joy. Travelling from island to island over bridges I slowly worked my way north. I later passed Yoya, one last time, sitting on a bench having some lunch. She would very soon be catching one of the many ferries that cross to Tønsberg or Sandefjord to continue her route around the North Sea, eventually going to Lerwick on the Shetland Isle and on down the east coast of Scotland and England.

As I travel north the coast is beautiful. Many official campsites are in this area, sandwiched between Hunnebostrand and Strömstad. I stopped at one not far from Långeby, west of Tanumshede called Saltviks. Although it provided a hot shower and a meal, it was crowded and noisy. Today, June 23rd was my last in Sweden. It was also my wife's birthday. Over the years we had been apart on such occasions several times, usually because of my selfishness of either being halfway up a mountain or cycling. The weather in June usually favours these outdoor activities.

I had avoided the E6 main road from Gothenburg but after an early lunch in Strömstad and my first coffee of the day that afternoon from a supermarket dispensing machine, proving that I am not addicted to caffeine, I rode for a mile or so on a fast road before passing the Nordby shopping centre, strategically placed for marauding Norwegians (old habits die hard) to raid from across the

Swedish/Norwegian border which was just up the road. I turned down a small lane leading to Saltbacken. On both sides was a dense forest. I found a gap in the trees sufficiently wide enough for grass to have grown and pitched my tent. What a contrast to last night. Only the sounds of nature and the delight of having deer visit me with seemingly no fear. An enjoyable and memorable last night in Sweden. I had also avoided being killed by a drunk driver who could hardly stand as he got out of his car.

Daily Blog: What is a bit of rain? June 20th

Woke to the sun this morning, was the forecast going to be wrong? Would it stay dry all day? Would there be no need to dress in wet clothes tomorrow morning? And other profound questions went through my sleepy head without being answered.

I was away from Fran's B&B in Gothenburg by 7.30 am and having decided to try a new offline mapping app, rode with a watchful eye on the direction. Pleasingly it took me away from the main road, through country lanes, cycleways, and quiet housing estates. Later there was no alternative but to ride the excellent path beside the main road. Later I crossed the main road to join a quieter one and, having forgotten that the new app gives a 50 m distance warning of a change of route, had turned too soon. It was on returning to the correct route that I met up with a solo cyclist, Michel, who was well wrapped against the deteriorating weather and was also well kitted out and knew what he was doing. Living in north Germany, he had cycled through Denmark and although he has plans, they are wonderfully fluid. His only deadline is to be in a new flat before starting his master's degree in September. Michel, if you read this, I wish you every success, it was great to meet you and to share the experience of getting drenched together. I think the two girls in the bakery who made us coffee thought us crazy to be cycling in such rain.

I have not intended cycling far today, ironically to avoid the rain. What unfolded after Michel rode on to wherever he is wild camping tonight, was a 'comedy of errors'. Anne had kindly booked me into a B&B in Tollenäs. On arriving I bumped into Yoya, who had ridden up from Gothenburg in the winds yesterday and is staying in the campsite which surrounds the cabins. She had had to work hard cycling into the wind. So, wind one day, rain the next, perhaps better is to follow.

She and I saw the site owner together. It was then that I was told there was no accommodation for me and that no booking had been made. She kindly suggested that it was at another location to which I cycled in less than pleasant conditions. Two hours later I am back here, confident that this is the place that was booked. My tent is pitched, I am showered and no longer shivering and have yet to see the lady. Who knows what went wrong? No photographs today, just too wet.

Daily Blog: *Bridges and ferries. June 21st*

As the day with the longest daylight hours, today has had time to deliver a variety of weather, which it certainly has. A calm daybreak and early morning sunshine with heavy clouds. The wind became stronger and by lunchtime was blowing hard from the NW. The skies darkened to an impressive deep grey and the first persistent rain arrived late afternoon, followed by heavy showers ever since. Those of us who are maturing in years will remember the phrase, 'blazing June', because usually each year you could guarantee a hot June in the UK. Now the month is usually wet, perhaps global warming, Mr. Trump!

Last night's evening meal had been baked beans on toast, with a hard-boiled egg and two cups of tea, made by Yoya. My breakfast was an open sandwich of prawns, salmon, and caviar, with the best cappuccino I have tasted for weeks. Two different but equally good meals.

Shopping is done for the day, (not sure that there would be another opportunity), family phone calls made, I headed off in high spirits and with great expectations for the day.

Breakfast fit for a touring cyclist.

I am in the Swedish province of Bohuslän. It is an archipelago covering several thousand islands. Not un-naturally it is a popular holiday destination, as reflected by the quantity of traffic on the larger roads.

I went west from Stenungsund, a town with a large and immaculate marina. As a cyclist, I was directed around a short traffic tunnel that ran onto the first of three bridges leading to the island of Tjörn, one of Sweden's largest.

Stenungsund marina.

The first of three bridges.

The second bridge is impressive and has a history. Whilst the new bridge is of a suspension design, the first was the longest arched bridge in the world. In 1980, twenty years after it was completed, tragedy struck. In thick fog the MS Star Clipper struck the arch causing the bridge to collapse. No one on board was hurt, but sadly with communications disabled, vehicles using the bridge were unaware of its collapse, and eight people died.

As soon as possible I left the busier roads to enjoy the quieter, quintessentially Swedish countryside. Scores of tiny inlets and coves, which are homes to all manner of small sailing craft. Smooth granite rock rising straight out of the water. Pine trees growing on steep-sided hillocks and everywhere small timber cottages painted in bright colours.

My first ferry was small but played an intrinsic part in providing an effective transport network. One car and another touring cyclist waited for the cable ferry to arrive. The cyclist was a businessman from Hamburg on his annual cycling tour, continuing to work his way around the North Sea cycle route. The second ferry had one car and two other cyclists, one being a German from Hamburg. All these ferries are free as they are considered part of the transport system. The countryside before, between, and after these ferries was a joy to ride through.

Ferry cable winch.

The postman does not have to work too hard either.

The last ferry was a different beast.

Capable of taking many vehicles and high-tonnage lorries, two ferries worked simultaneously to take traffic to and from the Lysekil area. I then took the busy 162 road northwards away from Lysekil, and it was here that those menacing dark clouds ejected their contents.

Now perhaps some have heard of the pastime of 'Bus Shelter Hopping'. Usually, an activity performed during periods of intensely high precipitation. The mode of transcript is not specified, only that there is no roof to the vehicle. The objective is to endeavour to remain as dry as possible. It is a fun game that usually has participants soaked to the skin and rather cold.

The bus shelters in Sweden are effectively weatherproofed and it was these that I hopped along the busy 162 road as the rain lashed down.

I have pitched my tent near the tiny hamlet of Myran Gistad, where only an occasional vehicle passes. The peace is all the better due to the heavy noisy traffic during parts of today. Now there is just the regular passing of a tractor towing a slurry tanker from right to left FULL and smelly and from left to right empty, but still smelly.

The Swedish flag, a yellow cross laid over blue, flies as frequently from homes in the countryside as the Stars 'n' Stripes do in rural America. Substantial poles support flags that remain rigid in the wind, way above the immaculately painted timber boarded houses. Gardens are pristine, frequently with a nearby outcrop of red granite rock towering about the property.

Last night was another wet one. The first thing I saw when opening my eyes was a large adventurous slug about 400 mm long with four tentacles. None had invaded the inner tent and could easily be flicked off from the inside. This game is called 'Slugs and Ladders' as they climb up and down the tent. However, one wanted to hitch a ride and was in the process of stowing away on my bike.

A slug hitches a ride.

It was windy from the outset, but a wonderful morning. Rolling roads, small meadows fringed with trees and outcrops of red granite, with a handful of cattle and friendly young horses grazing.

Gerlesborg is a typically beautiful hamlet on an inlet much like hundreds of others, all appealing and holding a quiet, timeless serenity.

Gerlesborg.

This is a holiday area, and cars, or should we just substitute the word 'Volvos', were loaded with all things to make holidays more enjoyable. Every fifth car was a Volvo and sometimes the wave of traffic released from the ferries solely consisted of this Swedish icon.

My second stop today was the small town of Hamburgsund with its ferry that bridges an 80 m water channel. An excellent coffee accompanied with a prawn and egg sandwich was had from a bakery that surpassed most to date. I even asked whether they had a job vacancy.

Arriving in the upmarket town of Grebbestad, with 'its places to be seen' quayside restaurants and 'moored to impress' yachts. I visited the tourist information centre to find out where the UNESCO Iron Age burial site was. Marauding Scots had visited the area to pillage, and all had paid the price, being killed, cremated, and buried in individual urns beneath standing stones. There are in all about 200 mounds dating from 200 to 600 AD. Travelling had made them weary, maybe it was seasickness, but they need have only bought a single ticket across the North Sea. Like other cultures of the late Iron Age, they appear to have believed in an afterlife, perhaps in the Asa mythology.

Iron age burial site.

Whereas my wild campsite last night was fit for purpose, there are many official campsites in the area, and as I monitored the dark leaden sky the thought of a hot shower was tempting. The first site was a 'mini town' of camper vans, caravans, and second homes. No tent was in sight. The second site, ditto and the third, but this one is beside the sea and there is one other tent. Hundreds of people are here. Returning from a shower I saw a football kicked by a dad playing with his son. The ball travelling at speed knocked my bike over. He looked around, saw me returning, collected his ball, and walked off. The bike remained on the grass. There are many reasons why wild camping is attractive. Not least because I am paying 30 pounds for a shower, to charge my devices, and make my usual indentation on the ground.

But I also will be able to listen to children playing past their bedtime, drunks talking rubbish that I will not understand and vomiting, dogs barking, maybe even a domestic argument, that again I won't understand, and the absolute necessity for camping, a heavy rock band playing slightly off-key at 110 decibels. I think there is a preference for the barking deer. What a difference a night makes. Surely, I am not becoming a 'grumpy old man'.

There is a postscript. Later, walking back from the restaurant to my tent, one of two in an area that has twenty or more designated tent pitches, I find a third tent. Two seats are a few feet from the entrance to my tent with a table neatly laid for two. Our guy ropes cross over as the new neighbour's tent peg threatened to puncture my flysheet. Just maybe they forgot to lay a third place at their table. Bodily functions may be heard tonight in addition to the cacophony of other sounds.

As it is the summer Solstice, there is a Swedish festival today. Many people are wearing flower garlands, and some are dressed either all in white or traditional national dress. It is also the start of a five-week school holiday.

One of six Cadillacs on the campsite.

Daily Blog: Last night in Sweden. June 23rd

What a great day this has been. OK, the partying did continue till the small hours and the singer has agreed to take singing lessons. The campsite was silent save for the sounds of snoring coming from most directions as I walked to the showers.

Having packed up, I phoned my birthday girl, Anne. I am feeling guilty that I am cycling and not being a dutiful husband. It is good that she is coming to Oslo on Wednesday.

Today's ride was easy and in near- perfect weather. The temperature has been ideal, resulting in a thoroughly enjoyable day. Only 70 km ridden, but I have three, nearly four days to do 140 km. So, some devious routes and sightseeing are on the agenda before arriving in Oslo. Yet again I have underestimated the daily distances.

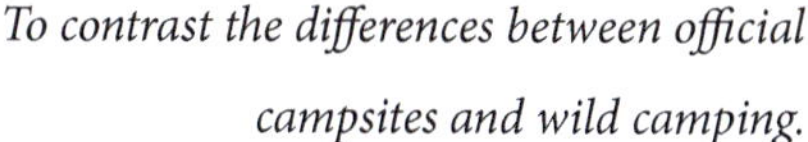
To contrast the differences between official campsites and wild camping.

I had hoped to do a little island hopping first thing today by going to Kalvön and onto Hamnsundet and Galtö, but there is no ferry across to Kalvön. I had to retrace my steps of yesterday almost back to the Iron Age monument and headed north on the nearly deserted road that runs west and parallel with the 110 dual carriageway. Up to Vik then into Strömstad via Stare. At the junction where I turned to Stare, a man was getting out of his small van, or should I say falling onto the road from the driver's seat. He got to his feet and, using the van as support, arrived at the rear doors, removed a signboard from the van and staggered, almost running backward and fell over – again! How had he managed not to crash? He was utterly inebriated, unable to stand yet had been driving a car!

Rounding the corner leading into Strömstad I was by a ferry parked beside the road.

Had the ferry berthed or crashed? Its tail end (stern) was discharging many vehicles, all heading in the direction I had come from.

Strömstad has a busy port and marina, a handful of fishing boats, but the main business is tourism, with boat trips around the numerous islands that lay to the south and of course the 'city sailors', lording it on James Bond-style floating palaces, where raised voices are a necessity, heaven forbid not to attract attention, solely to be heard when talking from the poop deck to a 'I'll never eat so many oysters again' person suffering in the heads. Jealous, me? Never! Although the 'centrum' of town thrives on tourists, only a few streets away all is peaceful.

Playboy harbour at Strömstad.

A church in Strömstad.

I was in danger of getting ahead of myself and arriving in Norway today. To avoid this, I opted to visit Hällestrand. A small collection of timber-boarded houses dotted the hillside leading down to two jetties with small craft moored there. Whilst I was there, three men arrived in a car, jumped out enthusiastically, each tested the temperature of the water with their hand, continued to talk in excited tones. Jumped back into their car and drove off. I can only assume that the water was too cold for a swim. On the other side of the inlet, two teenage couples had stripped naked and were persuading each other to be the first to jump in. As I cycled back up the hill, they were still naked and still dry.

I cycled under the E6 before heading west again. The road remained quiet until reaching Nordby, where a continuous and constant flow of vehicles came from what looked to be like Sweden's own Meadowhall (Sheffield, UK) shopping centre. I waited several minutes before being able to take a right turning towards Saltbacken, where I am now camped.

It feels as though I am leaving Sweden too soon. Two nights in Gothenburg, two wild camping nights, and two of only four nights on an official campsite since leaving Tarifa a 'decade ago'. Must be getting soft.

Tomorrow I will cross the Idefjorden at Svinesund and continue to head north to Borgenhaugen. I have decided to head northeast towards Rakkestad rather than to Moss. This will avoid the congested corridor that leads to Oslo and enable continued enjoyment of open country till Fetsund, east of Oslo.

- NORWAY -

CHAPTER TWENTY-ONE
Oslo Arrives Too Soon

'Twenty years from now you will be more disappointed with the things that you did not do, than the things that you did. Throw off the Bowlines, sail away from the safe harbour, catch the Trade winds in your sails.' Mark Twain

And into Norway, the final country of this trip. I did not want it to be over and it certainly was not. With over 2,500 km still to travel there was plenty of adventure to be had. Mountains, bridges over fjords, tunnels under the sea, up-close reindeer, aggressive raptors, snakes, folklore, and history of trolls, kings and queens. Roadside honesty libraries and architecturally stunning toilets. All these waited for me further up the road.

The bridge between Sweden and Norway.

Bridging the water between Sweden and Norway.

It was a Sunday and although aware that the Norwegians' approach to 'The Day of Rest' was, well, restful, I had not yet gauged how restful. From Hafslund I turned towards Varteig before Sarpsborg, a sizeable town where I could probably have got some food. It was midday, the sun was out, roads dry and undulating through peaceful countryside. I stopped at a small, white-painted church on the crossroads at Varteig. Beside the graveyard was a spotlessly clean public toilet. When you are wild camping and, on the move, you learn to recognise opportunities. This convenience had hot running water with large hand basins and no one around for miles. A little while later I emerged, smelling a whole lot better than when I went in. Clean, refreshed and with replenished water bottles, what more could a cyclist want for?

There was no rush to arrive in Oslo. Anne and I had decided that joining up in this wonderful city would be a great birthday present for her and, yet again, the geriatric legs were speeding me along. Perhaps in some way, the lack of any serious hills was also contributing, although there were a few punchy ones. I detoured into Askim for food and, whilst sitting on a low wall eating, a man on a mobility scooter approached. His story is covered in the blog. On his recommendation, I altered my intended route to travel into Oslo.

Now most Norwegians we all know are orientated to outdoor sporting pursuits. It is deep within their DNA. Since 1957 the 'Right to Roam' has been part of the Outdoor Recreation Act. It permits anyone to camp either in a tent or under the stars in almost any place, provided they are more than 150 m away from an occupied house and remain there only for one night. To date all the other countries I had travelled through had had stricter rules regarding wild camping and, apart from one incident involving an angry man with a rifle, I had encountered no real difficulties.

For some reason finding a suitable place to stop for the night had become elusive. From the isolated churchyard where two ladies were tending a grave, to the woods with hordes of hungry mosquitoes, to the numerous evenly spaced small factories and agricultural outlets, I could not find a suitable camping place. Although I could have camped quite openly in one or two places the experience of having a rifle pointed at me in Denmark had made an impact. I had developed a preference for covert camping.

I had made a mistake. Oslo was calling, I had cycled about 150 km with 1,600 m of elevation and had eaten little. Today cycling had become a perfunctory act. I should have stopped sooner but had not. It was easier to continue than to stop, but continuing would have to end at some point. I found a campsite on my mapping system and headed for it. Food and a hot shower would be welcomed. The campsite was marked as being on the lakeside. Having cycled along a no-through dirt lane for several kilometres to Torshov, I knocked on an outbuilding door from behind which someone was working. There was no response, so I carefully opened the door and got a surprise.

The detour to find the campsite had been unfruitful and, with open flat cultivated land all around, I still had not found a place to sleep. I retraced my tyre marks and on heading up the hill to Enebakk asked a couple of walkers where the campsite was. They were locals but knew of no campsite in the area. In my own little world, my mind reflecting on the day, I was resuscitated violently back to the present by the fleeting sight of a flying ball of fluff with long ears and rear legs passing close to my face. A hare had decided to go airborne rather than be ridden over. I had not registered it until it was an arm's length in front of me. The incident was over in milliseconds. In Flateby, with roadside industry increasing, I decided to turn down a steep hill with no intention of cycling back up it until the following day. Fortunately, I found a field and camped in long grass looking over the water below. A hard day but a rewarding day that showed the importance of correctly fuelling the 'engine'. Tomorrow June 25th I will be at the Oslo camping site and Anne will be arriving late on the 27th. Two days to look around Oslo to find the best to show her.

Daily Blog: And into Norway. June 24th

This morning I rode into the ninth and last of the European countries I will be visiting on this trip. It will, however, occupy more of my time and demand more effort than any of the previous (even Spain with its rain, wind, ice, and snow).

I will be cycling in Norway until July 28th. Anne and I have planned an additional visit, she will be joining me in Oslo on Wednesday. So, from then until July 2nd my legs will have a welcome rest.

Cycling across the Svinesund bridge early this morning was a pleasure. Once again, the border crossing was deserted. This route in and out of Norway is reserved for 'Nothing to Declare' travellers. It was interesting to note that, particularly on the Swedish side, the shops were the objective of many cross-border shoppers, with a strange emphasis on E-cigarettes outlets and garden summer houses of all sizes and designs. They all used the other bridge, the 'Items to Declare' bridge. The climb up the hill once in Norway was perhaps an indication of what is to come. The morning was most enjoyable; however, the day turned into a bit of an epic. The final distance covered was nearly 145 km and 1,600 m of elevation.

I have mentioned previously the requirements of a good location for wild camping. One is that the site is not in 'line of sight' of any dwellings, another is as few mosquitoes as possible. Today I surpassed my previous travel distance in search of such a place. Houses are spread out everywhere and having ventured into woods on two occasions, only to emerge very rapidly with a pint of blood donated to the local population of mosquitoes, woods are a 'no go' area in Norway! But more later.

I saw my first moose sign within an hour.

The language is quite different to Swedish, but 'hey, hey' is still the usual greeting and the Co-op supermarket is still pronounced 'coup'. So, you can get both groceries and 'eggs' there.

The countryside is beautiful, rolling hills (some not so rolling), woods, horses and Hereford cattle and bright PINK or YELLOW plastic shrink-wrapped silage bales stacked in fields that blend so un-naturally into the green fields and the deep blue of the fjords and sky with white fluffy clouds.

I had cycled for a while on Cycle Route 1 and from Mysen had intended taking the east side of the fjord up to Lillestrøm via Skjønhaug. Having gone to the larger town of Askim to ensure getting food on Sunday evening, and while eating a pizza, started chatting to a guy on a mobility scooter. Maybe mid-thirties, he had fallen off a ladder from three metres and had broken both legs in multiple places. From an X-ray he showed me the metal within his swollen left leg – it resembled a ladder inside his leg. If ever you needed an example of positive thought, here was your man. 'I will be walking again next year,' and 'They can't do me for drunk driving on this thing.' He made my day. He also recommended cycling the west side of the fjord and not the east. I took his advice and started looking for a place to pitch my small tent and was still looking 40 kms later. I was hanging onto that gentleman's positivity by diminishing thin threads.

Now that the evening was progressing, I became a little concerned. Were desperate measures needed? I walked around a churchyard. The idea of sleeping with the dead did not worry me, I live next door to a churchyard.

A potential wild campsite.

This would have been ideal for a camp, had two elderly ladies not being tending the final resting place of their loved ones. To see a cyclist pitching his tent between the gravestones may have resulted in a midnight visit by the village folk. I even considered a football pitch. The problem was players were still busy kicking a ball around. Even a builder's yard was considered.

An official campsite was marked on my map, near Enebakk and only 5 km off *my route. Let's go for that! Strange there were no signs. Nearly at the shoreline on a dirt track and still no sign of anything remotely resembling a campsite, I turned and retraced my tyre marks. I heard some regular hammering from a shed near a house. 'Let's ask,' I thought. I could not get a response. Finally, I opened the door from where this industrious worker was hammering away. He was of medium build, brown hair with large ears under which was a large head and a long tail that he flicked to keep the flies from him. Engrossed in kicking his stable door, the horse did not notice me as he continued to kick with vigour.*

Twenty minutes later I was cycling down a steep hill and had a second encounter with an animal, this time a hare as it jumped in front of the bike.

I finally found somewhere to camp just south of Flateby. I descended a hill towards a fjord and found a place to pitch the tent in long grass overlooking the water. The mosquitoes, although not so many, did eventually drive me into the tent, where I slept soundly until the morning.

Quite a first day in the last country of my journey.

Anne had booked me a campsite within the city of Oslo. Andrew Sykes had stayed on a campsite in the city, and I believed I was heading for the same site. Entering Oslo from Fetsund, as probably from any other direction, you cannot help but be impressed. To say the centre was a building site would be accurate but would convey the wrong image. Although cranes punctured the skyline, and many buildings were in various stages of construction, the whole atmosphere felt positive and rejuvenating. A small seed of doubt was entering my mind as I travelled further into the centre. Surely land occupied by a campsite in a city centre would be better used for some of this development? It did not make economic sense. Yet here I was opposite a building that clearly said 'Oslo Camping'. I locked the bike and went in. Several people were playing crazy golf on a course set out on the ground floor. The penny dropped. This was a city hostel, and the rooms would be on the upper floors. I approached the lady behind the bar and said, 'You have a room for me,' and gave my name. Although eighty percent of Norwegians speak English, it is wrong to assume that every Norwegian could, so the puzzled, slightly taken aback look was put down to not understanding a foreign language. I rephrased, digging the preverbal hole deeper. Then, fortunately, another older lady, maybe the manageress stepped in. She was laughing and was jovial about the situation. Several onlookers, some showing expressions of humour, others of disapproval. The 'manageress' explained that not for the first time had a camper arrived asking for a bed for the night. It was an ongoing misunderstanding. I cannot for the life of me think how there would be any confusion about the name of the place and what is provided. Obviously, 'Oslo Camping' is going to be a crazy golf course. I left with directions to a campsite that I was assured was in a field. It was out of town up on a hill. A hill that could be taken directly but steeply, or a longer meandering route. I chose the former – idiot! The next two days were spent scouting the city and enjoying the vibrant atmosphere enhanced so much more by the Oslo Pride festival that was in full swing. Relaxing, drinking coffee and watching people, and waiting for my wife to arrive.

Daily Blog: Oslo arrives too soon. June 25th

It was a good night's sleep. A deer barked a few times then moved off. In the early morning, the sun was warm on the tent, the fjord was like a millpond and apart from bird song, there was complete peace. I surveyed the previous night's bloodletting. Maybe a dozen decent meals had been taken by mosquitoes. Being morning, they were sleeping in and did not bother me. Breakfast was muesli and custard (mistaken in the shop for yogurt). Off up the hill onto the main road with a promise of caffeine at Flateby, a few kilometres away. I had intended to charge up my devices at the cafe, so had not put the mapping system on. I had missed The Town. Returning to the Spar shop that I had been directed to, 'up the hill', I had earned a hot Danish pastry that was waiting for me. The sign said, 'CLOSED ON MONDAYS', it was Monday! The expletive, not understood by a passing Norwegian, was justified. Back down the hill with a certain disregard for safety and a desire to 'go fast' brought a smile back to my face.

A fast 30 km into Strømmen, with a short stop to protest my innocence to two police officers who had set up a speed camera at the top of a hill. It is unlikely that an over sixty-year-old riding a cycle the weight of a double-decker London bus and sharing the same aerodynamics would have the ability to exceed the speed limit. Must have been the Volvo that overtook me. The three of us enjoyed the joke and they wished me a successful journey.

All good things come to those who wait. An excellent café was found in Strømmen. The coffee was particularly good, as was the second, as was the muffin and New York cheesecake. The cafe was that popular, Viserys Targaryen from Game of Thrones popped in. He is the one with long straight white hair, or was it Jonny Winters or even Rick Wakeman? Who knows?, but I'm sure this character enjoyed the attention the similarities brought him.

I wove an intricate route through the pleasant suburbs of Oslo before picking up Cycle Route 7 which ran first beside a motorway then the main arterial road in from the east and into the heart of the city and to Oslo Camping. There was little point in looking for a wild camp so near the city. There is also a thin line between wild camping as a long-distance cyclist in rural areas and being a vagrant on a bike in a city.

I walked into Oslo Camping a little suspicious. Indoor mini golf! The reviews had been good. 'I have a room booked,' I told the attractive lady behind the bar. Oh dear, how easily things go wrong. It was not until another lady intervened that the situation was resolved with a degree of humour. She laughed and told me that so many come in asking the same question. It was then she told me about this campsite, at Ekeberg. More intricate route finding and a sustained 17% hill to climb.

Hot after climbing the hill, I met Iselin, from Nordkapp, who told me that it would cost me fifty pounds to pitch my tiny tent for two nights, and did I want a shower? She was an excellent receptionist, taking my comments of astonishment at the price in her stride. She also perhaps had a keen sense of smell. 'A shower would be good,' I responded. 'Well, that will be a further ....' 'What! SO, I GET A TOWEL, SOAP AND SOMEONE TO APPLY AND DRY?' Iselin smiled and shook her head. I said I needed to think about it and waited and waited in silence for a reduced price to be offered. I broke the silence and here I am, clean and enjoying a beer.

The view of Oslo from near the hilltop campsite.

Daily Blog: *The positives of the unforeseen. June 26th*

Having arrived in Oslo too soon and not wanting to go sightseeing before Anne arrived, the day was either going to be cycling in circles or drinking coffee and people watching. Having found which train platform she will arrive on and where our accommodation is, which did not have indoor mini golf on offer, I opted for coffee in a city known for its indulgence with 'The bean'.

Getting my bearings required cycling down the hill from the campsite and slowly meandering through the crowded streets. Again, as in Germany, Belgium, Holland, Luxembourg, Denmark, and Sweden pedestrians and cyclists mix well with mutual respect and understanding that is also adopted by the many tourists. It really is quite pleasant.

On returning to the campsite, via a different, longer, and less steep road that I probably should have taken last night, I have just had a great chat with a German gentleman. It was one of those conversations where it wasn't necessary to ask each other's names, just an exchange of 'bits' of our lives. He has been retired for as long as I have and travels on his BMW 1200 motorcycle. His wife also joins him sometimes and when he sees something special, like the Northern Lights, they return together.

Not much else to say about today. Sitting here in the shade with a gentle breeze, watching the seagull's squabble over the food they have stolen from a barbeque, the world is relaxed and positive for this long-distance cyclist.

Food intake today had been negligible, as has calorie burn. So grilled chicken and salad followed by fresh strawberries and yogurt accompanied by a delicate white wine – vintage unknown! – is the menu for this evening.

A few photos were taken today:

The Royal Guard change, every day at 1.30 pm at the Royal Palace.

Trades person's entrance to The Royal Palace in Oslo.

King Harald V of Norway and Queen Sonja's entrance to the Royal Palace.

Some completed modern buildings near the massive development area.

A civilised campsite.

There is a phenomenal amount of building work going on in Oslo from avant-garde high rise to subterranean road systems.

Oslo, a vibrant city.

The cruise liner belonging to the Holland America Line was in town. How many thousands of passengers it had disgorged into the city, who knows? – but the Americans were in town big time. She is sounding her horns now as she departs.

Cruise liners from around the world bring thousands of tourists to Oslo.

Oslo's beach.

And finally, to the fleshpot of Oslo, the 'beach', where the endeavour is to get as near to an all-over suntan without being arrested by the patrolling police. And I thought my pulse was only going to race as I cycled back up the hill to the campsite.

Having returned to the campsite, three separate couples arrived.

The first couple – out of the car, working as a team put their tent up in 15 minutes, the epitome of efficiency.

The second couple – a car pulled up, guy gets two chairs out of the car boot; the lady gets two beers. Both now sitting drinking, looking at the tent in the bag on the ground.

The third couple – guy gets out of the car, gets one chair out of the boot and one beer. Opens beer and starts to drink. Lady gets the tent out of the boot and is putting it up. He drinks his beer. Next time let us hope he will be putting the tent up or, given the facial expressions on the lady's face, he will be drinking and camping on his own.

On June 27th I rode down the hill into Oslo from my campsite and headed to the apartment we were to stay in. Cycling along Wergelandsveien, which borders the northeast side of the Royal Gardens, my sunglasses fell from my helmet. In the time it took to return to pick them up, they were just disappearing into a guy's pocket. I thanked him for picking them up as he pulled them from his pocket and handed me them. Anne and I were staying in an apartment on Parkveien, just round the corner to the Palace gardens. As with Lourdes and Hamburg, I had arrived early which again gave me an opportunity to both clean the bike, the rider, and his clothes. We had been given a large, elegant room with high ceilings, to the front of the building. Opening the windows brought memories of Bremen flooding back – noise, trams, and traffic. I asked for a quiet room and with great understanding, was given a room of equal style to the rear of the property overlooking a cobbled courtyard. My bike needed more than general maintenance. Fortunately, a cycle shop was just around the corner. Endre at Bike Brothers on Pilestredet offered to do the job while we were in Oslo. New rear cassette and chain.

That evening I met Anne at the impressive central railway station, where near the entrance there is a statue of an oversized tiger, the randomness of which escaped me. Over the next five days, we indulged ourselves in excellent wines, good food, great coffee, and sightseeing. A belated and memorable birthday present.

Historically Norway had established a reputation for hardcore drinking which has resulted in some strict legislation, not least drinking in public places or even on private property where others can see you, is illegal. Considerable research has been done on the most effective ways to curb excessive consumption of alcohol in Norway and indeed the whole of Scandinavia and what has resulted has largely been accepted by their societies.

All alcohol is taxed heavily, some say it is a 'tax grab' by the government. The solution to minimising abuse is a package of measures, not least reducing the purchasing availability. There are tax bands for all levels of ABV, for example, 4.7% to 22% attracts 5.11 Kr per volume or litre. Far more than in the UK or the USA. Supermarkets are only allowed to sell alcohol up to 4.7% (in Sweden it is even less, at 3.5%) and no alcohol can be purchased after 8 pm on a weekday, 6 pm on a Saturday, and not at all on Sundays. Supermarket checkout systems will reject any attempted alcohol sales after those times. Then there are the Vinmonopolet shops, the State wine monopoly shops, of which there are only 272 in the country. They too have strict opening times, closing at 6 pm during the week and 3 pm over the weekend. Many of us jest about alcohol, so many jokes, so many greeting cards orientate around the subject. In moderation it is fantastic, but misuse is often life-changing and even fatal. Norwegian society has tackled this issue and, as would be expected, not all agree but there has not been the shout of 'You are denying us our basic human rights,' as perhaps other societies would have. Now, a taste of what is on offer. There are a few well-known alcohols in Norway. Aquavit is made from potatoes and grain with herbs and spices. Brennevin, a strong brandy. Punsch, from the Hindi word meaning five, representing the five ingredients and is drunk hot, as is Gløgg. Fruit beers and Pilsner and Bayer lager, or the stronger lagers such as Juleol and Bokko. Given the climate in Norway, most wines are imported but there is a wine that contains blackberries called Krekling. Having planned and applied a modicum of decorum, Anne and I were stocked up with our needs and headed off to do some sightseeing. On our first day we visited the following:

The Royal Palace

We purchased our tickets for this immensely popular tour for 135,00 Kr and together with about 20 others started our timed tour. No photography is allowed, and they are very vigilant about this. Designed by Danish-born architect Hans Ditlev Franciscus Linstow and built for King Carl Johan, it was not completed until after his death on March 15th 1849, somewhat bad timing. King Oscar I was the first monarch to live there from July 26th that year. The fabric of the palace was completely restored through necessity in 1999, with the furnishings and décor being completed in 2001. The most recent works were completed in May 2011 which involved the main wing of the palace. As we were taken around and shown the rooms, we became aware that the whole building seemed larger than its outer appearance. This deceit was by design. Visiting dignitaries were taken through the building via a devious route to create a feeling of exaggerated grandeur. It was an informative and interesting tour that gave us an insight into Norwegian and Swedish history.

The City Hall

A building of a city hall was first suggested in 1906 but construction did not commence until 1931 following an architect's competition. There were forty-four entries with Arnstein Arneberg and Magnus Poulsson being selected for their design so obviously inspired by the Stockholm City Hall. Perhaps a politically motivated decision or maybe they were in awe: after all, imitation is the sincerest form of flattery (and an assured way to win a competition). Two of the jury that decided on the winners were architects, one had designed the Stockholm city hall and the other the Copenhagen city hall; both buildings were monumental brick structures. The final draft was presented in 1930 after financial problems, with the addition of the two towers. By the time it opened on May 15th 1950 to celebrate the city's 900th anniversary to the sounds of specially composed music, the style was out of fashion, with steel and glass taking the place of brick.

This enormous square brick-built, twin-towered building, with mathematically positioned windows that fail to extend to the full height of either the main building or the towers, does not first endear the casual looker to look any further or for any longer. However, its sheer size with few other buildings around dominates the scene. Why one clock face on one elevation of one tower? Maybe so the ships in the harbour could see what the time was. Maybe there was no need for the townsfolk to know the time. Anne Grimdalen's sculpture of Harald Hardrada on horseback is on the western wall, with various other sculptures that adorn the exterior, including the Oslo Girl by Joseph Grimeland. Walking up the steps to the main entrance there is a feeling of minimalistic grandeur. Inside the 'wow factor' is immediate. The main hall is truly enormous, some 40 m long and 30 m wide with a ceiling of 30 m in height. The whole floor and parts of the walls are of marble, which further adds to the grandeur. Decorated by Henrik Sørensen and Alf Rolfsen the series of wall paintings depict the Norway-Sweden war and the occupation of Norway by Sweden (an occupation that grew into a partnership). The commercial development and rise of the labour movement, monarchs, and city patrons are all depicted on large bold murals that grab the eye and demand attention. In all, seventeen sculptors and eight painters provided the art pieces. Whether you are an architect or an admirer of architecture, Oslo City Hall will no doubt impress most. Some, however, like viewing an art masterpiece and, knowing it to be so, will remain unmoved.

The Vigeland Sculpture Park

I first met Tim when climbing Aconcagua, a mountain on the Argentinian-Chilean border between Mendoza and Santiago. Since then, he and I and our wives have become good friends, taking climbing and hiking vacations together and visiting our respective homes in California and Yorkshire. 'American' Tim is an intelligent gentleman, whereas 'English' Tim is not. One of the many things I must thank Tim for is his suggestion to visit the Vigeland Sculpture Park.

The Park is one of Norway's most visited attractions and the world's largest sculpture park made by a single artist. Oslo has many sculptures, from the tiger near the central railway station to the Glove Fountain on Rådhusgata, to the more traditional, there are so many dotted around the city. Contained within Frogner Park there are 200 sculptures by Gustav Vigeland in bronze, granite and cast iron. He also designed the park in which they stand.

Born in 1869, Vigeland lived for 74 years with much of his life devoted to sculpting the two hundred figures within the park. Although besotted by the human form, he did not limit himself. Other projects included a bridge, fountain, and spectacular circular staircase, a mosaic labyrinth, and a stone forest of carved figures. All impressive in their own right, but the masterpiece of 121 figures carved from a single solid piece of granite 17 m high, surrounded by 36 groups of people that portray the cycle of life, must be the pièce de résistance.

His father was a carpenter and Gustav was apprenticed to a woodcarver in 1884, but wood was never to be his favoured medium, preferring granite and bronze. Schooled in Oslo, he also spent a few months in Paris in 1893 where he met and was impressed with Auguste Rodin's work. Vigeland's early work was subsequently influenced by Rodin, resulting in an emotional style. Later he adopted a simpler and more stylised approach as he delved into medieval sculpture. For anyone visiting Oslo, Vigeland Sculpture Park is a must-see place.

The Kon-Tiki Museum.

Anne and I took the ferry from the City Hall pier across to Bygdøy where we immersed ourselves in all things to do with Norwegian history. The Kon-Tiki Museum had been our first objective. Since a young boy of eight, I had been fascinated with the Kon-Tiki story. My mother had told the tale with such relish and realism at a time in my life where I was beginning to understand that I had a serious problem with reading and writing. The heady mixture of excitement, travel, and culture were all ingredients that I was to become addicted to as the years passed into manhood.

The Kon-Tiki expedition was a journey made in 1947 across the Pacific from South America to the Polynesian islands. The leader was a Norwegian called Thor Heyerdahl. The Kon-Tiki was a raft made from balsa wood and the expedition was to prove that peoples from South America could have travelled to Polynesia during pre-Columbian times. Although only materials and technology that would have been available at that time were used during this successful expedition, the Kon-Tiki was fitted with modern equipment for life-saving purposes. The museum had the complete raft set up as though it were afloat and in action. All the boyhood mental imagery returned. It was as though my mind was reliving a memory of having been one of Heyerdahl's crew. Whilst we sat absorbing the atmosphere, three ladies sitting behind us started talking. Anne turned and said to them, 'I recognise that dialect, how is Sheffield?' The city of Sheffield is a few miles down the road from where we live in Yorkshire.

The Fram Museum

Within a stone's throw of the Kon-Tiki Museum is the Fram Museum. MS Fram, meaning 'Forward', was a ship designed for the Arctic and Antarctic oceans, the first ship in Norway to be built specifically for polar exploration. Three times the enervative skills of the designers and the shipwrights, combined with excellent skills of navigation and seamanship, saw the Fram survive perilous voyages from uncharted seas.

The last of these voyages is probably the best known because Roald Amundsen was the expedition leader pursuing Captain Robert Falcon Scott, who was unaware that Amundsen had elevated the expedition to a competition to be the first to reach the South Pole, another story every adventurer should read about from all perspectives.

The first of the Fram's adventures was in 1893 to 1896 with Fridtjof Nansen, over the Arctic Ocean. The second was in 1898 to 1902 with Otto Sverdrup to the Arctic Archipelago west of Greenland, and finally with Amundsen on his South Pole expedition in 1910 to 1912, from which he returned but Scott did not.

I sometimes think our expeditions to the 8,000 m Himalayan peaks are long at two months. Two, three, and four years must have seemed an age and without satellite communications.

Following Amundsen's successful expedition to the South Pole, the Fram sailed north from Antarctica to the South American continent in tropical seas, where she remained throughout the First World War. Not surprisingly the Fram soon looked a sorry sight. After the First World War funding was raised to enable the near-wreck to be towed back to Norway and restored. It attended the 1930 Trondheim exhibition and subsequently arrived in Oslo in May 1935 where the museum was built around it and opened a year later. For an initial build cost of 280,000 Kr (£24,000), MS Fram provided an incredible service to Norway, whilst enabling us to understand the world in which we live just that little bit more.

The Scott/Amundsen story is a fascinating one of hardship, determination, and bravery, which from the beginning attracted two differing views. Only by reading accounts of the expedition from both perspectives can we accurately understand why both men made the decisions they did. History is selective. Records mirror the bias of the writer and may even be rewritten.

The Maritime Museum

A second short walk led us to the Maritime Museum, a brick-built building in stark contrast to the Fram Museum with its steep triangular-shaped pitched roof and no walls. The Maritime Museum contains the near-complete history of Norwegian maritime activities. Exhibitions of maritime travel, from the opulent cabins to the hammocks slung in the damp dirty lower decks, reflect an age where class and status divided society as it does so frequently to this day. Shipbuilding and the technology through the ages is the common thread throughout, from the Stokkebåten, which is Norway's oldest boat dating back to 200 BC, to three of the best-preserved Viking ships in existence, the Oseberg, Gokstad, and Tune. These ships were discovered between 1867 and 1903 and had been buried for a thousand years. Other ships on display include the Stavanger and Svanen. Another worthy of note is the Gjøa, the first vessel to make its way through the Northwest Passage with a crew of only six in Roald Amundsen's 1903–06 expedition.

The Viking Ship Museum

Considered as part of the Maritime Museum, this high-profile period of Norwegian history deserves its own building.

As you enter the high-ceilinged light museum built in the shape of a cross you cannot help but be impressed by what you see. The centrepiece, the Oseberg, built in 820 AD, is wider than expected and looks magnificent. The museum was proposed by the Swedish professor, Gabriel Gustafson, in 1913 and now houses the Oseberg, Gokstad, and Tune, with most of the artefacts from the Oseberg. This ship was used as a burial ship for two powerful women on their journey to the afterlife. Onboard to make their next life a better one were elaborate sleighs, five beds, and the skeletons of fifteen horses, six dogs and two cows. The Gokstad was built in 900 AD and saw ten years of service overseas before being used to transport a powerful man to his afterlife. The Tune was the first discovery in 1867. A fast, ocean-going vessel probably built around 900 AD and again finally used as a transporter to the afterlife.

The Norsk Folkemuseum

The Folk Museum is a short walk north of the Viking Museum and is as impressive as any of the previous. We miscalculated the time we needed to enjoy all the exhibits. As we walked through the ages mainly from 1,500 AD to the present day, basked in the sunshine it was easy to imagine that we were being transported back in time. There are 160 historic buildings including the famous Gol Stave Church built around 1,200 AD. The museum is one of the world's largest and oldest open-air museums.

After our day of Norwegian culture, July 1st was taken at a steadier pace during which we visited the Nobel Peace Center, The National Opera and Ballet, Oslo's cathedral, and the Akershus Fortress. We did not manage to see Edvard Munch's *The Scream*, previously called *Der Schrei der Natur* or *Skrik*, perhaps with regret. Oslo has so much to offer, we had only 'cherry picked', but the rest is there for our return.

Oslo was buzzing! The Pride festival ran from June 27th to 30th, themed as 'Love and Respect', there were concerts, shows, political debates, and the fantastic Pride Parade all in an atmosphere of happiness and acceptance. We had been fortunate to be in Oslo at this time.

Daily Blog: Discovering Oslo. June 29th
The life's work of Gustav Vigeland, born 1869 and died 1943, consisting of more than 200 sculptures in bronze, granite and forged iron, rightfully attract over a

million visitors a year. The total works are a complete study of human life and behaviour. They represent Vigeland obsession, and a lifetime of work dedicated to the human form. It is hard for me not to put too many photos of these works of art on this blog, such is their impact. The following are only a taster: -

Bad hair day!

Playing with the kids.

Storytime.

Baby Boom.

A Life Appreciated

Yesterday we blitzed the centre of the city. The City Hall was one venue we visited.

Akershus Fortress.

To stay focussed on why we are here, the Trek cycle that has brought me 7,000 km to Oslo from Tarifa needed a new chain and rear mech. Not surprising as they have taken a hammering, particularly through the Pyrenees mountains and the kerb 'bouncing' on the German cycleways. I took the bike to Bike Brothers, around the corner from where we are staying. Endre could not have been more helpful. I am now confident that no mechanical problems will stop me from arriving in Nordkapp in a few weeks. Today we also called into a Trek cycle shop, Spinn Sykkelshop, where Sjur kindly donated some lubrication and mobile wash, (for the bike, not me!).

A statement so often made about Norway is, 'it's so expensive'. Well, this is only my view. Yesterday I paid 100 Kr (£10) for less than a pint of beer. Today I paid £1.50 for a pee. So, £10 to put it in and £1.50 to let it out! The beef burger and chips were also very tasty at £20. There is another aspect to all this regarding GDP per capita that helps put matters in perspective, but Norway is still the fourth most expensive country in western Europe and the cost of living is more expensive than 90% of all other countries in the world. The problem for the visitor is that the country is such a fantastic place and, given the opportunity, who would not want to continuing visiting?

Tomorrow we will take the ferry to see Fridtjof Nansen's polar ship and Thor Heyerdahl's Kon-Tiki that crossed the Pacific in 1947, and hopefully the Viking and Folk museums.

Daily Blog: Born too late. June 30th
Today has been an education and the day I fulfilled a boyhood ambition.

We have spent the whole day in museums. Something my limited brain function has never previously coped with. However, the adage that with a personal interest in a subject, learning becomes a pleasure, is certainly true.

Norwegian Folk Museum.

Viking Ship Museum.

Kon-Tiki (and Ra) museum.

Fram museum.

Any one of these museums would have occupied us for hours. Each is splendid in its way and thoroughly recommended!

Since my mother first introduced me to the world of Thor Heyerdahl via his Kon-Tiki expedition when I was about eight years old, I have been interested in all his adventures, and in part, this has contributed to my sense of adventure. It has been a lifetime's intention to visit this remarkable museum. Today, I fulfilled that dream.

Some of you will know that I have been fortunate to have climbed on all the continents and as such been privileged to have been to Antarctica. This incredible environment is one of the last frontiers of our planet and holds a special place in my heart. The Fram's third expedition of 1910 to 1914 took Roald Amundsen, a crew of 20 and 116 dogs to Antarctica, and on December 16th 1911 he and four others raised the Norwegian flag at the South Pole. The Fram, designed and owned by Fridtjof Nansen, himself an accomplished explorer, was a new innovative design, with a hull engineered to rise above the ice when the ship otherwise would have been crushed, as previous ships had been. I flew in a Russian transporter plane from South America to Patriot Hills, landing on an ice runway. Exciting, but how much more exhilarating would an expedition on the Fram have been.

I am in grave danger here of launching into a script about explorers, men and women from past eras of not so many years ago, who through skill, determination, and willpower achieved the seemingly near impossible. It is these people who provide inspiration and encouragement for us who follow them to push ourselves to our limits. I have drawn much from them and in full knowledge of the hardships they endured, in some ways I would have liked to have lived in that era of extreme travel and developing technology.

Today we are enjoying the benefits of lightweight everything, advanced knowledge of nutritional needs, and instantaneous global communication. Sometimes, just sometimes I think I was born too late. Frontiers are becoming harder to find. And to put it all in perspective, I am now past my 'youth'. There may be a desire to return to the 8,000 m mountains, but the body definitely says 'no!'

Statues of Roald Amundsen, Sverre Hassel, Helmer Hanssen, Olav Bjaaland, and Oscar Wisting. The five were the first to stand at the South Pole.

This whole lighthouse is made solely of waste pulled from the sea! No comment is needed.

Daily Blog: Intensive sightseeing in intensive heat. July 1st

Another enjoyable day in the great city of Oslo.

We spent a captivating morning in the Nobel Peace Centre. A wonderfully compiled exhibition about Alfred Nobel, his life's work, his legacy of prizes, science, and mathematics and of course the Peace Prize, the only prize administered by Norway.

As you walked around the museum your movement activated a presentation of each of the Nobel prize winners.

In contrast, there was a temporary photographic exhibition of modern-day materialism, the negative impact of social media, and the grotesque appetite for extreme wealth.

Next up was the Historic Museum.

Anne is surrounded by gold. As the Nazis invaded Norway, the country's gold reserves were smuggled out of the country.

Oslo Cathedral.

However, for us, the most impactive must be the tour of the Royal Palace, a building that is both functional as a working administration centre, housing 140 people, and the home of Norway's monarchy. This grand but by no means opulent building strikes a good balance between the historical ceremony and modern perception of where a monarchy sits in society today.

Anne and I have again learned so much. Today it has been about those who have done good works over the past two hundred years and how a new country was created, born from the friendship and acceptance of its neighbours and one of Napoleon's military generals falling out of favour with his boss and accepting an invitation to become Crown Prince of the new Norway.

Gardens to the rear of the Royal Palace.

National Service of one year is compulsory for all men in Norway. With France fleetingly talking about reintroducing National Service, perhaps the UK should do likewise.

We also went for a walkabout and saw the following:

Oslo's opera house.

City development.

A further reminder of how we pollute our planet. This creature is made solely from what has been taken out of the sea locally.

Tomorrow Anne heads home and I head north towards Lillehammer, where extreme weather warnings persist, as fears rise over possible wildfires starting.

CHAPTER TWENTY-TWO
All the Senses Satisfied

'Journeys, like artists, are born and not made. A thousand differing circumstances contribute to them, few of them willed or determined by the will.' Lawrence Durrell

The next time Anne and I planned to see each other would be in Tromsø after I had finished this adventure. We left Oslo on July 2nd walking together until the Cathedral where Anne headed to the railway station and I headed towards the Munch Museum, where Edvard's second painting of *The Scream* is on display, through the botanical gardens east to Lillestrom then north to Kløfta and Jessheim. Anne would already be at the airport as I cycled around its perimeter. Waiting in the hot sun, pushed into a small tree that provided a degree of shelter, I waited sandwiched between the end of the runway and a prison. If her flight were on time, I would be able to take a photograph of her plane taking off. A police car drove past with both officers looking at me with suspicion, or perhaps pity. Anyway, they did not stop. After Anne's plane had taken off, I cycled towards Stensgård and looked around a quaint church at the southern end of a lake. It would have been an ideal place to camp had it been at the end of the day. What a fantastic afternoon riding along the western shore of the lake to the northern end and then a steep climb to Byrud at the southern end of Lake Mjøsa. I could have made my way through the mountain roads to Lena and Kapp, but the path of least resistance was more inviting in the late afternoon sun than a multiple hill-climbing challenge. Within a few kilometres of joining the road that hugs the western bank of Mjosa I had found a near- perfect place to camp. So perfect was the area that there were signs around saying, 'NO CAMPING'. Moving away and into a mown field that looked like the extended grounds of a school summer camp that ran down to the lakeside, I pitched my tent and went for a refreshing swim.

The feeling of complete freedom and happiness continued one day to the next. In Gjøvik while drinking coffee I met Alistair, an Englishman living in Australia, cycling through Norway. As kindred spirits we hit it off straight away and for an hour exchanged yarns. Not un-naturally he had done plenty of cycling in Australia. With one of my daughters and her family living south of Perth in Western Australia, I am a regular visitor and have invested in a cycle that I keep there. How different cycling is in WA than in the UK. In the UK, the seasons dictate more. There is rain, wind, hail, wet leaves on roads, potholes wait to unsaddle you and of course the occasional dry and sunny day that makes it all worthwhile. WA is hot, usually, it can be a little windy and occasionally wet, but usually hot, a dry heat that is far more tolerable than humid sticky heat. The near certainty that your ride will not result in being drenched to the skin is uplifting. The only hazards are the dive-bombing crows that swoop viciously down on you like Spitfires or Hurricanes should you cycle too near their nests. Some Aussie cyclists place cable ties in their helmets so the bird hits them instead of the helmet. Sadly, cyclists have been unbalanced by these birds and died under the wheels of other road users. Then of course there are the snakes. Home of the most poisonous snake in the world, the Western Taipan, known by the Indigenous People by the name of Dandarabilla, Australia has more than sixty species of poisonous snake. Fortunately, most of these are not aggressive. On previous cycling trips I have encountered snakes in Slovakia, Thailand and America and can confirm regardless of them being venomous, they do not like being ridden over and will predictably bite.

Alistair and I went our separate ways and I cycled on and booked into a campsite that Andrew Sykes had been impressed with. It had been a free campsite for tents when he had stayed and although I had only wild camped for one night since leaving Oslo, it was an opportunity for a hot shower at Yorkshire prices. I was politely informed that the management have a few specific days in the year that no charges are made. However, guess what, this was not one of them. No matter, it was a good site and having arrived early, I pitched my tent in the exact place Andrew had done for a photograph in his book looking over Lake Mjøsa.

Daily Blog: Exiting Oslo. July 2nd
Anne and I had a morning coffee at one of the excellent cafés in the Oslo suburbs. This one was in an area that had the feel of having its own identity or community,

a little like Notting Hill in London. Oslo is one of the world's acclaimed coffee drinker meccas.

At twelve noon we left the apartment. We walked for a while together then Anne turned right for the city centre and the railway station and I turned left for Nordkapp. Although I am very much looking forward to the cycling, I have been away a long time and there is still 26 days of cycling to be done and, depending on my route amendments, up to 2,000 km to ride.

Oslo was to date the easiest city to evacuate, not that either of us wanted to leave. It really is an incredible place. By following the 'Route 7' signposts and in places where they were noticeably absent, a good sense of direction was used, and I was soon clear of both the city and its suburbs.

I had decided to change my route from going to Lysekil to head NW from Jessheim and cycle past the end of the airport runway, although I doubted whether Anne would see an old git on a bike beneath her. Oslo airport is a busy one and whilst I took photos of planes taking off, I was watched carefully by police in a patrolling car. Mainly because I was sheltering from the sun under a small tree, or was I getting ready to help a prisoner escape from the prison that was immediately under the end of the runway too? What a fantastic location for a prison, with aircraft constantly taking off. A little further down the road was a military training area. Could the

Stensgård Church near Oslo airport.

two interests be useful to one of the parties? Perhaps a different take on the phrase, 'live firing'!

I had not intended to cycle the west side of Hurdalssjøen until a few weeks ago, but what a treat! A deserted road led to its southern end and the beautiful church of Stensgård. Bathers were swimming in the lake, 100 m from the church.

The road that ran beside the full length of the lake was deserted, with stunning views all around. At the northern end, another beautiful church, and a bathing area. After Brustad came the long climb SE. Although nearing the end of the day, this was a fantastic climb up to some small lakes, before a fast and careful descent negotiating numerous hairpin bends down to Byrud at the southern end of Lake Mjøsa.

The 33 road along the fjord of Mjøsa was cool in the evening shade provided by conifers on either side. It was time to find a place to sleep.

As I get into rural Norway, I am adopting a less stringent attitude towards what is an acceptable wild campsite. The 1954 Act permits wild camping provided it is not within 150 m of a residence or on land where damage would be caused, such as cereal or root crops. At Svenstad I saw a sign saying, 'picnic and swimming'. Cycling down a 17% hill, I took the chance and found an idyllic location.

The no camping area resulted in finding this idyllic place in the grounds of a school summer camp.

However, there was a notice saying, 'no camping' in many languages and obviously those who had placed it there meant what they said. I ate my evening meal beside the lake and contemplated. A little way back up the hill there appeared to be a school's holiday village with mown grass fields leading to the lake edge. The place was deserted and one small patch of grass with a view across the lake became my home for the night. I swam in the cool water before sleeping soundly for a few hours. I am far enough north now for the nights never to get totally dark. I can read without a torch until 11 pm and full daylight returns by 3.30 am.

This was a particularly enjoyable day that covered over 110 km and 1,600 m of elevation. The weather is set fair for the next two weeks and I am about to cycle through some of the world's most beautiful countryside. I am a fortunate person.

Daily Blog: A room (tent) with a view. July 3rd

I awoke at 3.30 am with absolutely no objections. The outer tent had been left open during the night and when I opened my eyes the sun was just clearing the trees on the distant eastern bank of the lake. I watched as a shaft of light was cast across the still water. This was near perfection.

An early breakfast, a quick cycle back up to the deserted main road and a ride in the cool morning air took me to Skreia and a warmer and busier ride into Gjøvik.

Cycles are routed around this tunnel. It was on this stretch of old road that I saw a large fish breach out of the water.

The museum in Gjøvik.

Whilst having a coffee in Gjøvik and deep in thought a voice asked, 'Where are you heading?' An hour later I said cheerio to Alistair Sinclair. It is amazing that after such a short time you can identify kindred spirits. With no trace of an Australian accent, Alistair lives in Canberra and has done so for the last ten years. He is an Englishman who left the UK over twenty years ago. Every year he goes on a hardcore cycle tour. In 2012 he cycled across America, a different route from Andy Hill's and mine (Seattle to Boston). Alistair cycled from Virginia to Oregon. He has also done long distance rides in Australia, something that until now has not held my interest. Alistair, if you read this, it was a pleasure meeting you and I hope our paths cross again in the future.

My home for tonight.

I am sitting beside my tent on an official campsite, five metres from the lapping waters of the northern left arm of Lake Mjøsa. Sveastranda camping is no longer free to single tenting cyclists as it was when Andrew Sykes stayed here. Still, for the equivalent of £15 the views are very pleasant. Accompanied by fresh strawberries and IPA beer, a light breeze and unbroken sunshine, life again would be hard to improve. Following this trip, like several before, I may require a degree of reintegration into normal society.

July 4th, American independence day and a sunny one as I continued north to Lillehammer on the 'less trodden' road beside the E6. With high expectations I crossed the bridge and cycled up into the town that had hosted the Winter Olympics in 1994 and was the most northern town to have done so. It was also the first year that the winter Olympics had been held in a different year to the Summer Olympics. The year that saw Jayne Torvill and Christopher Dean return to gain a bronze medal for their ice dancing ten years after receiving gold at Sarajevo in what was then Yugoslavia.

I stopped for coffee in a large and characterless café and weighed up whether to explore the town. On the surface it seemed void of anything special. Although I knew there was a highly regarded arts centre that included paintings from the Matisse School and the Maihaugen outdoor museum of 200 buildings and an 800-year-old Garmo Stave church, perhaps the stay in Oslo so recently had satisfied my curiosity. The road was also calling, and the weather was pleasant. Cyclists are not permitted in the E6 tunnel, so I hugged the eastern bank of the Gudbrandsdalslågen to re-join the E6 as it arrived in Tretten. In Tretten, parked outside an American styled diner was a large truck adorned with the Stars and Stripes and Marilyn Monroe. Seen on the July 4th, this has to be appropriate. Keen to avoid the E6, I headed uphill on roads that became ever smaller and more rural, only later to return down a steep hill several kilometres further north on the E6. Well, it seemed a good idea at the time. That afternoon was to see considerable effort being spent in gaining little progress. It was hot. Arriving in Ringebu, I sought out shade provided near the entrance of a Rema 1000 supermarket and, having shopped to buy an evening meal and breakfast, sat on the carpark kerb, and drank to rehydrate.

My second faux pas, although not embarrassing, because it is hard to justify how a sweating man of certain years dressed in lycra can be concerned about embarrassment, was a serious 'can't be bothered to check the route' moment. Cycling past a larger-than-life weird-looking chrome snake randomly placed as a feature beside the road, I had taken the next turning to the right to Atna, a wrong turning. Already hot again and with the heat having drained my energy, my mind pushed my body up the steep and long hill that lay in front of me. Who knows how far up that hill I had gone when that sixth sense surfaced to conscious thought? 'This does not feel right.' 'Ralph, you are only thinking that cos it's a bloody hard hill and you're knackered.' 'No, I'm telling you, it's the wrong road.' Unclipping cycling shoes at exceptionally low speed going up steep gradients whilst maintaining minimal speed so as not to fall off, must be a quick operation, perhaps another reason I had continued climbing for so long.

Returning down that hill was, not surprisingly, quite different. There was no annoyance, only self-disappointment. Had I not learnt the lesson many times both on the bike and in the mountains, that it only takes a couple of small errors to collude for a serious mistake. I returned to the 387 road, straight through the green traffic lights that allowed vehicles to cross the narrow river bridge in single file and resumed climbing, this time having taken the correct right-hand turning on the 388 that soon joined the 27.

I stopped to look at the isolated small white steepled church at Venabygd. To the rear of the church are the graves of five Second World War servicemen. The Nazis invaded Norway on April 9th 1940. The invasion was sudden and total. Norway was considered so strategically important that a disproportionate number of Nazi soldiers remained to occupy the country throughout the war, effectively removing them from operations elsewhere in Europe. Allied operations were covert involving the Norwegian Resistance and the Commonwealth air forces. The Resistance were highly effective, whilst those who escaped to England returned either as pilots or as members of Joint Operations. Unlike many European countries there are no Commonwealth War Graves in Norway; those who died there were buried in civil churchyards. The five graves were just that, only five. Unlike the thousands in the enormous cemeteries in Belgium and France. Standing beside those five graves reading who lay in them was no less poignant than seeing row upon row of white crosses. Each grave contained a body of a person who had been a father, a son, a brother, to a family. The five who lay here were all from the 8th Battalion, Sherwood Foresters (Notts and Derby Regiment) and had all been killed between April 23rd and June 8th 1940. They are: John Rook, Leonard John Jones, George Ernest Stanton, Walter Summersgill and Reginald Cleary.

Daily Blog: A fitting tribute to an American ride. July 4th

It is only appropriate that today saw me cycling up a never-ending hill. An average gradient of 10%, this climb started immediately after leaving Ringebu. Andy Hill and I have fond memories of our Seattle to Boston trip. The climb today was like the Washington Pass in The Northern Cascades. Incredibly hot, seemingly endless, with wonderful views. However, I was not on a 7.5 kg lightweight Bianchi road bike with a credit card. I was on a 7700 Trek with my tent, worldly possessions and the evening's meal just purchased from Rema 1000.

I had completed 95 km from last night's beautiful campsite Sveastranda Camping, spoilt only by an Audi fitted with 37 doors. Three teenage girls had arrived in it and having wedged their tent between mine and a family, they started to enjoy themselves – loudly. At around 11.30 pm the 37-doored Audi was put to use. One of the girls had probably lost something. Instead of a methodical approach, each of the girls in turn searched the car multiple times, each opening and slamming a door in turn. A door was in motion about every minute for, yes, 37 minutes! It is amazing no one screamed at them, drowned them in the lake, or hung them from the nearby tree. I left early this morning, as quiet as a mouse.

The weather was perfect as I rode the cycle route parallel to the west of the E6 below me.

After three months cycling, I am only a shadow of my former self and the cracks are beginning to show.

The cycle bridge into Lillehammer.

Arriving in Lillehammer, over the impressive pedestrian and cyclist bridge that must be two hundred metres long, this was another place I have wanted to visit, mainly due to the 1994 winter Olympics.

The cycle paths were good, then when the E6 dived into a long tunnel south of Tretten, the road contoured around for the prohibited cyclist.

American diner in Tretten.

On leaving Tretten I had decided to avoid the E6 and take a series of country roads to the east. This was my first mistake of the day, but not without some benefits. The road kicked up to quite a gradient. After some climbing, I took a well compacted dirt road and got to see some very rural homesteads and some old farming methods in practice.

Logging viewed from a rough track diversion.

It became apparent that the effort taken to avoid the busy E6 was not proportionate to the benefit. So, from a deserted dirt track I rejoined the E6 and trusted other road users not to end my life prematurely. I was able to maintain a speed of around 30 km/h, perhaps due to the slipstream of passing lorries.

It was a hot afternoon as I found some shade in the supermarket car park amongst the vehicles that had been left running with their air con on. Having loaded my evening meal into already seam-stretching panniers, now carrying additional equipment for northern Norway, I took the 'back door' out of Ringebu. The climbing was steep, very steep, hitting 19% on one tight bend. It was hot work! The sun prevented me seeing the map screen, progress was painfully slow, and I was clipped into the pedals. The road did not turn to the north as expected, just continued going east and UP. Something was wrong. I was not angry with myself, just disappointed. I was halfway to Øksendalen. The ride back down was refreshingly cool. Ironically, the traffic lights were on green for me to start the correct ascent from the 'side door' out of Ringebu. Not quite as steep, but with no let up, the body again started leaking! How like the Washington Pass.

Some way on, it is a little blurred as to how far, there was an excellent reason to stop.

A traditional church sits to the right of the road at Venabygd.

A family had just been tending a grave and as they left, they told me there was a water tap to the rear of the building. I must have looked in need of a drink ÷ cannot imagine why. After a 15-minute break there was no postponing the inevitable. The hill continued up still at about 10%. Right-hand bends were even steeper and with a busy road, there was not the option of taking the wider bend on the left. After a while, the first of two campsites arrived. A tent wash and baby wipes were not going to be adequate tonight. I never arrived at the second campsite; this one is perfect.

I have just spent 45 minutes chatting with a Norwegian local. He spoke little English and we both uttered approving sounds as we pawed over my map. There are many places of beauty to visit in this region, let alone the rest of Norway.

So today the benefits of living and cycling in hilly Luddendenfoot, in Yorkshire, my home village, enabled me to 'get stuck in' and in a weird masochistic way, enjoy the climb. Overall, there was 1,535 m of climbing over 106 kms.

Although less steep now, I was weary and was looking for a place to camp, but not wanting the effort of stopping, so continued turning the pedals. Fortunately,

Trabelia Hyttegrend and Camping arrived on my left. A congenial gentleman about my age said I could camp anywhere. He spoke little English but insisted that I spread my maps over the picnic table that was to be next to my tent. He then proceeded to talk rapidly and enthusiastically about where I should be going. He stabbed the map in various locations and, not for the first time, spoke in the absolute belief that I could understand every word he was saying. With no other campers in sight, I chose a spot beside the picnic table with a long reaching view to the west and with the air cooling, watched the sun disappear from a challenging and enjoyable day. Having showered, eaten well and enjoyed a good night's sleep, I left the campsite the following morning with a smile on my face. The next few days were to be immensely enjoyable.

In anticipation of another warm day, an early start was prudent. I felt little of the effects of the heat of the previous day. The views were far-reaching, early morning mist lay in the valleys as if held down by some unseen weight. This was a beautiful landscape. I travelled along the road, absorbed in the isolation that surrounded me. A brief look through the windows of a solitary church, then moving on to arrive at the Sohlbergplassen viewing platform. This stunning piece of architecture was designed by Carl-Viggo Hølmebakk and completed in 2002. Made of concrete and steel it curves its way through the trees and leads the eye out over lake Atnsjøen and the mountains beyond that were the subject of Harald Sohlberg's painting called Winter's Night in Rondane. Although the mountains had no snow today the Rondane National Park is stunning throughout the year. I was that early, I had to wait for the café perched high above the lake to open. It was worth it, a caffeine loading only added to what was turning into a special day. Further up the road when taking a rest from the heat of the sun in a bus shelter, I met Elie on her mountain bike. We shared the shelter for a while and chatted. She reminded me of Helen, my youngest daughter, although an established nurse and not training as Elie was. There were similarities, both engaging and enthusiastic for what life could offer them. Having turned east at Folldal another campsite presented itself opposite a Joker supermarket, Yes, there is a chain of grocery stores in Norway called Joker. Jokers together with Rema 1000s and the Co-op provided most of my calories throughout the trip in

Norway. The Gjelten Bru campsite was another quiet site, this time set beside a large river and again I was able to make use of a picnic bench.

The next day, July 7th the weather had changed and presented a headwind as a challenge. High spirits remained, I felt alive and strong. Knowing there were several campsites along the route my loyalty to wild camping was being challenged every time I immersed myself under a hot shower and sat at a picnic table to eat, rather than on the ground where ticks sought me out for their evening meal. These sites were inexpensive and good. Four sites were on the road ahead, three too soon to stop at but one at 90 km would be ideal. Although marked on my map, none were there! I stopped for coffee in Berkåk and took the 700, turning off again onto the 510. I felt as though I was in the heart of the Norwegian countryside.

Daily Blog: All the senses satisfied. July 5th

The hill continued from last night but, refreshed after a good night's sleep, it was a delight. Within a few kilometres the gradient eased and in the early morning light the views were outstanding. Some of Norway's finest mountains are immediately to the west, Skjerellfjellet, Hornflågan and Blåkollen. All around 1,500 m ASL with snow still laying in the cories.

Isolated, deserted, and beautiful.

It was a good decision to stop near the top of the climb last night. The camp site was perfect. The second commercial campsite beyond the climbing was big. Shops and a café catered for the RV owner's needs. I far prefer the more natural approach to camping and with fewer people around the connection with nature is more fulfilling.

My head was constantly turning, absorbing the views. At 1,000 m ASL and further north than Scotland, even the Orkney Islands, this area is under snow from November to April, yet the road surface is unbelievable, not a pothole to be seen. The weather was perfect, with a following wind and sun on my back.

The next delight was a viewing platform over lake Atnsjøen. Not something that would normally grab the attention; however, this was an architectural masterpiece.

A quirky quality café in the 'back of beyond'.

A coffee and pancake at this café were enjoyed by two motorcyclists and four locals and me, who were knocking on the door at 11 am, when they opened.

The viewing platform over lake Atnasjøen.

There have been several further climbs and descents, one notable descent at Gunstadsætra allowed the bike to hit 78.9 km/h. I could have pedalled harder and sat on the cross bar with my chin on the Garmin, but the stability of the bike would not allow me. OK, I bottled out! Now on road 47 heading north to Folldal it continued through still beautiful countryside. I stopped at a riverside centre to again admire the views.

A bridge near a riverside centre.

It was shortly after this, whilst having a quick bite and drink in a bus shelter, Evie arrived on her mountain bike to share the sparse shade. Starting her final year of training as a community nurse, she lives 10 km up the road and confesses to loving the area. Who possibly could not? As we chatted, she said the area saw the coldest temperatures in Norway last winter, when they dropped to minus 40.

At Folldal, I turned east, then southeast, then south to Alvdal, directly away from my destination. Since leaving Tarifa I had rarely travelled in a southerly direction. I had decided that going through the mountains on dirt tracks to connect up with the No. 3 road near Nytrøa was not a good idea. Although it would cut the corner and reduce the distance. Best to do the longer route around and maintain some speed. After all, I had chosen this more eastern route to avoid the zero enjoyment of cycling the E6 up to Oppdal.

Today has been one of my most memorable cycling days. There has been something for each of the senses.

Sight:- so many incredible things to look at, the long views of mountains and upland moors, the rivers, lakes all bathed in near-perfect light.

Sounds: the skylarks, snipe, and a curious eagle. The water of a broad shallow river running over pedals.

Smell: the pine trees and fresh cut hay, even the fields of strawberries.

Taste: that morning coffee, (a particularly good one), accompanied with a pancake and tonight's IPA beer.

Touch: the viewing platform that invites you to run your hands along its surface. A piece of art that was created to enable something else of beauty to be admired, is itself a thing of beauty.

And the Sixth Sense? There was little need for it, given the diet the others had feasted on.

Daily Blog: A windy night. July 6th

Last night the tent was buffeted by strong gusting winds that rapidly brought in heavy cloud. This un-forecasted change in weather was a surprise. However, the heavy cloud did not result in rain, but remained brooding with the strong wind.

It has been quite different to yesterday. No perspiration, no need for sun block or copious quantities of liquid intake. The sun did win two battles with the cloud for a few minutes, but the war was won by the thickening cloud. It remained cold and windy. Whereas the wind had pushed me along yesterday, it had a concerted effort at pushing me backwards today. There were also many kilometres of low gradient climbing that switch-backed over several hills eventually getting to 733 m ASL.

My plan had been to go east then south, for reasons mentioned in yesterday's blog. The whole morning was a workout on a near empty 'tank'. A bowl of muesli and a drink of fresh orange did me for 68 km. Over the past few days, I have been carrying food unnecessarily as shops have subsequently always been available. Yesterday there was a Joker at the beginning of the day and one opposite the campsite at the end (they are a chain of supermarkets like Rema 1000 and the Co-op). Road No 3 was void of anything apart from the occasional farm. Not until 15 km from joining the busy E6 south of Berkåk was there a filling station and café. A Burger Whopper was consumed with a strong black coffee, very filling and a sarcastic gift at only £14.

Now, I might be getting soft, but a hot shower and a mosquito-free tent pitch must be worth a tenner. That is the very reasonable price paid for the last two nights at official campsites. It had been my intention to repeat the pleasure this evening. However, each of the three campsites marked on the map did not exist. Now having cycled over 100 km, all into the wind, I enquired about the site in Berkåk. Well, it is not really in the town. I was told it was about 5 km further NE on the E6. Tomorrow I travel NW on the 700. I decided not to seek it out.

Shopping done, I descended the steep hair-pinned hill down to the wide River Orkla and having left the 700 for a minor road, happened to look left and saw this: -

A special find at the end of a long day. The size of the cottage can be judged by the picnic table.

I am writing looking out of the window of a tiny Hansel and Gretel-style cottage, with traditional soil and plant roof which covers a cosy room beneath containing a 50 cm x 1.5 m wooden cot bed and a long since defunct wood burner stove. Numerous artefacts belonging to a past era are also in here. There is even a rug on the floor. With a picnic table just outside, no lock on the door and a notice without any exclamation marks written in Norwegian, I think I am not the first to have used this historic little cottage as a venue for a sleepover.

The night of July 6th was a special night. The blog says it all. I came across a 'Hansel and Gretel' cottage, so small it made Bilbo Baggins' home seem massive. So small there was not room for me to sleep on the bed and have my bike inside at the same time. I slept on the floor and the bike was propped up on the bed.

Built from tree trunks that had been rough sawn lengthways into halves and placed horizontally for the walls, held with cross struts, and packed at the joints. The roof made from timber and stone had long since been covered under lichen, moss, and grass. Inside, the interior had a timber floor and a small wood burner in a corner. The bed replicated a Medieval bed, deep-sided and roughly made. Two small windows to the front elevation provided the only light. Inside this quaint house, it was impossible not to focus on how people lived a few centuries ago.

It was not until a few hours later after it had become darker that I noticed lights on in a house just a little further up the hill between the trees. Blissfully I was left in peace to enjoy my stay and be thankful for the afternoon's elusive campsites. That night was one that was easily remembered for its uniqueness.

The following morning, I rejoined the larger road that is Cycle Route number 7. I cycled north past Løkken Verk, avoiding the 65. The countryside was pleasant and the agricultural building typically Scandinavian.

Daily Blog: Reward for effort. July 7th

The route that highway 700 takes from Berkåk north to Orkanger is easy on the eye. Nothing stands out as spectacular, it is all very pleasant with many traditional timber buildings supported on raised timber, stone, or concrete plinths to minimize the effects of the snow that lays for many months each year.

The barns have the timber door lats painted the same cream colour as many of the houses. Huge elk antlers whitened with years in the sun hang high above these doors. Each barn has a ramped access to the upper floor for animal fodder to be loaded into the barn for the animals beneath to eat during the long cold winter months. It is nearing the end of the summer here and the flower boxes and hanging baskets are full of geraniums and have been placed both on the houses and barns alike.

Ochre painted houses and barns are numerous.

Immaculate farm animal barns.

Quaint and ornate shelters accommodate the refuse bins and milk churns are ready for collection on raised covered platforms. A couple of houses have miniature replicas of themselves in their well-tended gardens. And all the while there is the soft sound of bells ringing as the sheep graze. The common thread that runs down the valley is the river Orkla, wide with shallow rapids and deep pools; this is a Mecca for fishermen.

I saw a fox and a hare, but not understandably together. Both were beside the road and both took little interest in a lone cyclist.

Arriving in Orkanger at noon, it is five days since I left Oslo, although it seems longer. Nonetheless it has been a thoroughly enjoyable experience. I have met several interesting people, notably Alistair Sinclair and Evie. The weather has been very warm until a couple of days ago. Today, like yesterday, the cloud is heavy and it is chilly.

I am currently in Orkanger and intend camping at Flakkvegen tonight, where I will take a ferry across to Rørvik, having first visited Trondheim tomorrow.

En route to visit Trondheim.

It has turned into a wonderful evening. The sun is warm, and I have pizza, chips, and beer from the shop at the ferry terminal. There was so much, I shared it with the camp receptionist.

Even burning high calories, the white flag went up on this meal.

CHAPTER TWENTY-THREE
Snakes and Cycling

'When I was five years old, my mother always told me that happiness was the key to life. When I went to school, they asked me what I wanted to be when I grew up. I wrote down 'happy'. They told me I did not understand the assignment and I told them they did not understand life'. John Lennon

Arriving in Orkanger, known more for its port and sea orientated industry and being one of the main industrial centres of central Norway, I sought out a particular Stave church. I had seen several and all had been impressive. This particular one, known as The Norway Building, the Pavilion was built in 1893 and was Norway's contribution to the Chicago World Fair. It used prefabricated house building methods of its time. M. Thams and Co. in Orkanger was the pioneer. After being transported to Chicago for the World Fair it remained in America for 123 years. This monument to Stave churches and Orkdal's wood carving traditions had only been re-erected two years before I was fortunate enough to see it in Orkanger.

From Orkanger I headed east, hugging the coast, through Viggja, Børsa, and Leinstrand before taking the 170 north to Rye and finally Flakk. This was a pleasant afternoon's ride, rolling hills with views north and west over the sea. A Hurtigruten ferry reflected the sunlight as it travelled from Trondheim. I pitched my tent in a small neatly mown field next to some small trees that provided shade. The ferry that was to take me across to Rørvik the following day was within a stone's throw next to a pizzeria that also sold beer. What a great way to end a good day.

In the morning I left my tent up and cycled into Trondheim, unhindered with paniers, to explore the city. I was to catch the ferry later that afternoon.

On the approach to Trondheim.

Trondheim is steeped in history. The name derives from the old Norse word Þrándheimr, meaning home of the strong and fertile. Founded by the Viking king, Olaf Tryggvason in AD 997, this interesting city holds a special place in Norwegian culture. It was Norway's first capital and to this day is the nation's coronation city where kings, since Harald Hårfagre in 872-933 to the current king, King Harald V in 1991, have been crowned and blessed.

Trondheim has moved with the times whilst preserving much of its history. The main 706 road is predominately subterranean as it heads both south and east from the city. In the centre of the city is the Stiftsgården, the Royal residence and Scandinavia's largest wooden palace built in 1774. At the time of my visit, it was nearly surrounded by extensive road works. I spent the day visiting several of Trondheim's better-known tourist attractions.

The Nidaros Cathedral

The world's northernmost gothic cathedral and an important pilgrimage site. The first foundations for the cathedral were laid in 1070, but it took 150 years before it became the cathedral of the diocese. It was built over the burial site of King Olaf II who reigned between 1015 and 1028. Olaf was killed in 1030 at the Battle of Stiklestad, and he was later canonized as Saint Olaf.

As so often is the case with historic buildings, it suffered several fires, one in 1337 and another in 1531, and in 1708 it burned to the ground, struck by lightning in 1719, and consequently it suffered a further fire. It appears the cathedral has not enjoyed too much divine protection over the millennia. Certain parts of the cathedral may have been designed on both Canterbury and Lincoln cathedrals in England.

Having looked around the cathedral and the adjoining Archbishops Palace, I took the short walk to and crossed over the River Nidelva on the Gamle Bybro bridge.

The Gamle Bybro

Constructed in 1681 at the same time as the Kristiansten Fortress, following the great Trondheim fire. Both the bridge and the fortress were of considerable military importance.

Gamle Bybro is also known as Lykkens portal, the Gate of Happiness, after the lyrics of *Nidelven quiet and beautiful you are*, composed by the Norwegian Kristian Oskar Hoddø in 1940, whilst he stood on the bridge. Hoddø was in the Resistance movement against the Nazis and was executed by them in Trondheim on November 17th 1943, together with eight other Resistance fighters.

Standing on the bridge looking downriver, views of the old timber wharf buildings are spectacular, painted in contrasting colours standing majestically on their stilts. Coming off the bridge you are walking on cobbles. Opposite, in Brubakken, a road takes you steeply up to a fortress.

The Kristiansten Fortress

Named after King Christian V of Denmark and Norway and built in 1681 to protect the city from attack from the east, and was ready to receive action in 1685 and was further fortified in 1691. In 1718 the Swedish invaded Norway and laid siege to the fortress and the city. Armfeldt, the Swedish general, was not successful, withdrawing his troops on hearing that the Swedish king Karl XIII had been killed at Halden.

Being a Sunday and in Norway, shopping for food needed to be planned. None of the supermarkets were open. Fortunately, I found a corner shop and was able to buy some needed food for the efforts that lay ahead. There would be no facilities at the ferry drop-off point and little opportunity to buy any food until I reached Mørriaunet.

I returned to my campsite, packed up and boarded the ferry for the small hamlet of Rørvik Fergeleie. I had decided not to go to Hell, a village east of Trondheim. The weather was breaking down, rain was on its way. I rode off the ferry with care, spawned from seeing other cyclists slide and fall on the slippery steel vehicle ramps. Soon the few cars that had accompanied me over the water had disappeared into the distance and I was left in isolation to cycle up a long hill. Deep in thoughts of a busy and enjoyable day, this daydreaming cyclist and a solitary wild strawberry picker hidden in the road verge startled each other. With mutual apologies in English and Norwegian and over-emphasised smiling, we returned to our separate worlds. The hill carried on, going up. On reaching the plateau it started to rain. Taking refuge in a bus shelter from a surge in the constant rain, I mulled on the thought that I was about to embark on 'The World's Most Beautiful Journey'. I had been given a small and disproportionately heavy guidebook of this journey FV.17 Steinkjer to Bodø. The route covered the middle third of Norway's south-north length and I was excited at the prospect of what lay ahead.

Rain, like all weather, is just an ingredient in the recipe for outdoor pursuits. Ideal conditions are rare. The ability to draw enjoyment from conditions that are far from ideal is an acquired one. Fairweather sportspeople hardly ever achieve too much. It is the acceptance of the cold, being soaking wet, but knowing also that it will not last and tomorrow sweat will be running off you, legs screaming as you push up a hill, or you will enjoy a sublime day in the saddle, feeling strong, smiling as you absorb the beauty that is around you. This is what makes cycle touring so fulfilling. Variety gives us a benchmark to measure enjoyment. We need the hardship to appreciate the special days.

The rain passed as it always does and with white clouds chasing each other across the increasingly blue sky, I came across a campsite near Ånes. Having pitched the tent just off the beach facing west across the water, I relaxed on my collapsible chair and drank a beer as the sun settled on the horizon. Soon the sound of the lapping waves stopped as I slipped into sleep.

Daily Blog: A Michael Fish day. July 8th

Note: Michael Fish was a UK TV weather presenter, who notoriously assured a viewer on October 15th 1987 that the UK would not be hit by a hurricane. It was!

'There is no precipitation forecast for the next two weeks.' That was the forecast.

I left the tent up at the campsite and took an easy ride into Trondheim, arriving just as the first two tourist groups were, one American and the other Japanese. Apart from them, the city was all still on a sunny Sunday morning. I enjoyed a relaxing sightseeing day before returning to catch the ferry.

Nidaros Cathedral, the world's most northernmost gothic cathedral, and an important pilgrimage site.

The Gamie Bybro bridge that spans the river Nidelva to the historic Bakklandet.

Within this part of the city, all the houses are of timber.

A ride up the steep Kristianstensbakken takes you to the 1681 fortress. Sadly, this was a place of execution of members of the Norwegian resistance during WW2.

Stiftsgården is the royal residence in the city. Built in 1774, it is Scandinavia's largest wooden palace.

A quick 12 km ride back to the campsite to collect the gear and onto the ferry.

Having crossed on the ferry, I travelled north (as always) to Åfjord. The first hill was long but not steep, the only excitement being a man standing up from behind the roadside barrier alongside me, giving me a 'rit good fright'. He was picking wild strawberries. Then came 'The Hill', on and on between 8 and 10%! It finally flattened out as it started to spit with rain whilst it decided what to do. By my reckoning, it made the wrong decision. Three hours later the numerous lakes were still being filled very rapidly with one extremely wet cyclist arriving in Åfjord at 7 pm, having cycled 92 km with 1,260 m of ascent.

Today was to be another enjoyable one. A stunning coastline and so much more. The roads are excellent, no need to be constantly looking out for potholes. So much time to look around on this sunny day. Parking the bike, I climbed a staircase attached to a cliff to see a cave, the roof of which had collapsed, and signed the 'visitors' book kept in a tin box. It reminded me of a secret cave in the English Lake District. That cave also had a visitors' book kept in an old WW2 ammunition box. One of the entries wrote, 'Been looking for this cave for eight years, I found it today'. The cave had an almost biblical atmosphere about it, as a stone had to be rolled away from the entrance, and a secret remote wire needed to be pulled to gain access. On my first visit I had crawled in through the narrow entrance. It was initially black. As my eyes became accustomed to the light, I apologised to the person sleeping on a wooden pallet bed. He did not stir. Again, I gave my apologies and again he did not move. How long had he been there? There was no obvious smell of decaying flesh. His hair was long and unkempt. I touched him and still no response, I rolled him over. I did not complete the roll; his torso fell out of the sleeping bag as I fell backward. Laying on the floor in front of me was the upper part of a dress mannequin. I have since visited the cave several times. It was a secret cave, now it is not. The secret unusually leaked out from the climbing community and was the subject of an article in a climbing magazine a few years ago that unbelievably gave the mapping grid reference. Sadly, it is a quite a different cave today.

Back on my bike and a few kilometres down the road, another not-to-be-missed event popped up. A rickety planked bridge spanned across the water that separated the mainland from a small island. Climbing down the embankment over some animal bones that had been bleached in the sun, Tim, 'The old git' on a bike vanished, being replaced by Indiana Jones. Although dressed in lycra and with no whip or handgun, the similarities were questionable. There are elements in the male species that never mature. The lycra-clad Indiana Jones explored the island before returning to the real world.

Today was another warm one full of variety from snakes, elk, rock stars, and Trolls. Norway has three species of snake, the Huggorm viper, Slettsnok, and Buorm together with others such as the Green Tree snake. My encounter was with a Huggorm viper, Norway's only venomous snake. Not known for its aggression and although poisonous, it is not capable of killing a human but is a hunter and always uses venom to kill its prey of mice, small birds, and frogs.

Namsos is a functional town. I used the shopping mall to escape the heat of the afternoon and to recharge my devices. Evening meal and breakfast bought and loaded with caffeine, I headed for a place to sleep. I think the Blog paints the picture.

Daily Blog: *Trees, trees, and more trees. July 9th*

There were many trees this morning. If I were a certain member of the British monarchy (which thankfully for both you and me, I am not) one given to tree-hugging, my arms would have been very tired. There are many varieties of trees, however nothing but spruce here, all growing in straight lines. Was this going to be a boring 'tree only' day? It certainly was not!

Whereas yesterday afternoon had caused me to dig deep, this afternoon was an absolute pleasure, variety, scenery, and hard work on a series of long steep hills.

From Lonin onwards riding was a delight.

As a light alternative from cycling at Reppkleiv I climbed several staircases and scrambled up to what the information board proclaimed to be the largest granite pothole in northern Europe, with a diameter of 11.6 m and a height of tens of metres. The sidewall having collapsed years ago had exposed what had been the remainder of the internal walls.

I later saw an Indiana Jones-style cable bridge that just had to be crossed (several times). Without a whip, revolver, school satchel, or a cowboy hat, I did not drown. However, I was not running for my life or having to rescue a damsel in distress.

The collapsed cave near Reppkleiv.

Not everyone had made a successful crossing.

After the lakes came the fjords. Now fjords were around long before the straight line was invented. So, when first putting in a destination into my mapping device, it may say 40 km. Now that is ok for a bird, but not a bloke on a bike. Ask it to identify a route and that 40 km could jump to perhaps double that distance. From here on, 'straight' does not exist. However, cycling on such beautifully maintained roads (and Norway, I am told, can be a little colder in the winter than in the UK – take note, UK Highway Maintenance, Norwegian roads rarely have potholes) and with such stunning views, who cares if you need to cycle in a near circle?

On nearly reaching Osen I looked across the fjord and saw a campsite. The fjord stretched away both to the left and right of me. The tide was out, would it be possible to wade? No, it would not even look plausible in a Monty Python's sketch. So, around another fjord and up another hill.

Daily Blog: Snakes and cycling. July 10th

I am sitting on the edge of a wooded glade three metres above the Blikkengfjorden, 25 km north of Namsos. It is 9 pm and the sun is still high in the sky. A breeze keeps the flying nasties away and the only sound is the lapping of water, the bees, and the leaves on the trees being gently blown. There is one large, solitary mosquito trying to take my blood, but sadly for it, he has a distinct sound, so he will die before he drinks, or even as he drinks my blood. The other sight and sound I have never seen before, numerous jumping fish. Some of them quite large, they clear the water and splash back down. Very much like miniature whales breaching. Strangely enough there is no bird song, none, very weird.

My pitch tonight after a cold swim.

I packed up my gear this morning at the same time as a guy in his late twenties packed up his, some twenty metres from me. He had arrived late last night, and we had not spoken. I asked which direction he was going. He was heading south to Trondheim. On hearing I was heading north, the route he had used, he advised me that I was in for some serious climbing on the 715 road before meeting the 17, going up to Namsos. I similarly advised him that there were a few 9% hills for him to enjoy on his way to the ferry across to Trondheim.

Using the bus shelter at the junction of the 715 and 17 for shade as I ate the remains of last night's gargantuan pizza, I reflected on those hills I had cycled on the 715. The late twenty-something year old on his electric bike may well by the end of his day have a different definition of 'hard hills'. However, he was carrying more gear than a fully loaded Pickford's removal lorry. The 715 was a beautiful road to cycle, and eventful.

A female Huggorm viper. Norway was not a place I expect to encounter a snake.

If you are a touring cyclist, please tell me whether you regularly come across snakes? I am starting to lose count of my encounters with these creatures. First, there was Hungary with Andy and Luke, then the Badlands in America with Andy. Australia, whilst cycling in WA, to be expected as Australia plays host to an extraordinary number of very venomous snakes and other critters. Then there was North Vietnam earlier this year, and now today.

The route today was over rolling hills. More ups than downs as elevation was gained. Some impressive waterfalls running over smooth red granite rock. Then came the deep blue lakes, numerous and like mirrors reflecting their surroundings.

The hills did require constant gear changes. So numerous were they and so nearly uniform, a pattern of gear changing evolved using every gear, a little like Valentino Lisitsa's performance of Ballade, that used all the piano keys. The ride along the 17 was a pleasant one and I arrived in Namsos sooner than expected, even though I had stopped for a rare drink of Coke for the 'sugar rush'.

After a coffee, prolonged so as I could charge my devices, and making good use of the iced water provided to fill my bottles, and the paper towels in the washroom to dry myself after a quick strip (partial) wash, (this was to be a wild camp night), I headed into Rema 1000 to buy my evening meal. Having mounted up I was heading out of town and I nearly bumped into Norway's rock idle, or to be precise a bronze statue (yes, another one!) of him. Åge Aleksandersen, born 1949, is the Norwegian compatriot to Paul McCartney. So influenced was he by Paul's music he formed a band called 'Prudence' after that Beatles song.

Åge Aleksandersen

To date, this is the only elk I have seen.

Humour abounds.

He seemed friendly enough, but at three metres high, I did not hang around.

Immediately after leaving Namsos, I turned up the hill and was presented with a 600 m tunnel. My first of any length. With lights on, I entered. They were right, every vehicle sounds ten times as loud, and the direction of that sound is also unclear. The whole tunnel was on an incline, which made for a baptism of fire.

The ride to where I am now was stunning. Two bridges both steeply ramped, arched, and curved, and the third, not 100 m from here, is a classic steel girder bridge.

Admiring the view from one of several elegant bridges.

Having taken a quick dip, I can also confirm that fjord water is extremely cold but invigorating.

CHAPTER TWENTY-FOUR
Norwegian Police Like Cyclists

'Do not go where the path may lead, go instead where there is no path and leave a trail.' Ralph Waldo Emerson

July 11th, another great day cycling along smooth roads, little traffic, looking to left and right at gently rolling hills with green pastures and woods. The roads are usually quiet, and I see no other cyclists for days on end. As a mirage floating on the tarmac, Michael approached from the opposite direction. With a centre point of gravity millimetres from scraping the road, his cycle was heavily loaded. Now my journey from Tarifa in Spain to Nordkapp is 8,000 km. Michael had started his journey from Beijing and was nearly home, as he put it. Home was Germany. I suppose distance is relative to what is travelled. Please do read the blog about Michael.

Bridges linked islands like Garsøya and Hestøya. The 769 road threaded a path connecting bridges and ferries. I arrived at the ferry near Lund to see it heading across to Hofles Fergeleie. Unlike some ferry waiting areas, here there was a large café. Sitting in the morning sun, not a care in the world, drinking coffee and eating cheesecake, I noticed that a cyclist had pitched his tent on the lawned area next to the café. Norway is so 'outdoors'. On the other side of the water, I had wanted to take the 771 but there was a landslip that had closed the road, so I took the 770 along the northern bank of Innerfolda to Foldereid then the 17 that hugged the waterside of numerous fjords travelling east then north, then west and east again, to the next ferry at Holm. I could have just eaten at the Vennesund restaurant and cycled off to a quiet spot for the night, but I did not, the shower and shave magnet was strong. Having pitched in a quiet area of a site that catered for RVs, caravans, some chalets, and one tent, I ate a mediocre meal and slept well after a near 160 km day that had seen some tunnels, bridges, and ferries.

July 11th was to be a treat. An early morning start resulted in seeing some wildlife, including an elk. How gracefully these creatures are, and how large.

They cover the ground at speed with little apparent effort. A low growling noise approached from ahead that increased to a roar as a posse of police motorcyclists passed in strict formation and sounded their horns and nodded their heads towards me. It cannot be often a cyclist gets an acknowledgement from eight police riders; this made my day! The early morning mist lifted for a fine day. Long-reaching views of mountains, quirky front garden decorations of dolls riding trikes, and in the middle of nowhere two bus shelters standing, side by side.

I cycled ever northwards and would become well acquainted with the '17', the road that took me to Bodø.

Daily Blog: Two ferries and three tunnels. July 11th
The ferries 'book ended' the day's cycling. I was away early from an ideal wild camp and covered the 25 km in the cool air to the first ferry. The scenery remained jaw-dropping with bridges using small islands as staging posts as the road hopped from one island or peninsula to the next.

A beautiful day.

As I cycled alone, I imagined seeing another cyclist approaching. Having not seen any for days the image seemed unreal. Michael rolled up beside me from the direction I was heading. His bike was that laden, it made any house removal lorry look like a Tonka toy. Unshaven, thin as a lath, Michael had been travelling for a while. Friendly and easy to talk to, we fell into conversation. Living in Germany, he had flown with his cycle to Beijing last September and had been cycling since. He was returning from northern Norway having arrived there via Finland and was on his way home. I wonder how many kilometres he has travelled during the last twelve months, and how many tyres he has worn out. Michael, if you read this, you are an inspiration. I was smiling for hours after meeting you.

Michael, 'nearly' home after leaving Germany a year before.
Note the beer cans! Man after my own heart.

And this is what Michael and I photographed

The first ferry of the day. A strong coffee and cheesecake were consumed in the sun while I waited for it to arrive.

This evening I am in Vennesund and having cycled 140 km today, have finally caught up with my itinerary, having spent some additional quality time in Oslo with Anne, my long-suffering wife.

Daily Blog: Norwegian Police like cyclists. July 12th

No, I did not get stopped for speeding, reckless riding, or not wearing a helmet. On my way up to Horn, the first 60 km of the day in grey, misty conditions, around a corner came eight police motorcyclists. In perfect formation, each one sounded their horn and nodded their head in acknowledgement. Now, how is that for setting anyone up for the day? It made the early morning start even better. First having seen two cranes strolling over a field (the' feathered' type not the 'lift heavy objects' type), a deer leapt out of the verge in front of me and shot off into a wood where it started to bark with alarm. Then a double treat, both a deer and my first sighting of an elk. The deer took off as the previous one had, but the elk stood motionless. The thing that struck me was its height; it was about the size of a large horse. Unfortunately, she was too far away to take a good photo. When she did move it was with both speed and grace, covering the ground quickly, but with no obvious effort. To complete the morning's safari, a red squirrel ran across the road about 20 m in front of me.

Like yesterday, today I would be taking a couple of ferries. The first from Horn to Andalsvågen, 20 minutes, and the second from Forvika to Tjøtta, an hour.

Yesterday's ferry at Vennesund.

Ferry at Horn going to the Vega Archipelago.

This area of Norway is sparsely populated: small industries and agriculture are the mainstays of the local economy with some tourism. However, most tourists are self-contained in their own RVs. There are campsites, but hardly any hotels. So, the need for public transport, which is good (I see many empty buses on the roads), is minimal. Strange that I should see two bus shelters side by side, maybe the supply has exceeded the demand, or who knows what pressures are placed on the system during the 'rush hour'.

Perhaps some over-provision of bus shelters here.

The second ferry to Tjøtta was an hour of visual feasting on grand views. The sun had come out and the light playing on the remaining mist was impressive.

Under the upper jaws of the ferry's bows.

A Life Appreciated

Having disembarked from the second ferry and back on road 17 up to Sandnessjøen, there is a remarkable granite escarpment that runs for several miles. A climber's paradise! It was near here that I saw this little girl.

"Mummy, Daddy, when I grow up, I want to do something stupid, like cycle from Gibraltar to Nordkapp".

Nearing Sandnessjøen at the end of another 100+ km day, I saw the Seven Sisters mountains.

Today has been a particularly good cycling day and the forecast, although the wind is from the north, does not include any rain.

July 13th, a Friday. What a great day this was, nearly perfect weather apart from the flies going up the long hill near Longset. Not even looking across the short distance of water that separated me from my destination and requiring a near-complete circle of several miles around Sørfjorden could dampen the spirits. Why would my spirits be dampened when it was the journey and not the destination that provided the enjoyment? Two long tunnels brought me ever closer to the Arctic Circle. Having stopped at a museum that stood in splendid isolation with the sole intention of loading up with caffeine and continuing my way to enjoy just being on a bike in ideal conditions, an instantly recognisable Scottish accent said 'Hello'. Brian and I were the only two people in a massively high-ceilinged foyer that doubled as a café and a museum. He, like me, was on a coffee mission. We chatted for a while, then he left. We both intended to catch the next ferry from Kilboghamn to Jektvik. So, with a loose arrangement to perhaps meeting up on the slightly longer than usual crossing, we were not sure if we would see each other again. We both stopped at separate times at a shop to collect provisions and fortunately, we again met up on the ferry. Brian kindly bought me a pint as we celebrated crossing the Arctic Circle. That night we camped beside a small fjord.

Daily Blog: Across the Arctic Circle this afternoon. July 13th
Fridays that fall on the 13th of the month are said by some to be unlucky days. Nothing could be further from the truth today. It has been a long day with so much variety and a chance meeting with Brian, a recently retired GP from Glasgow.

The event of the day rightfully goes to crossing the Arctic Circle. Brian and I had caught the 6.25 pm ferry from Kilboghamn to Jektvik. The captain kindly advised passengers that if we looked to starboard, we would see the Globe statue that marks the exact point at which the Arctic Circle circumnavigates the world.

The day had started with crossing the Helgelandsbrua, a spectacular bridge just NE of Sandnessjøen.

We cross the Arctic Circle.

The route today changed direction faster than a fly avoids being swatted, many of which I became acquainted with when climbing a particularly long hill. Passing motorists must have wondered why this lone-cyclist was waving a buff so vigorously at them. I was not – it was a failed endeavour to keep scores of flies off me whilst cycling up the hill. Why they should be so persistent on this particular hill was a mystery.

Before arriving at the hill there had been one ferry crossing. The hill was 9% up and 9% down. The down was enjoyable, at 80 km/h, my chin was on the handlebar and I was sitting on the crossbar. It was then that the bike began to wobble, as the panniers had an adverse effect on the bike's aerodynamics. A real thrill, but I was never going to get up to 100 km/h.

Having viewed the road around the fjord from the top of the hill, I knew that many km had to be cycled just to put me on the north side of the fjord. I rode east for some distance then around the head of the fjord and back west into a brisk headwind before diving into another tunnel. Inside it was very cool, but mercilessly out of the wind. I enjoyed the experience, which is just as well because there are numerous tunnels on the route ahead.

The view once having fought off the flies during the climb.

Hot, bitten by mosquitoes, pestered by flies, target practice for RV drivers, another hill never to be recycled, is completed.

Looking across and up the fjord to the road I'd be cycling from right to left an hour later, retracing my tracks, but on the opposite bank.

Norwegian roads and tunnels cannot be separated. This tunnel is prone to exhaust fumes.

Now when I say 'tunnels', these are not like the Blackwall tunnel near London. These were two or three km long. Vehicles are noisy when they pass through. However, not as loud as I had expected. During the times when I was the only tunnel inhabitant, I practised my best Placido Domingo operatic repertoire, by best I mean least awful.

Exiting the second long tunnel which had been driven through a granite mountain, there was a short rest from the wind in the lee of this impressive rock.

The granite hill through which the tunnel passes.

I pulled into a museum café for a strong coffee and a cake. It was here that Brian approached me. As we chatted for a while, we both shared a surprise at not encountering any other UK citizens. Brian had cycled up from Bergen and is going to Nordkapp. He is travelling remarkably lightly considering he is also wild camping. We decided to aim to catch the same ferry from Kliboghamn. After the crossing, we agreed that it would be a good idea to wild camp together this evening.

Brian and I find an ideal site.

Immediately the following morning, we were into two tunnels, followed by a short ferry to Halsa where we took the 'lesser trodden road' to avoid a long tunnel. The Svartisentunnelen goes beneath the small mountain of Glomssteet which is 1,129 m ASL. It runs from Kilvika to Glomfjord and was opened in 1986. At 7,624 m long it is the 12th longest tunnel of over 900 in Norway. The longest is a phenomenal 25.5 km long, completed in 2000, and goes between Lærdal and Aurland. We again travelled nearly full circle to reach Saura, hugging the coast to our left round to Vassdalsvik, where we caught another ferry squeezing between the mainland and the island of Messøya into Ørnes. As the 630 road had provided the main artery for me through Spain many weeks previously, so the 17 was in Norway. The main difference was that the 630 had run north/south via a line drawn by a ruler. The 17 road hugged the Norwegian coast. A coastline eroded and moulded by millennia. When checking my Garmin for distances, the initial calculation may say 5 km, then the route would compute to perhaps 50 km.

The following day Brian and I meet Paul on the road to Skaugvoll and later all three of us camped on a site offering a shower, a meal, and beer. A Welsh/Kiwi, a Glaswegian, and a Londoner turned Yorkshireman, a most unlikely trio.

Daily Blog: Life north of the Arctic Circle. July 14th

Life beside fjords.

Life north of the Arctic Circle is very much the same as immediately south. The wind had dropped, it was cool and heavily clouded, the day was ideal for cycling.

We also met up with Paul from New Zealand. Raised in Wrexham in North Wales, he is also cycling to Nordkapp. Having had a spinal fusion operation, he is cycling at a more leisurely pace.

Brian and I continued in a northerly direction. Actually, that is not correct, we cycled east, north, east, west, and north through two tunnels, (the Silatunnelen at 2,870 m and the Storvikskartunnelen at 3,200 m) and used two ferries. We avoided the Svartisentunnelen which is 7,624 m where no cycles are permitted, by using the coastal road via Saura and a ferry over to Ørnes. A further tunnel saw us to an official campsite beyond Oppsal, where a shower was very welcome. We are now only 84 km from Bodø and catching the five-hour ferry to the Lofoten Islands.

Left: I stopped to chat with this young man who was taking dog walking to the extreme, having walked from Germany. He had left home several weeks previously saying, 'Ich nehme den Hund einfach fur einen Spaziergang.'

Right: A memorial to the Norwegian and English submarine crew who all drowned having hit a Nazi mine just off this coast.

Arguably the most futuristic public convenience in Norway.

Brian outside one of several tunnels we have dived into.

July 15th and Paul had opted to stay longer at the campsite and, as the day wore on, I could see that Brian wanted to cycle faster than me. I was also conscious that yet again I was making faster progress than I had planned and at this rate would be in Nordkapp a week early. Anne and I had booked a return trip from Tromsø to Bergen with the Hurtigruten ferry company. Brian and I said cheerio, not knowing at that time we would see each other in Honningsvåg at the end of our journey and again in Glasgow months later. The acceptance of choosing whether to cycle with someone and when to leave them is unspoken. There is no animosity, only flexibility and from that there is companionship.

Brian was on a road bike, travelling light. He reminded me of David, who had cycled with me through some of France earlier on this trip, coincidentally another doctor, (who needs an expedition doctor when they can be cycling companions?). Both had the lightest of gear and the smallest of tents and have body frames of road cyclists, creating less wind resistance as they cut through the air. At the other end of the spectrum, you have an ex-rugby player as the 'bloke on a bike', (albeit old and decrepit), with two panniers and a tent mimicking the aerodynamics of a house brick being pushed through treacle.

Daily Blog: The world's strongest tidal current. July 15th

Brian decided that he was hampering the progress of an old git on a heavily laden cycle. He decided to leave early this morning so I could catch him up on the way to Bodø. Oh! I have got that slightly wrong. For the past two days, Brian has been waiting for me to catch up at the crest of each hill. His time scales are different from mine and whilst he is in no rush, I am again a day ahead of my schedule and in danger of becoming even more so. Hence, I am going to slow down a little.

Brian, it was great to ride with you over the past few days. When you pass through West Yorkshire and have time for a ride, it would be good to show you a few of the Yorkshire hills. We have a particularly engaging circuit called the Hell of the Worth.

We had already said cheerio to Paul at the campsite, so I continued on my own and headed up the hill and into three tunnels, Skaugvoll at 240 m. Vindvik at 980 m. and Sundsfjord at 750 m. The fjords were like mirrors creating perfect reflections. Traditional fishing boats looked serene in the still water.

Tunnels are all part of the experience.

Some 50 km later another bridge took highway 17 over something special at Saltstraumen, a maelstrom running between Saltenfjorden and Skjerstadfjorden. Under the bridge through the strait runs the world's strongest tidal current. Over 6 hours during the tidal changes, up to 400 million cubic metres of seawater push through the shallow sound travelling up to 37 km/h!

Saltstraumen, where the fish are enormous and the currents treacherous.

Saltstraumen is also one of the world's best cold-water diving sites. The fishing is beyond excellent, with pollock, cod, halibut, and wolffish frequently being caught. The world's largest line-caught pollock was landed here, weighing 22.7 kg.

Long distance cycling has the effect of distilling life down to basics. You are more able to appreciate and enjoy your surroundings without the clatter and demands that so often come with modern living. You need to drink and eat, you need

to keep warm(ish), you need to avoid getting lost and you need to be able to identify risk and danger. Flexibility and tolerance also come in useful. But returning to the subject of risk.

Risk concerns perception. A good start point is to be clear about what is a risk and what is a hazard. A hazard is something, anything, that may cause harm. It is the word 'may' that is critical. That ability to cause harm ranges from minute to absolute certainty. So, it is not particularly helpful to say something is just hazardous unless it is quantified. What one person believes through their perception that has been arrived at via their life's experiences, as dangerous, may in no way merit any recognition of being hazardous in another's. We need to add risk to that hazard. A risk is a chance of the hazard causing harm. Whether you are a cave diver or an ardent Saturday shopper or anyone between, you will face hazards and risks. People have challenged me regarding the safety of rock climbing and even more so of high altitude climbing. It can be argued that when taking a known risk in a hazardous situation you are more focussed, acutely aware of the consequences, and put measures in place to manage the scenario, note, not necessarily being able to minimise that risk. Complacency and repetition are killers. From crossing a road to failing to clip in before abseiling down a rock face or cycling away from a kerb without first looking behind you, are good examples. The society we live in today is becoming ever risk-averse, driven in part by the threat of litigation and the proliferation of a 'blame culture'. We see it everywhere, from overuse of traffic control measures that are deemed necessary when a small hole has been made on a wide pavement, to notices on country footpaths proclaiming care is needed as the ground may be uneven. The belief that an individual is responsible for their own safety is fast being bred out of us. Take the Coronavirus pandemic, as terrible as it is, some require rules to address all scenarios, even though the situation is dynamic. Where has self-reliance, pragmatism, and common sense emigrated to? Here, I refer to control of the virus and not the desperate financial hits that so many companies have endured.

So, some shy from risk and some utilise it to empower. It removes you from your comfort zone, you become bolder. The larger the risk, the larger the potential gain and loss. When you take a risk, you will always try harder than if no risk were present. When you take a risk, you know what the objective is, and you plan with realism and precision. Whether I am climbing on the Matterhorn or Denali or cycling down the Col du Tourmalet or Mont Ventoux, I am constantly taking calculated risks. Over time self-belief and confidence improves. Yes, on that journey there will be mishaps. I have reluctantly donated plenty of my skin to road surfaces, but to know your limitations, you need to visit the boundaries of your abilities and those boundaries can only be expanded by a commitment to improvement.

There is another dimension to risk. Largely unmanageable risk. I say 'largely' because all risk can be managed to a point, but some to little effect. Whether it is cycling in torrential rain on a busy lorry-laden road in Spain, watching an avalanche descend a mountain with an increasing awareness that life for you is about to end, or knowing that if you take a fall when climbing and a piece of 'protection' pops, you are going airborne. Some may say, why cycle, why climb? A response could be, why do anything that jeopardises your safety before you pass from this world?

When I first read Andrew Sykes's book, *Spain to Norway on a bike called Reggie* and started to read more about various routes, it was apparent that some cyclists had had safety concerns regarding the numerous Norwegian tunnels that need to be cycled through. Some found them at best unnerving and at worst frightening. I was not indifferent and was fully aware of the potential for disaster. Planning, as always, plays an important part in adventure and I knew that there had been relatively few accidents in tunnels involving cyclists and vehicles. That was not to say the non-existent 'Law of Averages', more probability, would not strike and I would be flattened under a truck that had to use my road space to avoid an oncoming vehicle. Although the risk associated with these tunnels can be managed to a point, ultimately the cyclist is largely reliant on the competency of other road users. For cyclists, this is the norm. However, tourists in tunnels that go on for miles do heighten the risk, and the consequences are considerable. Many of the tunnels in Norway have a warning system to other road users that cyclists are in the tunnel. All the cyclist must do is remember to press the button that activates the system before entering. Rear and front lights on the bike are a must. Tunnel lighting can range from excellent to near non-existent and Hi-viz clothing is a plus. The noise created by traffic in the tunnel is incredible. One vehicle can sound like a train passing at full speed through a railway station and a posse of motorcycles sounds as though you are standing next to a fighter jet when it takes off. Knowing this and the anticipated volume of traffic, the length of the tunnel, whether it is possible (or wise) to ride on the narrow-raised sidewalk, being aware that if the extraction fans are not working, the risk of carbon monoxide is increased, if there are emergency laybys in the tunnel, all helps to manage the risk and instil confidence.

There are those who say 'risk-takers are fools'. Let us not forget that we are all risk-takers, it is just the degree of risk. Surely, if by taking risks that are managed through knowledge and ability, we become more self-confident and braver, we are more fulfilled and happier. To quote Robert Mads Anderson from his book *Nine Lives*, 'I was not cheating death; I was controlling it. And in the process getting the best out of life.'

FACT FACTORY – TUNNELS: Norway has around 900 road tunnels. It is in the interest of all who use these tunnels to be aware of the risk, particularly as the vulnerability of the user becomes greater, like us cyclists. A survey of 587 of these tunnels covering five years found that there had been 26 fatalities, 99 serious injuries, and 620 slight injuries. No injury accidents were reported for 388 of these 587 tunnels. With these figures covering all vehicles that used the tunnels, the probability of a cyclist being involved in an accident is slight.

CHAPTER TWENTY-FIVE
Lofoten is Undefinably Unique

'Sometimes I saw what men have only dreamed of seeing.' Arthur Rimbaud

So, several days of cycling along 'The World's Most Beautiful Journey' had nurtured an inner calm in me. Why are we so often drawn into maelstroms of frantic activities to achieve aims and objectives that have questionable benefits? Some matters do require urgency; however, under that guise, ambition and personal agendas are often falsely injected.

I was approaching Bodø and a ferry that would take me across the Vestfjorden and on to the Lofoten Islands. Renowned for their beauty, I was certainly looking forward to continuing this remarkable journey.

A beautiful camp, but the reality is never far away as I silently heard youths dealing drugs in the isolated car park near me.

Although there are many bridges and tunnels, some of considerable length and depth, that link islands and landmasses to each other, there are still fjords that need to be cycled around. There were occasions when 300 degrees of the compass were travelled to arrive in a place two hours later that would have taken a rowing boat fifteen minutes to cross the water. One of these detours was from Saltstraumen to Bodø. Saltstraumen has a genuine claim on a world record. It has the world's strongest tidal current and although I mention the figures in the blog, it is worth doing so again as it is that impressive. Every six hours 400 million cubic metres of water flow through a three kilometre-long and 150 m-wide strait between Saltenfjorden and Skjerstadfjorden at a speed of up to 20 knots: for us landlubbers that is 37 km/h. Looking down from the bridge above the silent brooding power was all too obvious.

I was not sure what was to greet me on arriving on Lofoten and, knowing I needed to charge up my gadgets, I rode into a deserted and wet Bodø. I found a warm café near the ferry port. This was to become one of those occasions when having too much time makes you late. Call it the 'Airport Waiting Lounge Syndrome', 'AWLS'. The afternoon had turned to rain, and my right knee had been troubling me, an injury that has never fully recovered from a climbing accident several years previous, and although I only had a couple of weeks of cycling until arriving in Nordkapp, the condition of the knee was paramount to finishing the ride. My upbeat mood had evaporated a little so, unknowingly, a young lady called Catherine lifted my spirits with her enthusiastic chatter. She was a waitress in the coffee bar. The blog tells the story. My attempt at shortening my route and going to Stamsund, a compromise to appease my knee, was thankfully thwarted. And the reference to Catherine wanting to take her, as yet unborn children up Kilimanjaro came only from her enthusiasm for life, rekindling mine as she asked me about climbing mountains around the world. The ferry across to Sørvågen left in thirty minutes from us looking at the timetable. Certainly, an AWLS moment as I raced across to the terminal, with only a slight limp as I walked up into the cargo area of the ship. The five-hour crossing was relaxing, the meal onboard expensive and I had an opportunity to be a surrogate grandad for a few hours.

Arriving on the island was not the auspicious event I had anticipated. The sea crossing had been uneventful, the weather cold and dank and as I cycled away from the small terminal it was drizzling.

Now some places in the world should be visited solely because of the name they have. One such place would be Llanfairpwllgwyng yllgogerychwyrndrobwllllantysiliogogogoch. This is the name of a village on the island of Anglesey in North Wales and is the longest place name in the UK and the second in the world after a village on North Island, New Zealand. Translated from Welsh into English it means, 'St Mary's Church in the hollow of the white hazel near the rapid whirlpool and the church of St Tysilo of the red cave.' Understandably, Welsh speakers have the advantage of being able to pronounce this 'description'. As a youngster, I was once the proud owner of a railway platform ticket that was 150 mm long to accommodate the word!

To return to Norway. There is a small hamlet at the southern end of the Lofoten Islands, beyond where the E10 road terminates, that also has an unusual name: Å. Yes, this quintessential northern Norwegian village with its ochre-painted buildings with sky blue and white window frames is the village of Å. A village that has the shortest name in the world. Unspoiled, with around 1,000 inhabitants that source their income from smoked cod and tourists. Curiosity required me to visit, but it was late as I left the ferry and my idea of a treat at the campsite of a shower was doomed as large 'Campsite Full' signs appeared. As I left the harbour at Moskenes and cycled up the hill I started to look for a place to camp for the night.

FACT FACTORY: Pronounced 'AWE', Å is the last letter of the Norwegian alphabet and is correctly written with a small 'o' above the A. Having a vowel as the last letter in a language that uses Latin is exceedingly rare.

The tradition of air-drying cod continues from the days before freezers and represents a massive export for Norway. In northern Norway, cod is dried from February to March. To achieve the best results the correct combination of wind, sun and rain are needed. This practice was not the sole domain of the Norwegians, the process has been used in Newfoundland, Faroe Islands, and Iceland for over 500 years. We all know that an army marches on its stomach;

it would be accurate to say that the Vikings sailed on klippfisk, which is cod fish that has been sliced open, salted and air dried.

Arriving at the e10 junction I decided to turn north and abandoned the idea of visiting Å. It was a decision, a split decision taken at that road junction that I would regret. Had I not come on this journey to see as much as possible? It was not as if I was short on time, I had the time to visit but chose not to. It was certainly 'Å tråkke i salaten', as they say in Norway. I had 'stepped in the salad, made a faux pas! Was Lofoten going to be that enthralling experience promised? I found a grassy, but sodden shelf of land off to the right of the road just as one of the many road tunnels started. The sea could be heard beneath. I pitched the tent and climbed in to eat my evening meal. The drizzle developed into rain and became heavy during the night. On and on it rained. I awoke several times, and on each occasion, it was raining hard. In the morning it was still hammering down. I ate breakfast and felt dismal. Should I pack up a sodden tent, getting soaked within minutes, and cycle on north into the wind and 'admire' the views, or sulk in my damp bivvy tent? The rain eased at noon and an hour later, having cycled the old road around the cliff's edge to avoid the tunnel, the sun had dried my clothes and the long night was a fading memory with the true beauty of the Lofoten islands opening around me. Had the rain not been so hard and persistent I probably would have visited A and not been (to coin another Norwegian phrase) 'Å være født bak en brunost', 'To be born behind the brown cheese'. Stupid!

The village of Hamnoy coated in sea mist.

The sun was shy in showing itself as I cycled, looking from left to right and absorbing the beauty around me, travelling through three tunnels that cut their way into mountains and burrowed beneath the sea. I arrived in Leknes. Even in sunless light, this town looked impressive. Photographs adorn travel websites showing how stunning the visual impact is when the sun is out. I weaved my way around numerous recreational vehicles (RVs), many parked at random, others being driven slowly whilst hunting out parking spaces. The joys and benefits of cycling. After stocking up at the local supermarket I avoided the crowds and headed off on the quieter 817 that travels a southern route, hugging the coast to Sundklakk. The route that passed through Valberg was superb. The evening sunlight was glowing from behind me and was being reflected from the high sea cliffs. With so few cyclists seen for days, two younger men rode past me on road bikes, one pulling a small, wheeled trailer. This was the end of a special day. A rapid and well-practised camp was made beside a silage bale whilst being viciously attacked by mosquitoes, desperate for my blood. Wearing a peaked cap under the protective head net, although winning no fashion awards, is effective. This was perhaps the worst onslaught camp on the shore of Hognfjorden. My two cans of Frydenlund IPA beer drew a satisfying line under a perfect day.

The beauty of Lofoten.

Daily Blog: Lofoten is undefinably unique. July 16th

Yesterday cycling into Bodø on a Sunday afternoon I felt like Clint Eastwood riding into the deserted town in that excellent old film, 'High Plains Drifter'.

Although heavy cloud had persisted for several days it had until now remained dry. This was to change.

Having cycled up and down Bodø's deserted high street save for one solitary craftsman working on a shop front, I found the only sign of life in a café where Catherine worked. We initially talked about exactly what a flat white coffee is. I stayed safe and had an excellent cappuccino. Having spent several hours there, she approached me and started to ask about my trip and enthused about the Lofoten Islands, where she grew up. I had decided that because of my right knee again giving me 'jip', I would catch the ferry to Stamsund and not Moskenes. Moskenes is nearly at the furthest southwest point of Lofoten, and I would miss out on cycling 80 km, including the sea tunnel at Napp, which is 1,780 m long and has an 8% gradient down into it and up out of it. This would give my knee a much-needed rest. Catherine looked at the timetables. There was no information for the Stamsund ferry, so we presumed it was full, this being the school holiday time. There was, however, information on the Moskenes ferry. It departed in 30 minutes, so a hasty farewell to the extremely helpful Catherine, (and when your children are older, you will climb Kilimanjaro) and off onto the largest ferry yet for the three-hour trip for a reasonable £22. Onboard the usual limited and expensive food was available, the best value being beef burger and chips at another £22. I slept a little before being invited to become part of three young children's game of hide and seek. Once a grandad, always a grandad.

I rode off the ship at 10 pm and found a wild camp spot within 2 km overlooking a damp and gloomy sea. Where it rained throughout the night.

Waking this morning to the sound of heavy rain on the tent, a difficult decision was made to stay put. My travel advisor and internet browser (long-suffering wife) concurred that the rain would stop at noon. The last time I stayed in a tent for such a time was when a friend and I were trapped by a storm at Camp Two on Khan Tengri, a mountain that sits on the borders of Kazakhstan and Kyrgyzstan, which incidentally was when I injured my knee. The rain stopped at noon precisely. I had almost packed up by then, so was off by 12.15 pm.

Immediately, although still very much overcast, it was evident that Lofoten was a special place and as the weather improved its full beauty was revealed. There is a uniqueness about the place that is difficult to identify. The mountains are sharp, steep-sided, and green with plant growth. A little like the Mount Kenya region approaching Batian and Nelion, but that is where the similarity ends. The white and red timber buildings, the fish drying racks, with just the wind-dried heads of cod hanging from them. The traditional fishing boats floating on the crystal-clear seawater, all go to make a wonderful landscape.

Fish cod heads remain after the harvest.

I made good use of the old roads, now designated cycleways, to bypass the first three tunnels, including Hamnøytunnelen at 1.5 km long. However, there was no bypassing a tunnel that went under the sea. The Nappstraumtunnelen is 1,780 m long. You descend into it and ascend out of it. On the left side was a footpath which made the experience almost enjoyable. The vehicles were loud but passing under the extractor units was louder. The light was minimal, so I did not see what I did hear to be glass under the front wheel. A puncture in the tunnel would not be very pleasant. Fortunately, both tyres remained inflated.

Emerging from the tunnel I realised how wet and filthy both I and the bike were. Some cleaning of both is required.

Having bought provisions in Leknes, I turned off the E10 onto the 815 to commence a most enjoyable ride. It was mid-evening and most of the traffic had disappeared. With the sun still high in the sky, it was both peaceful and beautiful with the evening light on the calm waters and mountains.

Beautiful white sandy beaches with a plastic pink flamingo?!

I am pleased that the ferry to Stamsund was not available last night. And of my knee, well we will have to see how it copes, but with only 12 more cycling days to Nordkapp, I am not about to allow it to dictate.

So, a wet and dreary morning developed into a special day. I had to stop myself from constantly getting off the bike to take yet another photograph. I can only include a handful here. Hopefully, it is sufficient to give you the flavour of Lofoten.

Tonight, I am camped beside a stack of white plastic silage sacks and my hosts are scores of midges. Finding a piece of land dry enough for the tent was difficult. So, choices were limited.

FACT FACTORY: The Lofoten Islands, at 190 km long this archipelago of small fishing villages lies 200 km north of the Arctic Circle, with a backdrop of ancient granite rocks dating back millions of years. Enjoying the 'midnight sun' from June until late July, the 4,000 residents of Svolvær, the main town, can be inundated with holidaymakers, primarily in campervans from the mainland via the Bodø ferry during the summer months.

The days were losing their identity, they were all good. Merging together it was difficult to sometimes remember what was seen and experienced when and where.

The roads were empty. Where had all the RVs gone? I stopped for a coffee at an impressive hotel at the head of a fjord. Fully glazed to the high ceilings to make the most of the view, the place was deserted. I sat on reindeer skins draped over a leather sofa. Timber chairs, roughly hewn from local trees, were placed under the ubiquitous elk antlers that hung on the walls. Strangely I had the feeling from the waitress that I was perhaps not their usual type of customer, as she returned to vacuuming the floor. This was a posh hotel after all and a great place to view the Northern Lights.

Although the 82 road had been unexpectedly quiet, I was approaching

Andenes, which was a terminal for a longer ferry crossing and had the capacity for many vehicles. Anyway, why would you choose a busier road in preference to a peaceful alternative? Taking the road to Bø and Nøss, I headed to Bleik where an enormous slice of chocolate cake and a seriously strong coffee were waiting for me. I passed a concrete angular building with mirrors covering its walls that reflected the surrounding landscape. Isolated and sandwiched between the road and sea I was curious and had to stop to see what it was. Now, public toilets are not renowned for their architecture or aesthetic qualities, but this is exactly what it was. It drew the eye to it and not away from it and was not to be the only public convenience of interest on this Norwegian part of the journey.

That night I camped at Andenes official campsite. Not that I was aware of any other campers, with my tent on the grass a metre or so from a beautiful beach. I had watched the sunset over the Norwegian sea. Iceland lay southwest and the Greenland Sea to the northwest. The sun had been warm, and a gentle onshore breeze had kept the mosquitoes away. I fell asleep to the sounds of lapping water.

Paradise camping on Lofoten.

Pedalling fast, not to catch the 8.45 am ferry the next morning, but to arrive at some shelter before the dark grey clouds burst. I and a few other cyclists arrived on the large concrete apron and looked for some shelter from the rain that had started to fall. There was none, only a locked hut. Four cyclists sheltering on the lee side of a public toilet that was also locked trying to keep dry has a humorous side, although the humour did not reveal itself until we were on the warm ferry.

Crossing from the island of Andøya to Senja, a 40 km stretch of water, allowed me to charge my power pack, phone, and Garmin. Off the ferry across another bridge and into the Ballesvikskar tunnel on the 862 before climbing a steep hill. This road meandered across the palm of a 'six-fingered' peninsular. The island of Senja, like all the Lofoten Islands, has a bedrock of granite that is one and a half billion years old. Over the last two million years there have been over 40 ice ages, all of which have carved and moulded these islands into the stunning scenery we enjoy today.

Fortunately, the weather stayed dry long enough to see some of its features before the rain set in. The Senja Troll attraction boasted the largest troll statue in the world and many others besides. This family-run attraction had humour oozing from it and was connected to the Hulderheimen cultural centre. Even the owner's children dressed as trolls. There was also a cosy café with plenty of troll dolls for sale should you wish to own one. Sadly, on March 28th 2019 a fire broke out and destroyed this quirky entertaining attraction. Soon after leaving the trolls, the rain started.

July 17th and another day of pure enjoyment. The scenery, as improbable as it seemed, surpassed itself again, with mountains always in view, blue skies with white clouds passing over crystal clear water and deserted white sandy beaches. I took the ferry across to Melbu and continued my fantasy journey to Sortland, crossing two more bridges before setting up camp.

Daily Bog: Bridges, boats and bus shelters. July 17th
Another wonderful day, clear skies with a rising wind late afternoon. Today was very much about cycling over a series of stunning bridges.

Some have narrow pavements with high kerbs. My cycle is classified as a 'wide load', although some long-distance cyclists ride bikes that are seemingly as wide as they are long. This makes negotiating the bridges, which are narrow for two-way traffic, difficult. With the crosswinds and little margin for error, concentration is paramount. To be blown off the pavement at the wrong time would not be healthy.

I rode around 130 km today and having arrived in Sortland near the end of the day's ride saw this navy ship tied up beside the filling station.

Riding into Sortland a chance glance to my left revealed a fantastic and unique bus shelter. It was just like a mini sitting room, perfect and done with such charm.

All this with a backdrop of continuing mountains, crystal clear water, and an abundance of wildflowers, in air that is void of any pollution.

And my home for the night- simply perfect.

This beautiful creature lived at The Senja Troll attraction.

Trolls abound.

The sons of the owners dressed as trolls.

Note: Sadly, this family business suffered a devastating fire and I understand that it has now closed.

Having dried from the early morning soaking on Lofoten, we left the ferry, and all headed off north through the new tunnel south of Ballesvika on the 86 and onto the 862 just before Håverjorda. Here an 8% climb started and continued until it entered another tunnel.

Overlooking the village of Bergsbotn is a 44 m-long platform of sculptured beauty. I was able to see this just before the heavens opened on a fast descent that turned each droplet of water into a near skin-penetrating needle.

After a short break, the rain returned with a musical accompaniment of thunder and an occasional flash of lightning. It was particularly heavy and loud on the second long and steep hill. Would the 'old git' be found by the roadside having been struck by lightning, with scorched tyres and curly hair?

The rain did have a break, enough to trick me into delaying and allowing me a dry look at the Tungeneset rest area. A walkway made of Siberian larch permits uninterrupted viewing of the razor-edged Okshornan peaks, known as The Devil's Jaw, when the cloud base is high enough.

Another example of how architectural design can complement natural beauty.

Wet through. I surrendered to a second consecutive official campsite, where a hot shower was very much appreciated. The area had also been home to this massive elk, before a macho game hunter decided to shoot it.

Daily Blog: In the land of the midnight sun. July 18th

I am sitting beside my tent overlooking a golden sandy beach a few metres from me. Many small outcrops of rock protrude from a quiet sea. A shaft of light reflected from the sun runs across the water and cuts through the wildflowers next to me. With a gentle onshore breeze, I close my eyes and not for the first time realise how fortunate I am. On the right, a dark jagged line cuts the horizon. The high rock reminds me of the Alps without the altitude. I have just had an evening meal of creme fraiche potetsalat, chicken, cheese and biscuits and a beer.

The view from my tent.

Another day of around 100 km and another stunning one. The landscape had changed from Melbu and continued to be more open with the mountains less dramatic, but no means less impressive, as I rode towards Sortland. From Sortland, I took the 82, through extensive road works and on northwards to the island of Andøya, where I took the longer west route. The scenery was stunning.

Another architectural masterpiece for a public convenience. The mirrored toilet.

Today developed into a day of variety, so much happened. Here is a selection of some events. The bridge over the sea from Dragnes to Risøyhamn had the steepest ramped access to its apex to date. Beautifully engineered, the experience of cycling up it was further enhanced by one of the Hurtigruten ships setting 'sail' and going under the bridge, with many onboard waving. It was made all the better for knowing that in a few weeks' time Anne and I will be going under the same bridge on a Hurtigruten ship. I wonder whether an old git with a white beard on a cycle will be waving from it.

A Hurtigruten ship, an integral part of Norwegian coastal infrastructure.

From Bø, yes that is a place and takes twice as long to write as Å, near Moskenes, I did not want the day's ride to finish. The museum at Risøyhamn had been impressive, where I met up with two brothers on their annual cycle trip from southern Norway.

Bleik, with traditionally painted timber houses.

Arriving at the pretty little town of Bleik I was unexplainably drawn into a café supermarket. This shop was something out of the ordinary. The calories on offer exceeded those in Willy Wonka's Chocolate Factory. The cheesecake was exceedingly good and possibly better than Mr Kipling could make. Similarly, the coffee was good, and refills were encouraged. This 'necessary' delay resulted in me arriving at the Space Centre Aurora too late in the day to do it justice.

Space Centre at Aurora.

Tomorrow I take the ferry to Gryllefjord on the island of Senja. Again, I am a couple of days ahead of schedule, so Anne has booked me into a hotel in Tromsø for two nights. This will be an opportunity to clean and service the bike and deep clean its rider, before setting off for the final week of this adventure.

Daily Blog: A very WET Senja island. July 19th

The night was windy, very windy, some tents were misshapen by this morning. Having wrestled the tent into its bag and not lost anything to the wind, it was an early start to get to the ferry at Andenes. The first downpour arrived as I left the campsite. So, I circled about and took shelter in the campsite common room. The second deluge occurred after I had arrived at the terminal. Unbelievably, there was no shelter. This resulted in several foot passengers and cyclists sheltering under the eaves of the public convenience: very inconvenient. It was not one of these impressively designed loos either, just a bog-standard one.

The anticipated rough crossing to Gryllefjord did not happen. When we embarked there were about ten cyclists, the two Norwegian brothers, another Norwegian about to move to Manchester in the UK, and a Dutchman amongst others.

Arriving at an impressively designed viewing platform ramped out into thin air, the middle of three sections raised like a wave yet to break surf, I stood looking down the length of the fjord. Descending the hill that followed, the rain arrived in earnest accompanied by thunder and lightning. It is common knowledge that being on a mountain in such weather is not 'best practice'. The higher and more exposed you are, the greater the risk of being struck by lightning. I had descended the hill some way but was very much in the open in torrential rain and was soon soaked to the skin. There was no clothing that could hold out against this deluge. It would be a wet and uncomfortable night and my right knee was now giving me an increasing amount of pain. Fortunately, I had idly looked to my left. A campsite, it was a campsite, I am sure it was. I circled and in a few minutes was inside a log cabin booking in for the night. I sat at one of the few tables in the reception/café area for the next hour, slowly removing the soaking layers of outer clothes as I gradually warmed up under the watchful eyes of the huge head of an elk supporting his antlers. On one wall a complete set of commemorative plates of all the Hurtigruten ships hung, from Dronning Maud to Finnmarken and Kong Harald. As I left, I apologised to the receptionist for leaving a pool of rainwater beneath the table.

Putting up my small tent in the rain and strong wind would not have normally been a problem, I have put tents up high on exposed mountains in strong winds, but my knee was now dictating my movements.

I would have liked to have caught the ferry from Botnhamn to the island of Kvaløya and arrive in Tromsø from the west. Instead, I caught the 8.00 am Friday express from Lysnes, just! With numerous small piers and no signage, I had taken several wrong tracks before finding the unmarked jetty. I hoped that the two nights rest in Tromsø would suit my knee and enable me to arrive in

Nordkapp. The ferry was impressive, fast, and smooth with luxury seats. The weather outside was foul but in the company of Ryan, who I mention in the blog, it remained unnoticed.

CHAPTER TWENTY-SIX
Opened My Final Map Today

'Ride as much or as little, as long or as short as you feel. But ride.' Eddy Merckx

I would be returning to Tromsø on a Hurtigruten ferry from Honningsvåg and Anne would be flying in for a day before we set off south to Bergen. So, a day spent looking around the city would, like Oslo, be beneficial.

The sun was out as I cycled and strolled around Norway's eighth-largest municipality, which enjoys a relaxing atmosphere, resting my knee as best I could. So many things to see.

The Arctic Cathedral. This modernistic A- framed building completed in 1965, was designed by Jan Inge Hovig. It commands a significantly prominent position across the Tromsøysund Strait and is accessed by the city's longest bridge. The A- frames resemble the sails of sailing ships and there are massive stained-glass windows designed by the artist Victor Sparre, behind an equally impressive crucifix that is lit at night, after the setting arctic light that cascades through has disappeared. Late night concerts are held for those who visit the city on the cruise ships.

Tromsø Cathedral. The city's other cathedral. Famous for being Norway's only timber cathedral, it was built in the Gothic Revival style, it stands in the centre of the city and is the northernmost Protestant cathedral in the world. Again, stained glass is a prominent feature. The other remarkable feature is the wooden altar which is a copy of Tidemand's stunning Resurrection.

Elverhøy church. This church did occupy the site where Tromsø Cathedral now stands. The beautiful redwood structure was built in 1803 and has been dismantled on two occasions, once in 1861 and then a century later. Again, it has ornate carving to the altar, pulpit, and a beautiful wooden carved Madonna. Whether you are religious or not, all three buildings cannot fail to impress.

The Polar Museum. Tromsø is more than 130 km north of the Arctic Circle. Not surprisingly it has become known as 'The Gateway to the Arctic'. This museum shows the history from the first settlers to the whaling industry and the exploits of the numerous expeditions, not least of Roald Amundsen and his role model, Fridtjof Nansen.

Roald Amundsen 1872 – 1928

To write about Norway and Tromsø and their history and not to include one of the greatest explorers of all time would be remiss. Roald Amundsen, most famously known for being the first person to reach the South Pole, was an extraordinary man and should be remembered for more than that one deserving feat. The youngest of four sons born into a seafaring family of ship owners and captains in July 1872, initially he had no desire to become an explorer and under duress from his mother, studied to become a doctor. He was not academically minded and achieved little success with his examinations, preferring to ski and develop his nautical skills and ability to withstand conditions of extreme cold. He dropped out of medical school soon after his mother died tragically. Perversely his dislike for study did not stop him from being enthralled by Sir John Franklin's book about his unsuccessful expedition to try and find a way through the Northwest Passage. This daring story galvanised Amundsen and was to remain a lifelong motivation.

As with so many famous people, we remember them only for a specific deed or achievement. It is as though our minds prefer to distil a whole human life down to a particular occurrence. It is not that we are not aware that each had a whole life lived with so many facets, it has more to do with what our minds can absorb and recall. Amundsen was a driven individual, determined and calculating. Even his personal life reflected this. He never married, choosing to have many lady friends, most of whom were married, and choosing to leave them when matters became too serious - the wives of a British aristocrat and a Norwegian lawyer being two. However, at the time of Amundsen's untimely death he was engaged to be married to an Alaskan called Bess Magids. The marriage was to be the culmination of a long relationship and her more recent divorce. Perhaps he had decided as he grew older that stability in a relationship was worthy of merit. Sadly, he never did grow old.

This is not a book about Roald Amundsen but mentioning him and flagging that he was the explorer who beat Robert Falcon Scott to the South Pole, may interest some to go hunting for the true man.

His expedition to the South Pole came about by chance. He had originally planned to be the first to the North Pole and had attracted the necessary considerable financial sponsorship to try and achieve this. He was, however, thwarted by Robert E Peary and Frederick A Cook, who had just laid claim to reaching the North Pole. Amundsen's funding was withdrawn – after all, the objective was no longer a 'first' – and with it, his dreams evaporated. Amundsen decided to head south and persuaded his sponsors that the South Pole was an equal prize to the North Pole.

Robert Falcon Scott had already embarked on an expedition to the South Pole, knowing that Roald Amundsen was heading to the North Pole. Scott's expedition was not a race. It was a scientific expedition with dual aims, yes, to be the first to the South Pole but also to achieve everything possible to advance the understanding of our planet. Some accounts say that Amundsen was in no rush to advise Scott that he was heading his way. Scott certainly remained oblivious to the fact for many weeks as he indulged in various research projects. The motivation for Amundsen was that the sponsorship for the North Pole expedition had only been re-secured because the South Pole remained a 'first'. It was he who pitted the two expeditions against each other and started 'The Race'. Needless to say, you will find no references to this in Norway.

Amundsen's actions are understandable, although not gentlemanly, and put in context with his other achievements distracts little from his reputation as one of the world's greatest explorers, whilst taking nothing from Robert Falcon Scott's own achievements and unquestionable integrity in the face of extreme adversity. 'The Race', as so many see these two expeditions, can be likened to a cross country race where one competitor's sole aim is to win, whilst the other collects fauna and flora en route to the finishing line. As with all expeditions, whether to the Poles or to climb 8,000 m peak mountains, meticulous planning enhances the chances of success, but pure luck is always in the equation. Tragically Scott, who so nearly survived, had that luck desert him.

Amundsen's achievements were considerable. In addition to the 1910-12

South Pole success, he was the first to reach both Poles and the first to have previously traversed the Northwest Passage in 1903-06. He returned to the Arctic in 1926 to make the first successful crossing by air with 15 others in the airship, Norge.

In June 1928 he was part of a rescue team searching for survivors of the airship Italia that had crashed returning from the North Pole. No survivors from either the Italia or the search craft, the French Latham flying boat that Amundsen was on, were seen again. A memorial to the fate of this rescue mission is at the southern point of the island that Tromsø sits on.

Daily Blog: Opened my 18th and final map today. July 20th

The last of the eighteen maps covering the route was opened in my hotel bedroom this afternoon here on Tromsø. Just 550 km to cycle. I have mixed feelings about finishing this wonderful journey. I miss the company of my wife but will miss this life of new daily experiences and meeting so many interesting and different people. A bed surrounded by four walls feels slightly alien, having slept in a tent since Anne and I left Oslo.

Yesterday saw me wet and cold to the core. My right knee, that sustained an injury a few years ago, is not good. Any reasonable downward pressure on the pedal results in a stabbing pain. Fortunately, the upward pull is still good. However, any advice coming my way that suggests stopping now to avoid possible adverse effects will be ignored.

To avert the accusation I have Summit Fever, this old git decided last night to take the express ferry to Tromsø made in part due to the forecast of further heavy rain and the near certainty of cycling inside clouds most of the day. On reflection, I am pleased with the decision. Not least because I met a great guy from Vancouver, Ryan Sykes. Like Yoya, Alastair and Brian previously, I immediately liked Ryan. Kindred spirits with the same objectives in life. Ryan, if you read this, I wish you every success with your work/life balance, but it strikes me you have got it about right.

A different theme today. Andy Hill and I frequented a few excellent brewery pubs when we did our Seattle to Boston cycle crossing, starting with a great one in

Seattle and another in the Old Fire Station in Rapid City. Tromsø also has a valid claim to brewery notoriety.

Tromsø is different from other Norwegian towns. I am not talking about the big cities, it is Norway's eighth-largest municipality, but still holds a small-town atmosphere, blending old buildings with new ones, and part of that heritage is the Mack brewery. In 1877 an enterprising gentleman called Ludwig Markus Mack saw the potential for a brewery to quench the thirst of the increasing numbers coming to Tromsø to make their riches from the Arctic Ocean. Today's Ølhallen beer hall, or pub, is to be found in the cellar of the brewery and dates to 1928. The brewery also lays claim to being the most northerly brewery in the world.

I enjoy a pint under the watchful eye of a visitor from further north, a 2.5 m polar bear. At £15 a pint, every drop of beer had to have the full taste squeezed out of it, and indeed it was excellent.

The 'bear' necessities of life are costly in Norway,
one of 64 beers available at the Mack brewery.

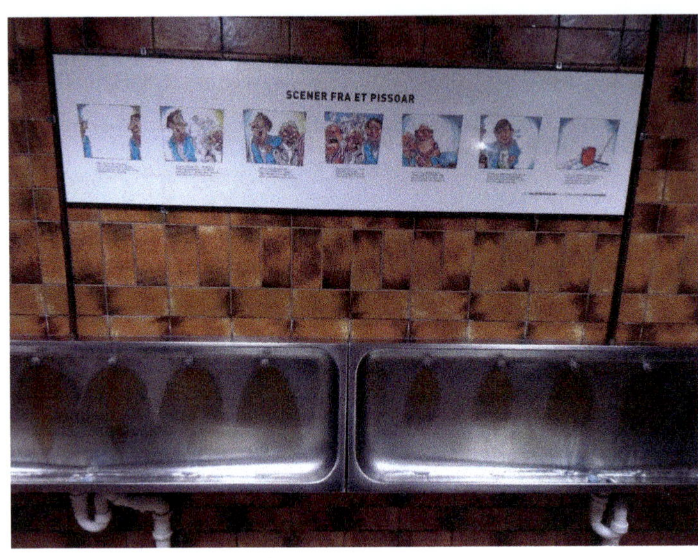

Restroom cartoons are usually highly amusing. Sadly, wasted on me this time.

Tromsø is full of worthy places to see and I certainly could not do justice to them. The Tromsø Folk Museum, The University Museum and The Town Museum, all places to spend several hours.

A 'must visit' place was Skansen. Previously a Customs station from 1789, Skansen is the oldest house in the city and now a café serving excellent coffee with relaxing surrounding grounds. A little way north of the city, past the extensive fire station, is the Arctic-Alpine Botanic Garden. For the botanists, this is a treat that includes the rare giant Tibetan blue poppy. Last, but not least, although I have not included all that Tromsø offers, is the most northern brewery in the world, The Mack Brewery. This small award-winning brewery was founded in 1877 by Ludwig Mack, who emigrated to Norway from Germany with his parents. He was trained as a baker but having visited his uncle in Bavaria who was a Brewmeister, strangely enough, decided to abandon flour for hops. Many of the impressive range of beers that are on offer to this day have their origins in German beer. After 130 years of brewing in Tromsø, operations have been moved to Nordkjosbotn, 70 km south of the city. When I visited the brewery pub, walking in off Storgata, I was impressed with the array of beers on offer and the polar bear that awaits your arrival.

Earlier in the day, in the morning sun, I had visited a café and having 'parked' my bike next to a table in the café garden, gone to buy coffee and calories, only to find on my return the table had been taken by a young couple. There were no other vacant tables, so I asked if I could join them. The next hour was spent chatting with Runar and Kristina, a trainee nurse, and a special needs carer. My enthusiasm for Tromsø and Norway apparent from the start, they were also keen to enthuse. Young, happy, and vibrant, they told me about their country, the positives and some of the few negatives, such as the laws concerning the sale of alcohol. Basking in the sunshine talking with these two young people was a joy.

Norway has relatively successfully controlled its previous alcohol problem, resulting in a largely positive attitude from most Norwegians. In part, the problem was magnified by coping with the sun setting in late November and not rising until two months later. It is incorrect to say Tromsø is plunged into darkness during these months. The sun does not rise above the horizon but there is light. Neither is the winter temperature that cold, as the warming effect of the surrounding sea is ever present. Having ice climbed in Norway and Finland in early February, I can confirm that there is certainly light during the day, albeit for a short while. There is a word in Norwegian that describes how they as a nation approach the wildly varying seasons. 'Friluftsliv' translated to English means 'open air life' or 'free air life'. It reflects how Norwegians embrace their seasons, including the positive effect this attitude has on minimising Seasonal Affective Disorder (SAD), or winter depression. Removing the immediate availability of alcohol over weekends has also played a beneficial role.

Tromsø seems to have something for everyone, from the most northern university in the world and the most northern brewery in the world, a tried and tested symbiotic relationship, to cultural and an extensive variety of outdoor pursuits. I looked forward to meeting up with my wife here in a couple of weeks.

Daily Blog: Tromsø floats my boat. July 21st

Only my humble view, but Tromsø is certainly a cut above many other towns I have seen in Norway. Its heritage is very much on display, in part due to the many older buildings around the town. More modern buildings work with the older and add variety and enhance their character.

Anne and I will be meeting up here after the ride has finished. I tried not to look around too much. However, if our day here is dull and overcast, (the weather, that is, we certainly will not be), it would have been a shame not to have used today's sunshine and taken a few photos. So here is a mouth-watering taste of Tromsø.

One of the pieces of artwork done by minority group school children being displayed in the Folkeparken. This park contained numerous styles of buildings found in northern Norway.

An atmospheric shot of under the pier at the Folkeparken.

Nitty and Gritty make the London Cray Twins look like Pinky and Perky.

So much like my brother and me all those years ago.

Part of the 21-bay Fire Station. Even London has no stations this big.

The most northerly botanical gardens in the world, with a Hurtigruten ship berthed in the dock.

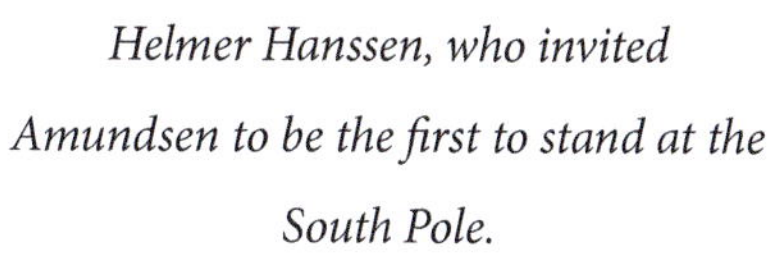

Helmer Hanssen, who invited Amundsen to be the first to stand at the South Pole.

The Mack brewery pub, the most northern brewery in the world.

Helmer Hanssen who, on 14th December 1911, as captain of the Andoya, ordered a stop to sledging as their expedition approached the South Pole and asked Amundsen to ski in front of the dogs. He thus became the first man to reach the South Pole.

I would also like to mention two young people I met today. My love of caffeine is well known, so having parked my cycle next to a table, I went into a very pleasant café to order. 'My' table being the only unoccupied one attracted a young couple. I returned to the table and asked if I could share it with them. What followed was a very enjoyable hour of chatting with Kristina and Runar. They both live in Tromsø, Runar is training to be a nurse and Kristina works as a special needs carer. I was not surprised to learn that Runar is into bouldering. For those who do not know what this is, it is climbing without ropes and gear at lower heights. It is both technical and demands strength. Runar was reserved about his abilities, but as is so often the case, our ladies support us, and Kristina confirmed that he is good. We talked about Norway, the honesty that prevails, the cost of living, jobs, cycling, and climbing. If you read this, guys, it was a pleasure meeting you. I am jealous of the lives you have ahead of you and wish you the best for your future.

This was the café where I met Kristina and Runar.

So tomorrow I mount up for the final leg of my journey. The forecast is as anticipated, changeable! Part of me does not want this to end, but very shortly I will be running out of land to cycle on. Beyond Nordkapp there is only sea.

CHAPTER TWENTY- SEVEN
Approaching 70 Degrees Latitude

'There are no laws that govern the will, the heart has reasons that the head knows nothing of.' Eddy Merckx

I left Tromsø on July 22nd and headed in a general easterly direction, my knee still letting me know it carried an injury. Refreshed, clean, well-fed, and with unexpected good weather, today was to be another especially enjoyable day. There was some underlying urgency to make progress as bad weather was forecast and some exposed and remote ground needed to be covered. Two ferry crossings, the latter from the pretty village of Lyngseidet, provided temporary rest for the knee.

Unlike on the Lofoten Islands where the cod fish are weathered and dried on stocks in their thousands on an industrial scale, further north, here single timber stocks can be seen near isolated homesteads, bringing home the fact that people who live here are more self-sufficient. These timber racks called stocks are used to air dry codfish, which are called 'stockfish', and hang from between February and May. I was now cycling through the best climate in the world for producing stockfish.

The scenery of these stocks in the foreground with fjords and mountains to the rear and bands of sea mist hanging in the air are quintessentially Norwegian. I cycled with a smile and a sense of wellbeing. I was coming to the end of my journey. Could I allow myself that feeling of achievement? My knee was aching, and I was becoming more reliant on pulling up with the leg of my clipped-in pedal than pushing down.

Leaving the coastal village of Ravelseidet and being prohibited from travelling the 2 km through the mountain tunnel, I took the 9 percent climb up into the mist of an eerie world of silence. A world where trees hung heavy with 'old man's beard' and white branches lay dead in twisted forms on the lush green grass. Small lakes with mirror surfaces, so smooth and ethereal you could imagine the arm of The Lady of the Lake reaching to accept Excalibur. I was alone in this world that seemed to border reality.

Descending to sea level again I re-joined the E6 as it emerged from the tunnel and headed southeast before northeast and Tretta. Having covered 145 km, I was happy to find a camping area for RV and tents beside the road. Essentially this was a stopping place for any traveller. I found a small, grassed area surrounded by hedges with a towering cliff face of granite above. As the evening grew on, so more RVs arrived, and barbeques were lit. Sitting at a picnic table next to my tent, with the last paper map laid out in front of me, I read it as if it were a book, absorbing the information it gave. Even with the arrival of sophisticated GPS and electronic mapping systems, these maps hold something special. Looking at the detail on a good map, the mind can transpose those contour lines and all the many features into a mental picture of what physically surrounds you.

Out on the road again this was to be a big day. A day I nearly lost not one, but four lives with RV drivers choosing to blow the sweat off my face with their passing slipstream. The blog infers that I may have lost my cool. Who would not have, when vehicles are passing at speed within centimetres of you? I was now 370 km to my destination. A destination that only three roads are headed towards. A destination that hosts 200,000 visitors a year. It would only get worse; I was heading for the northernmost point of mainland Europe.

Before the drama came the charity. Although now faded from having been in the sun for a couple of months, the printed route of my journey was still visible on the back of my shirt. Nearing the end of my travels, those who were curious could still see where I had come from. The destination of a touring cyclist heading north from now on would have only one finishing line in mind. Two coaches passed with the back windows full of people, some waving, some with the 'thumbs up' sign. Cycling up a hill, one that would contribute to the daily total of 2,000 m of elevation, an old car hardly making better progress than me, overtook and parked. A guy jumped out with a bottle of water and offered it to me. That deed was appreciated and balanced the later selfish near misses.

Arriving at the Gildetun hotel I enjoyed some high-calorie food and a coffee, whilst being asked questions about my trip. Even the boisterous schoolchildren, climbing on the petrified tree that doubled for a sign for the hotel and a mileage indicator that told me only 370 km left to cycle, were interested. From 400 m ASL, I descended over undulating tundra on near-perfect roads bordered by avalanche fencing placed strategically to try and stop snow from closing the roads. I passed Sámi roadside stalls selling all things reindeer, road signs advising that both elk and reindeer were likely to be on the road. The wet weather forecasted had not arrived; instead, the air was crisp and cool and so clean. The sun shone weak in the sky. My head was again turning from side to side, absorbing all that there was to see, including some interesting wood carvings, one of an enormously proud 'wood copper'. His creator had chosen not to remove a coincidently placed branch. I was existing in what seemed an improbable world. A world more read about than visited. A world I was privileged to be surrounded by and absorbed in.

The E6 branched left and over a long bridge before immediately entering the first of three tunnels and on to the town of Alta. I took a quieter alternative and passed through the hamlet of Kåfjord, stopping at an immaculate small, white-painted timber chapel with blue doors and windows. By the entrance to the graveyard was a notice that caught my attention. Every hamlet, village, town, and city has its history. This tiny place certainly had.

Daily Blog: Approaching 70 degrees latitude – further north than Iceland. July 22nd

On reaching Nordkapp I would have cycled across 35 degrees of latitude since leaving Tarifa. On occasions it has not been a straight northerly route, rather a meandering line frequently travelling both east and west and at times, south. Tomorrow morning, I should pass an unusual sign confirming that it is only 370 km to Nordkapp – more in the days to follow.

Today I have covered 145 km and have arrived in a remote area. Back on the E6 through necessity, as there are no alternatives. I pushed on to a tiny place called Tretta, NE of Storslett, in part because of the weather forecast for Wednesday, (three days ahead). The road from Alta, the last remaining larger town before Olderfjord and Nordkapp, is over 100 km of exposed and deserted tundra. The plan is to arrive at least in Skaidi by Tuesday night. Again, this puts me two days ahead of schedule, but better to be ahead of time than hunkered down in bad weather further south.

With a huge hotel buffet breakfast hardly confined in my stomach and a substantial lunch, from the same source that happened to find its way into my bag, I cycled over the bridge from Tromsø (the only bridge so far where anti-suicide precautions have been erected. Perhaps 'Friluftsliv' has its limitations?). Passing Tromsø's sail-like cathedral, I first avoided the E6 using Cycle Route 1, but was soon directed onto it again. Then came the peace and beauty of the 91 and two ferries. I successfully raced to catch the first. The second ferry was just arriving in the pretty town of Lyngseidet, so I had ten minutes to linger.

Now arrived at the point where any form of transport would be kinder on my knee than cycling.

The beauty of Norway.

Mist hangs on high marshland on a mountain route.

Raised salt bins indicate the depth of snow in winter.

Avalanche management to keep the E6 open for longer during the winter.

Tonight's 'home' is a large roadside rest area beside a broad river with picnic tables in amongst trees beneath an impressive crag. Even a loo is provided.

Daily Blog: Question: What is the width of a Recreational Vehicle (RV)? July 23rd

This question has been asked for a specific reason. To make it easier the answer is within one of the following multiple choices.

1. Is it the same as a Harley Davidson motorcycle with full panniers being ridden by a guy that looks that hard all vehicles give him as much space as they can?

2. Is it the same as your Ford Focus car or Mini (the classic iconic Mini, not the new massive Mini)?

3. Is it the same as a Volvo pulling a caravan fitted with extended wing mirrors the size of Dumbo's ears that are equally effective at decapitating a cyclist as Ben Hur's knives on his chariot wheels did to the legs of those who got in his way?

4. Perhaps it is the width of a 16-seater minibus?

5. Or could it be the width of a small lorry/truck?

Please forward your answers on a postcard to be placed on top of my coffin before I am cremated.

Most RV drivers are aware they are driving a vehicle larger than they normally do. But it only takes one! If you drive a small car a certain distance from the central white or yellow line, it follows that if you do the same in a wider vehicle the nearside of that vehicle will be nearer to the kerb or CYCLIST! To avoid hitting the cyclist it may be necessary to cross over that central line. There is no fine or tax for doing so and the cyclist will be immensely grateful to you.

Not to labour the point too much, but it is my life we are talking about, why did four idiots today choose to use my elbow to put a clean line down the side of their

RV? There was no oncoming traffic, were they texting, reading, or watching TV? – all of which I have seen on this trip.

Anyway, to change the subject. How many youngsters can you get on one bicycle? I saw four today. The rider, one behind her, one on the crossbar, and the fourth in front of the handlebars. As kids, we rode croggies, but not three up!

With my previous ramblings, you would be forgiven for thinking not much happened today. However, much did. Another 145 km nearer to Nordkapp involving 2,000 m of elevation, one hill took me from sea level to 400 m ASL.

At the Gildetun restaurant there was this sign. Confirming there is only 370 km left to cycle to Nordkapp.

Vehicles have slowed down behind me before overtaking, then with thumbs up, waves, or shouts of encouragement they drive past. At the Gildetun hotel, an Austrian group on a coach trip was interested to learn more about my kind of insanity. After one hard hill climb, a chap having driven past waited for me at the top of the hill and offered me a bottle of water.

I saw my first reindeer today.

A Life Appreciated

Near to where some Inuit people were selling antlers and pelts.

Tonight, I am again wild camping just outside the town of Alta, the last town of any size before Nordkapp and only 240 km from it.

As the E6 dived into a cyclist prohibited tunnel and headed towards Alta, I took the quiet lane that passes Kåfjord church and a striking bronze statue within its graveyard. At the beginning of the 19th century, copper deposits were found in the mountains around Kåfjord, and in 1826 Alten Copper Mines under English management started to mine the copper with eleven labourers from Roros. More than fifty years later the mine was managed by a Swedish company until 1909.

Many migrant workers were employed. With the company wanting a stable workforce they encouraged families to accompany their menfolk and in 1840 numbers rose to over a thousand. At the time this amounted to more than the total populations of three nearby towns. The government and the mining community worked together to build the necessary infrastructure, including the

Kåfjord church that was completed in 1837. There were many blasting accidents where people were injured and killed. Child mortality was high, and life was hard, made more so by freezing conditions.

Women had always played a central role in the community. It had been a woman who had first found the main ore deposit in 1826. Women worked alongside their men, crushing, and breaking the rocks. Both the victims of accidents and child mortality are buried in the graveyard, many in unmarked graves.

The sculpture made by Per Ung is in memory of the many who died in this harsh environment. It stands on slag stone from the copper mine. The only obvious evidence that there had been a community at Kåfjord is the church.

Having read the history on a sign near to the statue, I walked around the church listening to the utter peace and quiet. Through the silence, I imagined the commotion, poverty, and hardship these people endured, their ghosts forever here. Their need to believe in a better life must have sustained them.

Per Ung's sculpture to the copper miners of Kåfjord.

A little further on there was a sign for the *Tirpitz* museum. It was too late in the day for me to visit, it was closed. There is a museum both here and in Tromsø containing photographs and artefacts from this gigantic Second World War German battleship. The *Tirpitz* was 251 m in length and weighed over 50,000 tons when loaded, with a hull 30 cm thick. Coupled with an ability to travel at 30 knots, it was truly an enormous and formidable ship. The firepower matched its size with some of the largest naval guns ever built, including eight 38 cm (15 inch) guns. It had a crew of 2,600 that included 100 officers. The *Tirpitz* had played a major part in the northern Norwegian campaign. It was eventually sunk in November 1944 after many operations trying to do so. The RAF used 30 Lancaster bombers armed with Tallboy earthquake bombs to sink her. Two bombs hit their target and caused internal explosions resulting in her capsizing. Unlike *Tirpitz's* more famous sister ship, *Bismarck*, *Tirpitz* had proved to be an elusive prey for three years, whereas *Bismarck*, having sunk HMS Hood with a loss of all but three of the 1,421 crew, was herself sunk hours later only ten days after starting her maiden voyage.

I cycled on skirting the head of the fiord and saw a stretch of grassland beside the water just beyond Kåfjord. This was an ideal camping site. A few tents were pitched at random over about five hectares. As was now the norm, they were far outnumbered by RVs. There were perhaps twenty vehicles. I pitched my tent on rising ground overlooking the southernmost point of the Altafjord for a peaceful night, falling asleep probably among the souls of the miners and their families.

July 24th, another big day with two notable climbs and over 100 km of exposed riding. It was to be an enjoyable day with one notable surprise coming literally out of the blue. The Stokkedalen is not a place for a cyclist in bad weather. Fortunately, the forecasted rain and wind did not materialise. Before I headed out northeast, I needed to stock up and charge my power pack in the last large town before reaching my final destination.

I cycled early into the deserted town of Alta and found an open-fronted upmarket café/bar with patio burners and reindeer skins and rugs draped over the seating. Apple pie and coffee – why not?

I had just cycled past a striking piece of architecture. Alta's Northern Lights

Cathedral is either liked or not, there seems to be no middle ground, a Marmite structure. To me it looked like a stunning piece of sculpture. Designed by Schmidt Hammer Lassen Architects, who were inspired by the Aurora Borealis, and consecrated in 2013, it is made of concrete and cladded with titanium sheets that reflect the surrounding light. During the winter months when the Northern Lights are displaying themselves the Cathedral complements this natural light show.

A rough-legged buzzard screeches as it prepares to dive on me again.

The freedom of the road.

The blog describes the aerial attack that had me waving my arms above my head and wishing I had long cable ties attached to my helmet, Australian style, to fend off any direct contact from the diving raptor. The rough-legged buzzard is a moderately large bird of prey, with the larger female having a wingspan of up to 153 cm or 60 inches. When they have fledglings, they are protective and can be territorial. Although I had heard their alarm calls, a little like a slurred whistle, I had no idea an attack would follow. I had not even seen the bird before feeling the wind pass by me inches from my head. The display was both unnerving and spectacular and noisy as the bird's alarm calls were nearly constant. The road was deserted both in front and behind me for as far as the eye could see to the vanishing point, no likelihood of being run over should the bird have unseated me. Then as quickly as it had arrived, the skies became peaceful again.

I stopped for a quick energy intake at Skaidi and 20 km later arriving in Olderfjord, finally leaving the E6 that headed back south. I joined the E69 north before stopping at a campsite, where I met Lukas, a cyclist from Germany. Having pitched my tent near the water's edge looking out over the waters of Porsangerfjorden that was to be my view to the right all the way to Honningsvåg, I showered and crossed the road to the hotel restaurant and ate an excellent meal, returning to find a tent pitched about a metre away from mine. Maybe they had not realised the footprint of theirs when they started to put it up. As that night progressed and the pile of beer bottles and cans mounted outside, there was probably little realisation of anything. Any noise they may have made was drowned out by the heavy rain that had eventually arrived. With a wet tent packed, the following morning I had a relaxing coffee or two before the weather blew through and I hit the road: a windy day lay ahead.

There is now only one road that heads north to Honningsvåg and onto Nordkapp. At the restaurant the previous night, which had an enormous parking area, there was a realisation that coaches were to play an ever-great part in my cycling experience as I headed north. The roads remained in good condition and with only two tunnels to go through before the long subterranean tunnel that went deep under the sea across to the island of Magerøya and Honningsvåg, I remained upbeat.

Reindeer supporting massive antlers grazed beside the road and the water's edge. A group had waded out into the water to a small island to graze on the seaweed. This habit, that had previously been considered unusual, had long since become the norm. I even saw a white reindeer and her calf. These are not albino but have a rare genetic mutation that does not allow any pigment in the fur. The Sámi people believe seeing one brings good luck. I dismounted and walked slowly towards them to try and get a better photograph. I was permitted to approach so far before the mother trotted effortlessly to a safe distance, where her calf followed.

Cod stocks and isolated groups of small timber fishing boat sheds lined parts of the shoreline. The air was pure and clean, visibility was to the horizon. As the road contoured the shore there were views of waterfalls dropping from the cliffs. Sometimes these cliffs were set back from the road, other times the road was wedged between the cliffs and the sea. When the sun was shining the sea was a deep blue, turning a metal grey when clouds filled the sky, only to return to a cobalt blue as the sun returned.

On this penultimate day of cycling, I travelled through five tunnels with a combined distance of over 14,290 m. The first was Skarvberg at 2,980 m, closely followed by a shorter one. Just after Kåfjord, before heading steadily down towards the infamous Nordkapp tunnel, a mere 6,870 m long and which runs 212 m below the sea, a group of reindeer caught my eye. Again, they seemed as though they had made their way out to a tiny island but there was no obvious seaweed there to graze on. In recent years as climate warming has accelerated, reindeer have adapted and now eat seaweed as part of their diet, usually in the winter, but this change seems now not just confined to the winter months.

To return to The Tunnel. Resembling a massive rabbit hole from which only blackness exuded, it was difficult to comprehend that this 'tube' descended beneath the Magerøysundet Strait. The Nordkapp tunnel had been opened on June 15th 1999, and from that date ferries no longer travelled across the Strait. I had lost count of how many tunnels I had travelled through in the previous weeks and, contrary to the writings of many touring cyclists, I had no problems in applying the attitude necessary to maintain sanity whilst placing my life in the hands of other road users.

I took a few photographs of the entrance and the sign advising of the 9% downhill as you go beneath the waves. I layered-up, it was going to be cold. Daylight disappeared almost immediately and was replaced with regularly spaced but minimal lighting. The condition of the road was hard to make out: it looked wet, perhaps icy, and slippery. My fingers turned cold as did my face, which was made colder by my exhaled air condensing on my cheeks. I would normally have sought some thrills and accelerated down the hill, but a degree of caution was more appropriate. Squeezing on the brakes reduced the circulation to the fingers and the cold penetrated deeper. As contradictory as this sounds, I was enjoying myself. The here and now would not be repeated, I would not be returning this way, so 'indulge yourself' was the inner thought. Where was the traffic that was said to be so disorientating and frightening? Yes, the extractor fans were noisy, the fog that was promised lay only thinly. Then a car approached although I could not see it or guess from which direction it was coming. It passed from the rear, as did several others. The noise they made was unbelievably loud, only surpassed by a motorcycle. There were several laybys with emergency phone booths, and I chose to 'delayer' in one, removing some clothing, in anticipation of the 10% climb back up to the surface. It was a mistake to have cycled into the layby. Whereas the traffic on the road had prevented any ice from forming, a mixture of ice and oil had accumulated in the layby. Still travelling at a reasonable speed with the intention of stopping in the layby, I immediately and unceremoniously fell off and slid along the greasy road surface. I removed my now oily jacket, felt that the handlebar extension had broken under the sleeve, checked the bike over, and started the long 10% climb. Emerging back into the sunlight was like stepping out of an airplane in a hot country, having stepped into it in a cold one.

I was through the short tunnel immediately after the Nordkapp tunnel without really registering it. Similarly, the 4,440 m Honningsvåg tunnel through the hillside was uneventful. Straight in front of me as I emerged from the tunnel were some unsightly concrete towers that reminded me of a place Andy and I had cycled through in America. A place called Concrete, where we had sat on the kerb eating ice cream in temperatures approaching 100 degrees Fahrenheit. It certainly was not that temperature here. Honningsvåg was across the bay. Brian had contacted to say that he had been to Nordkapp and this was his last night in Honningsvåg before returning home on a Hurtigruten ferry early the following morning. I called in at the Rema 1000 supermarket for provisions and as I cycled into town Brian cycled towards me. It was good to see him. We ate early at Viva Napoli and chatted easily about our trip. He too had been swooped on by the rough-legged buzzard.

We could have left our bikes undercover before having our pizzas but had not, and the rain had done its work. We cycled towards the hamlet of Nordvågen, beyond which there is nothing but wilderness. We looked for shelter, maybe a derelict building, but found none, so Brian took us to a small, grassed area sandwiched between the little-used road and the sea, beneath the road barriers where he had previously camped. Having pitched our tents, we said our farewells. He was catching an early ferry from the town the following morning.

I awoke to the sound of rain on the tent. I certainly did not feel as though I was approaching the end of an 8,000 km cycle ride and did not consider my body needed a rest day, but it was raining, and I had every intention of maximising the enjoyment for the last ride north to Nordkapp. I also had several days to explore my final destination before catching the ferry that would return me to Tromsø; there was certainly no rush. Later, after the rain had cleared, I sat on a rock beside the sea that gently rose and ebbed on the lower rocks beneath. The small grassy patch that was to become familiar was in an ideal location. Out of town, but not too far, on a quiet road with splendid views southwards across the sea to the peninsular of Sværholthalvøya.

I cycled into Honningsvåg; a town that had been burnt to the ground under the Nazi's 'Scorched Earth' policy. A town that used to be called Little Chicago in the 1960s because it was so unruly and full of gangsters. A town that now looked at peace with itself, small, self-contained with a vibrant community. I spent some time in the museum learning about the sorcery laws, battleships, and whaling.

Witchcraft and persecution of those thought to be witches in the late 16th century and early 17th century abounded. Norway had Europe's strictest laws against trolldom. As remote as Honningsvåg is, it was drawn into the belief that witches were everywhere, threatening life, livelihood, and the divine order. In

1610 five members of the same family were condemned to death and a further one in 1626. Throughout Europe, over 100,000 people were accused of being witches, mainly women, with 40 to 50,000 being executed. It seems no part of the then known world was immune from this persecution, even in America where the Witches of Salem are notably remembered.

A newspaper cutting from the Daily Mail dated Wednesday 29th December 1943 was an exhibit covering the demise of the Nazi battleship *Scharnhorst*, also known in Germany during WW2 as '*Lucky Scharnhorst*' and a source of national pride, which was sunk by allied forces over Christmas 1943. Considered the most 'beautiful' battleship built and engineered to near perfection, she had taken eleven torpedoes and over a dozen hits from *HMS Duke of York*'s 8 and 14-inch shells and thousands of rounds from surrounding smaller cruisers. The sinking of *Scharnhorst,* together with the capsizing of *Tirpitz* a month before, marked the end of the Nazi surface navy.

Whaling is a highly contentious subject that continues to have the ability to ignite heated debate from both ends of the spectrum of views: on the one hand the Whale and Dolphin Conservation Group and on the other, the Norwegian government. This is not a book about whaling and the politics and ethics that are behind the issues. A part of me feels the need to become outspoken here and to express a view, but this is not an appropriate platform. Whaling in Norway started in the 17th and 18th centuries. By the 1800s unregulated whaling led to the depletion of the whales in Norwegian waters. So, whales were hunted around Iceland. It is primarily the Minke whale that is hunted today by the Norwegians. Norway caught more whales than any other country between 2010 and 2016. However, their whaling fleet has gone from 350 in 1949 to 11 in 2017.

I returned to the present world with some relief, knowing that modern day life, although immensely hard for millions and atrocities still occur with sickening regularity, has moved forward. Just perhaps not in the precise direction we would want it to.

The sun is out as I walk past a collection of brightly coloured Wellington boots with flowering plants having replaced the owner's legs and a framed collection of soles cut from flip-flop shoes (thongs). I like Honningsvåg with its brightly coloured timber housing and neat harbour. Small fishing crafts are moored on the quay. Neat lawns run to the quay edge. Three large old timber buildings supported on stilts that protrude from the harbour walls add character. One of the two schools in the town sits on a site that any medieval lord would have chosen for his castle. In the working area of the harbour there are many snow Skidoos and a few quad bikes parked up. Honningsvåg during the winter would be a quite different place.

My day was finished with a coffee sitting outside a café overlooking the harbour. There was warmth still in the air. There was only one other customer, a fellow cyclist and, as I say in the blog, my interest was instant. His name was Aldo Rock, probably not the name his parents gave him as a baby, but neither was John Wayne or Elton John given theirs as children. An Italian, Aldo has a radio station back in Italy, Radio Deejay. He has a perfect work/life balance, or to be more accurate, his recreation is his work, and he works hard at it. The blog explains. Whereas Andy and I had cycled at our leisure, albeit fast, across America, Aldo had competed in a race across the country. He was interesting and engaging, with personal stories of Eric Clapton and cycling. He gave me his phone number before heading off towards Nordkapp, where he was scheduled to do a radio broadcast at midnight. I headed back to my personal campsite, pitched my tent and, sitting looking out over the calm sea, drank a beer.

The sea was tranquil and would remain so until I left Honningsvåg on the 29th. Suddenly there was the sound of turbulent water. Looking over the edge of my small cliff down to the water there were no breaking waves. The commotion continued and became louder as I walked around the rock head. A circular shape of several metres' diameter was 'boiling' with activity. I could only guess what was happening. Small fish, somehow choosing to confine themselves to a tight space, were causing the water to bubble as if in a jacuzzi. I later found out this was a 'bait ball'. It happens when small fish move in a tightly packed sphere. It is a desperate defence against attackers. These small fish have many predators, hence the term 'baitfish'. This shoal of fish seemed threatened, so swam as a school, moving rapidly and closely together at the same speed. Very much like an aquatic version of a murmuration of starlings. The activity stopped as quickly as it had started. I returned to my tent. Today, as so many, had been a good one.

Daily Blog: Across the Stokkedalen and Repparfjorddalen. July 24th
Today has been a great ride with a feeling of having crossed over a large remote stretch of country.

The road tunnels leading into Alta from the west on the E6 had not permitted cyclists. All the detours added distance; however, the deserted roads and beautiful scenery more than compensated.

Alta is a reasonably sized town with a modern relaxed feel about it and an unusual and striking church. The café I found did an excellent cappuccino. The apple pie and ice cream were also good. No excuses needed – with 120 km to cycle and a 1000 m of climbing ahead, I was looking forward to today's ride.

The church at Alta.

The rain that had been forecast for tomorrow is now patchy, but strong winds and heavy rain is forecast for the 29th. Plans need to be flexible, so hopefully I will arrive in Honningsvåg tomorrow night, 25th. I had thought about cycling through the 7 km sea tunnel to Honningsvag during the night when traffic is light. This would have necessitated carrying two days' food to camp over, and I have not the room. Besides, I have quite enjoyed the previous tunnels and the reported loud and bewildering noise of vehicles has not been as expected.

Back to today. Many of the photos today were either taken using my Olympus 'from the saddle' whilst moving, as the light differential was too much for the phone camera.

There were two substantial climbs, not steep at 7% and 8%, but long. Sea level to 250 m at Sarves and 385 m at Sennalandet. These climbs were enjoyable. Once on the barren tundra, where the road in front ran for miles, straight to its vanishing point, there were a surprising number of small timber dwellings dotted around the undulating hills, each with a snowmobile parked adjacent. The sun was shining and the air cool. This was very enjoyable!

Then came a fright. I had heard the screeches of a bird of prey above me for a few minutes. Without warning, there was a loud swishing sound near my right ear as I felt the air disturbed. Looking up I saw a bird do an incredible rising turn and started to descend towards me again, screeching all the while. Fortunately, there were no vehicles around as I waved my arm and shouted, expecting him to make a strike. The bird subsequently flew around me, and I managed to get two photos of it, again on the Olympus.

Nearing the end of a remarkable journey.

Daily Blog: Nearing the finishing Line. July 25th

The patchy rain forecasted for today was 'patchless', seamless as it hammered down on my tent during the early hours. This did not bode well for the ride up to Honningsvåg. However, after a coffee in the restaurant attached to the campsite, the skies had cleared, and the signs were good.

The route from Olderfjord to Honningsvåg consisted of far-reaching sea views, open windswept country, sea cliffs, tunnels, and reindeer.

Approaching another tunnel.

Cod drying racks called hjell.

The calm sea was to my right as I cycled along the E69 hugging the coast, weaving in and out of numerous coves. With a brisk wind coming in from the west, there were times when it was blowing directly at me and others when it was pushing me at 40 km/h, depending on whether I was cycling the southside of the deep cut coves or the northside. Around Repvåg it is necessary to climb up over the northeast peninsula and head west into the wind before entering the Nordkapp sea tunnel. This was hard work, and I was willing the tunnel to arrive to give respite from the wind.

The long-awaited tunnel, a mere four miles long.

At 6,870 m in length and 212 m below sea level, with a 9% 'hill' down into it and a longer 9% 'hill' out of it, the tunnel holds a certain respect by cyclists. Some write having had frightening experiences and loathed every minute in it. This instils trepidation in all about to enter it. Having put both my rear lights and front light on and layered up, into the tunnel I cycled.

On reaching this far north in Norway every cyclist would have by now been through many tunnels. What made this one different was the immediate massive temperature drop, enhanced by the speed that you descend under the sea. Lighting provided in the tunnel is minimal and the noise of the extractor fans trying to remove the fog is loud. It is also true that sound is distorted, particularly with motorcycles sounding like trains. The ascent back out was long and, with vehicles passing, care was needed. My main concern, as it has been for many days, is the incompetence of some RV drivers – the problem being, it is impossible to identify those excellent drivers and those who should not be in charge of an RV. However, the overall experience was enjoyable and the relative warmth that greets you as you emerge is welcoming.

Inside Nordkapp tunnel.

A further two tunnels and the final one, the Honningsvåg tunnel, at 4,440 m cutting through a 400 m high mountain, brings you to a less than auspicious area consisting of a desensitization plant and derelict concrete silos before a supermarket, Rema 1000, welcomes you into Honningsvåg town. A town completely rebuilt after the Nazis burnt it to the ground as they retreated in 1945.

During the ride I saw numerous reindeer. I took some time to get reasonably close to this cow and calf.

Brian, the recently retired GP from Glasgow, who was great company for a few days, way back sometime somewhere, messaged to say he had been to Nordkapp and was now in Honningsvåg and suggested having a meal and drink together before he headed home early on 26th on one of the Hurtigruten ships. We enjoyed a *pizza and some beer together whilst our bikes got soaked outside. Not able to delay our departure any longer we headed off to try and find a derelict building to save putting the tents up, as he had to be on the ship by 5 am. Unsuccessful, we pitched the tents overlooking the sea, said farewell to each other, and slept through a wet night. I heard Brian's alarm but was back to sleep immediately.*

I now have four days until I board the MS Nordkapp for Tromsø to meet Anne for our trip south to Bergen. I think I am going to get to know the island of Magerøya very well.

Daily Blog: A day of R and R. July 26th

I could have risen early, packed up the tent in the rain and cycled into town to look around. But today was planned as a rest and recuperation day. Arguably I needed neither, but there is little else to do. The rain continued until 11 am and I continued to remain lazy until that time too. I have since looked around Honningsvåg and the museum.

Quirky things abound in unusual places. These 'souls' obviously survived the stormy seas.

Honningsvåg's main attraction is probably the museum. I spent an enjoyable time learning about the town's ancient dwellings and modern history, including the following. The sorcery laws of the 15th and 16th centuries, resulting in the death of both men and women, the 'Scorched Earth Policy' the Nazis operated in all villages and towns in this area and the rebuilding programme, the sinking of the German battleship 'Scharnhorst' by four allied destroyers, the past whaling and current fishing industries and future oil and gas production from the Barents Sea and a surprising piece of random information was the fact that Honningsvåg in the 1960s was known as 'Little Chicago', for its unruly and gangster racketeering.

Honningsvåg harbour.

Honningsvåg.

This evening I had a coffee where the only other customer was another cyclist. We immediately fell into conversation. Aldo Rock, an Italian with perfect English, was energy-loading before setting off on his road cycle to Nordkapp. Initially a 'dark horse' as we chatted about sport, it came to light Aldo has competed in the cycle race across America. He is also a triathlete and has a radio and TV station in Italy and is giving a radio interview from Nordkapp this evening at midnight, hopefully with the midnight sun shining. Now, that is how to mix work and play. Aldo, if you read this, I hope the ride to Nordkapp was not too arduous. The wind was particularly strong. It was good to meet you, I am sure one day our paths will cross again.

My home for tonight.

CHAPTER TWENTY-EIGHT
Today I Finished a Wonderful Journey

'I cannot rest from travel: I will drink life to the lees.' Alfred, Lord Tennyson

Stepping out of the tent, with the sea lapping beneath the rocks and while answering the call of nature, I saw a sea otter rise above the seaweed that floated on the calm water. It must have seen me but was unperturbed and went about its business ignoring me. I had never seen a sea otter so close and was mesmerised. These intelligent creatures are one of only a few non-primate animals that use tools like rocks and shells to gain access to their prey, such as crabs and mussels. It crossed my mind that this otter may have been the cause of the bait ball the previous evening. Although otters are usually interested in larger fish.

July 27th was already a special day. A 'summit' day. A day that I still remember so vividly. Like the day Andy and I rode through the rain-soaked streets of Boston to dip our feet in the Atlantic Ocean, having cycled from the Pacific Ocean. Like the day Robert Mads Anderson, Dawa Gyalze Sherpa, and I stood on the summit of Everest. The summits of Denali with Richard Scott (Scotty), Aconcagua with Tim, Chip and John, Mount Kenya with Sean, Angus, and Ben, Mount Vinson and so many more, some more easily obtained than others. These are the memories that never fade, the expeditions and journeys that make life so vibrant, and always the realisation of how fortunate I am, a life appreciated.

But I am not at my destination yet. I have 33 km to cycle and a few more hills. Like Ama Dablam, the 6,812 m peak in the Himalayas, the effort needs to continue to the end. As you arrive at the top of a mountain or the top of Europe, the realisation of achievement dawns. Whether looking from a mountain top and soaking in the views of Nuptse, Lhotse, and Everest, or looking out across the sea towards the North Pole, as I would do this day, and witnessing the curvature of our planet we live on, so plain to see, the feeling is ethereal.

I had packed up the tent at dawn and left Honningsvåg early. Enthusiasm and a desire to avoid the coaches that would soon be taking hundreds of visitors to Nordkapp were my drivers. The first climb started shortly after the turn-off for Kamøyvær. The condition of the road was excellent and would allow a rapid return whilst enjoying some silent movie slapstick comedy of seeing an RV with its rear doors open jettisoning contents as it drove uphill in the opposite direction, but that would be tomorrow. Today I travelled downhill, passing the road that went northwest to the Nordkapp Sea Park, up another hill, and past the turning for Skarsvåg, before climbing a further two hills.

On my return, I would turn off and visit Skarsvåg. This small village, where sixty people live, is the most northern settlement in the world that can be reached by a tarmac road, but not always, as the winter frequently isolates it. It is also where the world's most northern fishing fleet harbours, with its main quarry being cod. As I cycled ever closer to my destination reindeer could be seen grazing beside the road and out on the tundra.

It is now most appropriate to mention the Sámi people. Beside the road was a Sámi man holding the reins attached to a reindeer, both standing beside a traditional tent. Adjacent was a large parking area to accommodate the numerous coaches that were inextricably attracted to stop. Tourism comes in many guises and is an industry that provides a living for millions, but exploitation is ugly. Whether the Sámi people would wish to be so embroiled in tourism out of choice, I cannot say. The gentleman dressed in traditional clothing answering a barrage of questions, a minority of which were mildly sensible, seemed happy as he idly held the *reigns of a* dutiful reindeer. I hope he was. His ancestors have been persecuted for centuries and to this day they remain the target of discrimination. In February in Tromsø there is an annual festival cultivating the culture of the Sámi. Dressed in their strikingly colourful traditional costume, they race reindeer in the town, a spectacle not to be missed.

The Sámi are the only indigenous people in Europe. They are not confined to modern-day country borders and live in northern Finland, extensively in Sweden, and on the Kola Peninsula in Russia as well as Norway.

Out of the ten languages they speak, only one has been lost to history, a testimony to their determination to maintain their identity. When we talk about the Sámi it is impossible to ignore talking about reindeer. Societies and cultures are dynamic, what has in the past been acceptable may or may not remain so as time moves on. However, we need to temper our views and realise necessities and have respect for those whose lives continue to rely on what has become questionable to those of us having the luxury to do so. The Sámi people are inextricably linked to reindeer husbandry and all it entails. Their survival relies on the reindeer, from the meat to the fur, to transport. No other animal can survive the winter, no crops can survive. Yes, we have modern down jackets and pants (that require goose feathers sometimes plucked whilst the bird remains alive) that some say, contentiously, are equal to reindeer skin, but their durability and enormous expense make them wholly unsuitable. The Sámi have respect for the reindeer. Enshrined in folklore is a promise to the reindeer that they would feed and care for them if the reindeer provided for the Sámi, so long as no part of the reindeer was wasted. To this day this ethos prevails.

The Sámi people have been around a long time, nearly 3,500 years. Although recent history has them as Arctic people, there was a time they lived in southern Sweden and Norway. In more recent times they have been persecuted with sustained efforts to eliminate them. Sterilization and removal of children from their parents was practised. They were the subjects of eugenics, the now correctly discredited practice developed by Sir Francis Galton in the 1930s. Economic development in northern Norway also impacted adversely on the Sámi. The only acceptable language for business and financial transactions was Norwegian and as most Sámi spoke little of the language, they were ousted from their lands. In 1913 laws were passed permitting settlers from the south to take Sámi land.

The land that the Sámi live on today is known as Sápmi, it is rich in natural resources and is under constant threat of exploitation and endangers the ability for the Sámi to continue their traditional way of life. It was only in 1990 that the Norwegian government finally recognised the Sámi as an indigenous people, a people who have lived here for 3,500 years. It is hoped that their land, culture, and traditions can now be preserved.

The treatment of the Sámi people is not unique, indeed tragically historically it has almost been the norm. But, to lighten the note. The Sámi men have an ingenious way of letting the fairer sex know when they are single and available or when they are married. It is all about the buttons on his belt. A married man will have square buttons and a single man will have round buttons on his belt. I hope I have that the right way around.

A happy Sámi.

FACT FACTORY: In the 1990s the four countries where the Sámi people live, Norway, Sweden, Finland, and Russia finally recognised them as indigenous people and granted them special provisions. Norway granted special rights to ensure the protection of their language and culture, even allowing them their own parliament. However, few laws have been passed and little has been addressed regarding abuse and discrimination. In Sweden, it is worse as indigenous rights are banned. Although in 1998 the government issued an official apology for its treatment of the Sámi, discrimination continues. In Finland, the Sámi were recognised in 1995 but this is currently meaningless as the country has yet to ratify the ILO Convention 169 regarding Indigenous

Peoples. Finland also denies land rights to the Sámi. And Russia has yet to act on Article 69 of the 1993 constitution that addresses the anomalies and marginalisation of indigenous peoples.

Leaving the smiling Sámi gentleman wearing a blue and red three-pointed hat and oversized sunglasses, and unable to see if he had square or round buttons on his belt, I rode away from the vehicle park and the three coaches that were reabsorbing their human cargo, and continued to ride on a good road through rock-strewn grassland. The sea was calm, the low dark grey islands lay like half-submerged giant whales. The weather was kind. With no shelter to the surrounding horizons, there were thousands of miles for weather systems to build and explode onto the land. Here the wind can lift and throw small rocks: at times a human cannot remain standing.

As I approached the entrance to the massive parking area that serves the Nordkapp visitors' centre, another wave of realisation hit home. I was now within a kilometre of the end of my journey. I wanted it to be a private moment, a time I could later reflect on. I had met some wonderful people on my travels but had enjoyed the solitude and self-reliance as much. Robert Mads Anderson, who climbed Everest with me in 2010, puts this feeling succinctly in his book, *Nine Lives*.

Climbing together overshadows the mountain itself and the mountain becomes a stage where the human drama plays out.

Soloing is a completely different experience – it is only the mountain and you; the mountain dominated my world and my thinking.'

He talks of a direct relationship with his environment, whereas this relationship is elusive when not on your own. Unlike Robert, I have rarely climbed alone and certainly not 8,000 m peaks but most of my cycling is on my own. I very much enjoy the company of others. However, as Robert says, it does detract from the experience that you seek to immerse yourself in. You can indulge yourself as you please. When you feel powerful, you can cycle as fast as you are physically able. When you feel knackered, you can stop cycling. You can take photos as you choose. Sing out loud with joy (in deserted places) or scream with frustration, sometimes not in deserted places. Your achievements are your own, as are your failures. If you get lost, it is only you who has got you lost. There is no drafting behind another cyclist, sheltering from a headwind. Solitude builds self-reliance and your experiences remain unique to your memories only and the clarity of those memories is profoundly planted.

I push the bike, slowing past the statues of the Children of the Earth. There is time later to look around the attractions that draw 200,000 visitors each year.

I pitch my tent someway off to the right of the visitors' centre. The exact spot was decided on by the minimum number of rocks that need to be removed to secure a comfortable night's sleep. I later place rocks around the tent skirting and use them to secure the pegs still further from any wind that may blast this exposed landscape. There are no other tents to be seen and only a handful of people venture in my direction.

A few hundred metres in front of me, the cliff edge plummets to the water below. The sea and sky dominate. I look north and can plainly see the curve of planet earth and am reminded of the curving edges of the same planet from the summit of Everest, some 6,100 km away. With the realisation that I had now completed 5,000 miles of cycling, a blanket of contentment and satisfaction wraps around me. Northwards, there is no more mainland until Alaska. Only the archipelago of Svalbard, known as Spitsbergen until 1925, breaks the waterline of the Barents Sea and Arctic Ocean. The Dutch navigator, Willem Barentsz, discovered these islands in 1596, following which whaling, trapping, and mining have provided livelihoods for the hardy. Hardy, because of the extreme cold - the coldest recorded temperature being minus 45 degrees Celsius (minus 49 degrees Fahrenheit). Coupled with the sun going beneath 6 degrees below the horizon on October 26th and not re-emerging until February 15th, this is a land not for the faint-hearted. These islands lay equal distance between Norway and the North Pole. Directly north of me is the island of Nordaustlandet, covered in part with ice caps that are melting rapidly: this island is that remote it remains uninhabited, save for reindeer and walruses.

I am strangely reluctant to become a tourist and explore what the majority have come to see. Sitting next to the tent looking out to sea, watching a few small fishing boats, I see two reindeer casually stroll towards me. I am completely in the open and they are very aware of me. They continued to walk towards me. Not for the first time did I think how small these creatures are.

The iconic Globe was beckoning. This monument was erected in 1977 and is synonymous with Nordkapp. There must be millions of photographs around the world of the Globe silhouette with a dramatic sunset shimmering across the sea behind. Even in bright daylight it is dramatic and of obvious significance.

Later I walked over to see the visitors' centre. Built in 1959 and later expanded in 1988 and again in 1997, it can now accommodate a few thousand visitors at once. Much of what is there is underground to minimise the impact on the environment. Beneath there is a Thai museum opened in 1989 to commemorate a visit from the then king of Siam (now Thailand), King Chulalongkorn. There is an impressive exhibition of a variety of sea birds stuffed and presented in their 'natural' habitat, a chapel, a panoramic bar, and a restaurant, where the curry will not be the only thing making your eyes water as you punch your PIN into the credit card machine. I meander up and down the buffet bar searching for a meal that will not cause my bank manager indigestion. Marie, the happy smiling cashier, lets me know that my can of Coke is 48 Kroner, £4.80. I drink it slowly.

Too many people, I need some fresh air and there are some enticing statues and monuments to look for. The seven circular monuments set in an arc facing a young child who points to them whilst looking up at a woman beside him, her hair set permanently blowing in the wind, is striking. Each of the monuments was designed by a child from different parts of the world. In 1989 the children came to Nordkapp to see their work erected and in June every year, local children come to celebrate the values of friendship, hope, and joy across the world that first inspired the idea. The monuments are set away from the visitors' centre and can be best viewed sharing the backdrop with their wild surroundings. Another monument is of King Oscar II of Sweden and Norway. Raised in 1873, it was to mark the outermost limit of the union of those two countries.

A road only arrived in Nordkapp in 1956. Before that, visiting Nordkapp necessitated a sea voyage, a 'not without risk' landing, and a steep climb up the cliffs on a footpath. All within the probability of not seeing too much because of persistent sea fog. In 1875 Thomas Cook, a UK travel company, (sadly now no longer, following their collapse in 2019) took 24 tourists to Nordkapp. This was the first commercial tour to Nordkapp.

The world became aware of this magical place following an expedition in 1553. Three ships commanded by Richard Chancellor were looking for The North Eastern Passage and happened upon the towering cliff faces, which he named Nordkapp. The renowned 'globetrotting' Italian priest Francesco Negri, probably the world's first tourist, later arrived and said it was the end of the then known world. Two hundred years then passed before King Oscar, in 1873, climbed the steep path up the cliff face and sparked international interest. Two years later the Thomas Cook cruise arrived.

Daily Blog: Today I finished a wonderful journey. July 27th

I have pitched my tent 400 m from and parallel with the Globe that marks the furthest northern land point of Europe. So tonight, for one night only, I will be the most northerly inhabitant of Europe. To the east, I can clearly see the Russian coastline and the next landmass to the northwest is Greenland, which I certainly cannot see. Looking due north there is no mainland until the northern coast of Alaska. Quite a thought.

Journey's end!

The weather is perfect, with the sun shining and a gentle breeze. There is an uninterrupted 180-degree view of the sea with the occasional small fishing boat passing by with its tail of seagulls flying noisily behind. Somewhere out in front of me is the invisible dividing line between the North Sea and the larger Barents Sea, named after the Dutch navigator Willem Barentsz, with its huge untapped resources of oil and gas.

A pair of reindeer have just wandered past the tent. It is not often anyone can say that.

Children of the Earth. Created by seven children from around the world who came together for a week at Nordkapp to create a symbol for world peace.

A solitary figure stands looking west from the most northerly point of Europe.

It is beyond me to describe just how serene and beautiful this place is. However, and not only in the winter, it can also be a desperate place, with winds strong enough to pick up stones and hurl them through the air.

I have been here for some hours and yet the fact that there is no more cycling to do has not fully registered. No more maps to read, plans to amend or wild camps to find.

The curvature of our planet beyond the Nordkapp Globe.

This cycle ride has been an epic, longer than any trip to climb an 8,000 m mountain. I have met some fantastic people; some I hope will remain in contact. I have seen innumerable places throughout Europe, learned more than I ever thought possible, and whilst I have turned the pedals, sweated, hurt, and swore at idiot drivers and determined flies, mosquitoes, and ticks. …..

…. I have also shouted out loud with joy and exuberance, sung at the top of my voice in the darkest, coldest road tunnels, and pushed the boundaries of safety to gain the rush of adrenaline.

Whilst I thank everyone who cycled with me, whether planned or by chance and good fortune, the one person I want to thank is Anne, my wife. Who is not only my wife but also my weather girl, my hostel booker, and my link with the real world.

Tonight, with a continuing clear sky, the midnight sun will be very visible. I will sleep with the tent open to that sky.

The midnight sun casts it ethereal light.

Tomorrow I will cycle back to Honningsvag and perhaps do the hike to Knivskjellodden, provided I can secure the bike.

The statistics – I have purposely not delved into the stats. beyond each day's figures. I did not want to initiate any reoccurring thoughts revolving around, 'only another 1,000 km to ride, only another 6,000 m of elevation'. As a taster though, in July alone I have travelled over 2,500 km and climbed 31,898 m of elevation, nearly four times the height of Everest.

CHAPTER TWENTY-NINE
A Leisurely Return from Nordkapp

'My biggest fear isn't crashing this bike at 85 mph and losing my skin, its sitting in a chair at 90 and wishing I'd done more.' Graeme Obree, The Flying Scotsman

As I waited, leaning on the fence in front of the Globe, several hours before the sun would set below the horizon, I start to 'people watch'. Most are couples or small groups. Truly an international gathering with many languages being spoken. I chat with Frank, a BMW motorcyclist from Germany. Considering where we all are, the weather was kind to us. Views to the horizon, little or no wind, and much warmer than expected.

The hours passed; midnight came and went, and the sun still had not sunk beneath the horizon. All of us knew that this was a special day in our lives, one to be remembered. Frank and I said our farewells, not knowing that we would see each other on the road the following day. I walked back to my tent and stood beside it, not wishing to get into it, the light was ethereal, the peace total, and the beauty so vulnerable. An hour later, having warmed in my sleeping bag, still with the tent open with the view towards the North Pole constantly to look at, my meandering thoughts reflected on how an embryo of an idea, a passing thought of the possibility of cycling from the most southerly point of Europe to the most northerly point, had grown from scribbled plans to past tense. The journey was finished but the memories would remain. Closing my eyes, I realised that for just this one night I would be the most northern person on the European continent.

FACT FACTORY: The timeline of Nordkapp
1539 – The Swedish priest Olaus Magnus drew a map of northern Europe. He filled in the undiscovered areas with sea monsters attacking ships. Nothing like instilling confidence in sailors.
1553 – The Knyskanes rock was first named North Cape by the English captain

and navigator Richard Chancellor, in his search for his route to China.

1664 – Francesco Negri from Ravenna, Italy, visits and is subsequently considered the first tourist to the area.

1873 – On 2nd July King Oscar II of the Norway-Sweden union unveiled the royal monument to indicate the northernmost point of the Norwegian kingdom.

1950 – Olav V, beloved king of Norway, visited Nordkapp.

1956 – The road to Nordkapp was opened on 30th June, the first car having visited the previous year to start the Cape-to-Cape race to Cape Town.

1984 – On 7th June the Royal North Cape Club was founded, with the unveiling of the Midnight Sun Road.

Journey's end.

The Globe at Nordkapp.

POSTSCRIPT

I am cycling southwards, a direction that I have rarely followed since leaving the Mediterranean Sea. Heading back to Honningsvåg. Similar to the effort needed to summit a mountain and the briefest of time then spent on the top and, for like reasons, I chose to return to Honningsvåg. The weather had been a friend, but it is a fickle friend, and would not hesitate to show a less compassionate side. Wind, rain, snow, or hail were all possible and the exposure would be considerable.

The memories and experience would not be enhanced any more by staying a further night. It was time to start the return home. The weather remained perfect, my senses saturated by the surroundings, I appreciated every minute. Reindeer with calves at foot, some tourists sounding their car horns and waving happily as they pass me, cycling, cocooned in contentment. A photo stop before a long descent, where I was joined by a coach of adventurous octogenarians. The coach driver followed me down a long hill, staying a safe distance behind. Crouched on the crossbar with my legs and arms tucked in, adrenalin and happiness surged through my ageing body.

As the road levelled, the coach passed, and a rear window of beaming faces and waving arms looked back at me. Some of those faces could have smiled out of a coach window seventy years ago, I hope they had. I wondered how the world had treated them.

I arrived back at my 'private' campsite outside Honningsvåg. Lifted the cycle and threw the panniers over the road barrier and carried them down the short slope to the small grassy area that was to be my home for another night. I had inner contentment. Through 'Å ha bein i nesa', which translates from Norwegian to English as, 'To have bones in your nose', or 'To be determined and capable', that embryo of an idea had not only been born, but it had also matured into reality.

Daily Blog: A leisurely return from 71°10'21" to Honningsvåg via Skarsvåg. July 28th

Honningsvåg harbour.

Back at my Honningsvåg seaside residence, found by Brian (my thanks, friend), I had just opened my 'early' evening beer, a Mack, remembering the most northerly brewery in the world in Tromsø, when a man carrying a fishing rod walked through my back garden to the sea. Within fifteen minutes he had caught a sizeable fish. It would have taken him more time to go shopping for it. These waters must be teeming with fish.

On my return ride from Nordkapp, the anticipated feeling of anti-climax never arrived. With the weather remaining perfect, beautiful surroundings, reindeer with calves at foot grazing the hills, and a sense of achievement, I was feeling good.

The trusting nature of Norwegians is refreshing, cycles, vehicle snow tyres and other items of value left unattended and rightfully they are proud of their honesty. However, with hundreds of other tourists around I did not feel comfortable leaving my cycle and panniers unattended during the 20 km walk I had planned to Knivskjellodden, so rode back to Honningsvåg via a detour, to Skarsvåg, which is – guess, yes! – the most northern fishing harbour in the world.

Europe's most northern fishing community.

My previous less than complimentary comments regarding the competency of some RV drivers were borne out when I heard metal scraping on the tarmac as an RV re-joined the road from a layby and drove away from me up a hill with its rear door swinging open and access ladder scraping on the ground. Pots and pans falling from the open door, it was like a sketch from a Buster Keaton silent movie. Any following vehicles would have had to negotiate the debris to be able to overtake and advise the driver.

After a brief stop to take a photo with a coach party, both the coach and I set off down a hill. An exciting descent would be an understatement, pure enjoyment, topped by many of the passengers waving and clapping as they overtook me as the hill ran out onto flatter ground. The driver even sounded his horn.

Tomorrow will be a 'chilling out' day in Honningsvåg, a town I now know well. Then a 4 am rise on Monday to catch the 5.45 am departing MS Nordkapp to Tromsø, stopping at Hammerfest, the world's most northern city!

Heading south and homeward.

CHAPTER THIRTY
When the Traveller Returns Home

DEPARTED HONNINGSVÅG. July 30th

'When the traveller returns home, let him not leave the countries where he hath travelled altogether behind him.' Francis Bacon

Awaking early the following morning for the Hurtigruten ferry to arrive and take me from Honningsvåg to Tromsø, another cyclist was doing the same. Hugh from Bristol, England, a piano teacher and intrepid tourer was also on his way home. We boarded together and enjoyed a feast for breakfast. It was still early, and we had the impressive restaurant to ourselves and an even more impressive array of food. Anything that anyone had ever eaten for breakfast was on offer. Gluttony and guilt could not have been further from our minds. During the 78 days of cycling up from Spain, I had burnt over 200,000 calories. This 64-year-old had developed legs like pistons and a sixpack of a Thai boxer. The need to consume quality energy giving food was still paramount. As Hugh was staying on board and heading down to Bergen, he had booked a cabin, whereas I was on board just for the day. As we left the restaurant, we asked whether we could return later for a second breakfast, and a smiling waiter said we were welcome to do so. We never did. I spent the next 17 hours covering the 390 km south to Tromsø, relaxing and looking forward to seeing my wife. Anne would be arriving in Tromsø at 8 pm and I would dock around midnight. Remembering midnight was not night, it was noticeably light. We would have a day to enjoy Tromsø before our five-day trip, again courtesy of Hurtigruten, down to Bergen, this time sailing on the *Finnmarken*. Those few days were special, 2018 was the 125th anniversary of the Hurtigruten company, founded by Richard With in 1893. One evening a special celebratory meal was held during which Anne and I enjoyed the company of two strangers who became instant friends, Malcolm and Doreen from Inverness, Scotland, who coincidentally had recently returned from Cape Town, where they had met my sister and brother-in-law. It is a small world, with only 'six degrees of separation'.

The Nordkapp arrives to take Hugh and me to Tromsø. I later enjoyed a reflective pint.

THE TUNNELS OF NORWAY

The following is a list of the tunnels travelled through on my way to Nordkapp.

Name	Length	Lighting	ID number.
Mørretunnelen	154 m	no	828
Rødhammertunnelen	42 m	no	340
Bangsundtunnelen	169 m	yes	1071
Hestnesetunnelen	579 m	yes	342
Botntunnelen	38 m	no	344
Mølleviktunnelen	100 m	yes	343
Løviktunnelen	254 m	yes	345
Sjonstitunnelen	368 m	yes	333
Sjonatunnelen	2,796 m	yes	247 Prone to exhaust fumes.
Fornestunnelen	146 m	yes	334
Silatunnelen	2,882 m	poor	248
Kistatunnelen	412 m	yes	337
Straumdaltunnelen	3,232 m	yes	249
Storvikskartunnelen	3,100 m	yes	251
Skaugvolltunnelen	247 m	yes	319
Vindviktunnelen	980 m	poor	362

Sundsfjordtunnelen	772 m	poor	363	
Eivikhammerentunnelen	258 m	yes	364	
Nappstraumtunnelen	1,776 m	yes	266	Ferry as an alternative.
Rørvikskartunnelen	726 m	yes	268	
Nonshaugtunnelen	85 m	none	281	
Bygrensen	36 m	none	871	
Børratunnelen	133 m	yes	267	
Hattnestunnelen	165 m	yes	280	
Kleivatunnelen (Nordland)	100 m	yes	380	
Ballasvikskartunnelen	850 m	yes	1035	
Hamntunnelen	27 m	none	887	
Skalandtunnelen	1,890 m	poor	360	
Steinfjordtunnelen	1,265 m	poor	356	
Geitskartunnelen	2,147 m	yes	276	
Otervika raseroverbygg	607 m	none	980	
Hestentunnelen	350 m	poor	358	
Svartholla	310 m	yes	357	
Breitindtunnelen	920 m	yes	765	
Storuratunnelen	320 m	yes	808	
Garfjelltunnelen	162 m	yes	807	
Melsviktunnelen	2,467 m	yes	1085	
Storvikatunnelen	1,200 m	yes	1072	
Kåfjordtunnelen	1,208 m	yes	1032	Can be avoided.
Tyskhaugtunnelen	218 m	yes	1033	Can be avoided.
Aslakheimtunnelen	300 m	yes	1034	Can be avoided.
Skarvbergtunnelen	3,000 m	poor	260	
Sortviktunnelen	499 m	yes	734	
Ytre Sortvik	135 m	not sure	1173	
Nordkapptunnelen	6,900 m	poor	261	
Sarnestunnelen	195 m	yes	733	
Honningsvågtunnelen	4,500 m	yes	262	
Nordvågentunnelen	455 m	yes	985	

The Nordkapptunnelen was finished in 1999 and is 6,871 m in length and submerges to 212 m below the sea. There is minimal lighting which prevents accurate judgement of the road surface conditions. The extractor fans are loud and can affect judgement on which direction vehicles are approaching. The tunnel is usually extremely cold.

Cycle alert buttons are placed at the entrances to longer or heightened risk tunnels and some, such as the Breitindtunnelen, ID No. 765, have high viz jackets in containers at either end of the tunnel, to be used and returned by cyclists. By activating the cyclist alert button, all traffic is made aware that there is a cyclist in the tunnel.

MAJOR CLASSIC MOUNTAIN CYCLE CLIMBS

The following classic climbs were completed or attempted on the tour.

Mountain	Elevation Gain	Length	Country
Alto del Angliru	1,266 m	12.5 km	Spain
Lagos de Covadonga	962 m	14.2 km	Spain
Puerto de Urkiola	524 m	5.7 km	Spain
Col d'Aubisque	1,190 m	30.0 km	France
			Repeated 2019
Cirque de Gavarnie	1,585 m	30.9 km	France
Hautacam	1,223 m	16.3 km	France
			Repeated 2019
Col du Tourmalet	1,405 m	18.8 km	France
			Completed 2019
Col de Peyresourde	655 m	9.9 km	France
La Redoute	161 m	1.7 km	Belgium
Mur de Huy	128 m	1.3 km	Belgium

Other climbs of note included: - Col d Osquich 495 m, Col de Marie Blanque 1,035 m, El Escudo 1011 m, Erro 801 m, Etxauri 840 m, Mezkiritz 922 m, Mirador de Cabania and Palares 1,378 m.

Note: - Elevation gain is always less than the summit height of the mountain. Neither does it take account of the approach elevations of subsidiary climbs required to access the main climb.

STATISTICS FOR TARIFA TO NORDKAPP CYCLE RIDE – 2018

DAYS IN THE SADDLE	78
DISTANCE	7,946.91 km
CYCLING TIME	484 hours 5 minutes
ASCENT	94,816 m (10.7 Everests)
CALORIES	200,898 (25.2 per km cycled)
AVERAGE DAILY DISTANCE	101.9 km
AVERAGE DAILY ELEVATION	1,215.6 m
AVERAGE DAILY CALORIES	2,575.6
AVERAGE DAILY SPEED	16.4 km/h
FASTEST SPEED	80 km/h 5th July
AVERAGE bpm	91

PEOPLE MET WHILST ON SPAIN TO NORWAY CYCLE RIDE

Joanne from Tauranga NZ. Jim and Marianna from Freemantle, Australia. Bernadette and Paul from Deventer, Holland. Paul from Canada. Ryan from Canada. Aldo from Italy. Yoya from Holland. Alistaire from Glasgow, Scotland. Runar and Kristina from Tromsø, Norway. Frank from Germany. Malcolm and Doreen from Inverness, Scotland. Hugh from Bristol, England. Amerly from Paris. And my cycling companions, David Cronk from Cambridge, England, and Andy Hill from Ripon, Yorkshire, England. These and others I met, whilst our paths crossed only fleetingly, you all added to the enjoyment of my experience of cycling from the most southerly point of Europe to the most northerly tip.

FOOTNOTE: SCHOOLING

'The heights by great men reached and kept, were not attained by sudden flight, but they, while their companions slept, were toiling upward in the night.' Henry Wadsworth Longfellow

I hope by including the following I may inspire some young people who find academic study challenging. At my birth, I received less than an adequate serving of brain cells. However, I was blessed with a generous helping of common sense. There seems to be an ever-increasing magnetism towards a belief that personal gain should result without effort. An effort is always required to achieve, but effort alone is insufficient because the effort does not always translate to success. Commitment to determination will result in achievement.

My earliest memory of school is not a good one, it was frightening and a bad omen for my future education. Welldon Park Primary School in South Harrow, North London was my first exposure to structured learning. It was early September 1959 when my mother left me in a classroom and walked off down the timber-glazed corridor, still so vivid in my memory. She had gone perhaps half a mile and arrived at the Northolt Road before I caught her up, an emotional wreck determined never to return to any school. Twenty minutes later, sitting in class with my teacher, Miss Flower consoling me, years of frustration caused by a distinct lack of brain cells had commenced. David Griffin and his gang regularly picked on me in the playground. That was until one day by chance he and I met on the shallow wide-stepped path to the rear of a building. Without his supporting gang, equality reigned. It resulted in him never again getting his gang to beat me up. It had been unfortunate that he had lost his footing on what seemingly looked innocuous steps.

Learning – how do you learn when you cannot remember? I loathed school. My writing was neat, my spelling atrocious. Piece was pees, coal bunker was collbuncer, putting was pooting, height was hite and knocked was nockde.

We moved from South Harrow, not so far from the famous Harrow school on the hill, (as far as I was concerned it may as well have been on the dark side of the moon) to Cheshunt in Hertfordshire. Cheshunt's claim to fame is several.

Richard Cromwell, son of Oliver and the second Lord Protector of England, died in Cheshunt in 1785 at the then ripe old age of 75. A couple of centuries later we witnessed his ruin of a home going up in a spectacular night-time fire. A short while later a housing estate replaced it.

Jack Cohen, from Whitechapel in London's Eastend, had established the now massive supermarket chain, Tesco. From a stall in Hackney this keen businessman opened the first Tesco in Burnt Oak in 1931 and later in Cheshunt, it became the major employer.

My new school was Dewhurst St Mary. This school was old. A lawyer called Robert Dewhurst opened the school for boys in 1640. It was for poor boys to receive an education in reading, writing, and arithmetic. It was not until 1873 that a further building was added that would be the girls' school and in 1958, only a few years before I attended, both the schools were merged. Mr Grey was the headmaster, with Mr Huggins and Mr Evans supporting. Mr Evans, never without a cigarette between his lips or wedged between his yellowed nicotine-stained fingers, patrolled between our desks, exhaling smoke above us, and occasionally belting us about the head if he was displeased with our work. I learnt not to duck his swiping hand as to do so would attract further punishment. Ms Jones, perhaps the model for Giles cartoons 'Old Lady' dressed in Victorian black, minus the fox stole, was a formidable character who told gruesome tales of pupil punishments for misdemeanours involving pushing pencils up children's noses.

I had brought my inability to learn from my previous school and developed it with ease at Dewhurst. Whilst my brother was placed in a higher class, albeit he was fifteen months younger than me, I remained in the same class for two years. On leaving, he and my sister went to a grammar school, I went to a secondary school. Even the name infers inferiority. It was, however, to be a good decision.

'Dyslexia is a common learning difficulty that causes problems with reading, writing, and spelling.' This is one of several similar definitions that probably most know. However, in the early 1960s things were quite different. Tolerance, compassion, and empathy were not words used often in conversation. Remember, pencils had only recently started to be used explicitly for writing and drawing and the cane was in regular use as a corporal punishment.

I attended St Mary's High School; my first class was R1, the 'R' standing for Mrs Russell. What patience she had with me, and at home I have recollections of standing for hours beside my mother, who sat at a table trying to teach me words that a child, years younger than me would write with consummate ease. The saving grace of my appalling academic abilities that spanned, English, mathematics, and music, was sport and arts and crafts. Whilst sitting, sweating, and trying to be invisible in the English class waiting for Mr Martin to call my name to read aloud to the class, I would dream of being on the athletics track or playing rugby.

Academically, geography and history were the only subjects that attracted me; geography in particular. I was fascinated with our world, the countries, the cultures, how the human species could be so diverse. It was at the end of the fourth year that my mind started to absorb meaningful data, probably kick-started by interests in geography and a developing desire to travel.

I had realised that the only way of booting my brain was to saturate it with 'parrot fashion' learning and, as repetitive and time consuming as it was, the tangible progress drove me on. I had missed out on years of foundation learning and had to devise shortcuts to prop up those missing building blocks. With sport playing a big part in my life, badminton, taught by the strange Mr Meads and played with my great partner, Terry Coltman, we achieved some notoriety, and we are still friends to this day some five decades later. Basketball, athletics, and the beginnings of a lifelong love affair with rugby union. These were now testosterone-filled times, and the distractions were plentiful. I will not embarrass either the ladies or myself. They were fun times but a serious diversion from academic progress.

With the arrival in the fifth year at school and GCSE and CSE's, my teachers had in the main written me off. Roger Martin, English and history, John Courter, mathematics, and music, sadly I cannot remember her name, although the girls' PE teacher, Mrs Hurst used to fill in. Only Mr Davis who taught geography and rugby and Tony Instral, our PE teacher had faith in me. My only potential at this time was in sport.

I studied hard that year, hour after hour in my room. The most crucial part was the stringent self-testing that the 'grey matter' was absorbing information. Hundreds of hours were spent in self-study in the knowledge that others would achieve better results from a fraction of my efforts. Having sat my exams, I surprised both my teachers and me with top grades in all subjects apart from maths. Turning over an examination question sheet and reading those questions and feeling a smile come over my face, had until then been alien. I had for the first time in my life enjoyed sitting exams. This method of prolonged and intensive study is to this day the only assured method of achieving good results.

I suppose if there is a moral to this story, it is that nothing is gained without effort. For some that effort need only be minimal and for others, it must be considerable, and do not expect additional recognition for that additional effort, you will be disappointed, but the satisfaction of having achieved something that was previously beyond your abilities, more than compensates.

Looking back to my youth decades later, to a time when I believed my current age was ancient, like all of us, I had no idea which paths my life would walk me down. What I do believe is that we can be architects of our destiny, but to what extent can only be dictated by what comes our way. We should seize opportunities and make the most of our time on this planet and try to leave it a better place when we depart.

IRISH BLESSING
May the roads rise to meet you,
May the wind be always at your back,
May the sunshine warm upon your face,
The rains fall soft upon your fields and
until we meet again may your God hold you in the hollow of His hand.

About the Author: - Following his retirement from the UK Fire Service, during which he indulged in a few sports, including rugby, badminton, squash, white-water kayaking, and rock climbing, Tim divided his time between working for a charity for non-sighted people and as a retail 'boy' for an outdoor pursuits company. Already having ventured into high altitude climbing, he embarked on climbing the highest mountain on each of the seven continents. He achieved that goal in 2010 when he summitted Everest. A self-confessed sporting 'Jack of all trades and master of none', he became the oldest English 'old git', (as he calls himself), to have both climbed Everest and acquired elusive membership of the Seven Summits club. Tim has also climbed many other mountains around the world and in recent years has become passionate about ice climbing. Cycling had become an integral part of Tim's training regime for these climbs, as did dragging tractor tyres around his local area, whilst on land skis. Soon road cycling morphed into an integral part of his life. Trips such as the one from Seattle to Boston, a 4,000-mile, 40-day credit card journey with a friend, Andy Hill. Lands' End to John O'Groats, a month after returning from Everest with another friend, Luke Lengiewicz. Hungary, Slovakia, and Poland with both Andy and Luke. Solo trips around Ireland and Portugal and in Australia and Thailand. He is also slowly working his way through achieving all the European cycling classic climbs. With two further long-distance trips planned, it is unlikely Tim will be hanging his wheels up anytime soon.

Nordkapp, the northernmost point of mainland Europe.

All illustrations have been taken by the author.
Three photographs taken in Bergen-Belsen and two taken in Tromsø,
are of originals.

Nordkapp-
tunnelen
6870 m
212 m.u.h.
Storvika-
tunnelen
Lengde 1,2 km
Sundsfjord-
tunnelen
750 m
Skaugvoll-
tunnelen
240 m
Syklist i
tunnel
Sarnestunnelen
190 m
Silatunnelen
2870 m
Honningsvåg-
tunnelen
4440 m
Kuldeport
9 %
Low gear